PRAISE FOR *ALL IN STRIDE*

"A story of two athletic journeys intertwined, the complexities of becoming American while still embracing the culture that shaped you, and the power of running to change the course of a life."

—MOLLY HUDDLE, two-time Olympian, author, and mother

"*All in Stride* takes readers on a compelling journey of a truly modern American couple. It effortlessly weaves together stories of Kenya, the United States, the world of professional distance running, and the challenges of building a home in a new country. For millennia, the words 'athlete' and 'woman' didn't play well together, and the idea of adding 'mother' to that list was unimaginable. Women like Elvin want to change that narrative. Fortunately for all of us, she has the conviction to do so and a supporting family to make it possible. The world needs more stories like this one."

—SHANNON ROWBURY, three-time Olympian,
sports broadcaster, and mother of two

"For two people I have known for nearly a decade as some of the most positive and determined peers of mine, I have been blessed to learn so much more about their eye-opening stories in this beautifully written book. The perspective that Johanna Garton sheds on the character-building hardships these athletes faced chasing the American Dream makes this a must-read both within and outside of the running community. Utterly blown away!"

—NATOSHA ROGERS, professional distance runner,
two-time World Championship finalist in the 10k

"This story is truly inspiring. It's not so much about running as it is the struggle of life and overcoming it."

—NATHAN MARTIN, American professional distance runner

"*All in Stride* tells the incredible journey of Elvin Kibet and Shadrack Kipchirchir, from their childhood in Kenya to their collegiate days competing at the NCAA Division One level to their service in the U.S. Army and as professional runners in the Army's World Class Athlete Program. It's a heartwarming story, one that's infused with grace, courage, and determination about what it takes to chase a dream in sport and life."

—CHRISTINE YU, author of
Up to Speed: The Groundbreaking Science of Women Athletes

"*All in Stride* is a powerfully written account of pursuing the American Dream—that rough road that rides more like an obstacle course but consists of perseverance meeting opportunity to build the ultimate American hero. On every page, you'll find yourself cheerleading, empathizing, crying, or heeding wise advice."

—DEENA KASTOR, Olympic medalist in the marathon,
New York Times bestselling author of *Let Your Mind Run*

"I read Johanna Garton's *All in Stride* expecting a book about running, which it certainly is, but it's so much more. It's about joy, love, suffering, determination, sacrifice, and humanity. I just loved it."

—GEORGE HIRSCH, founder of the New York City Marathon,
magazine publisher, and chair emeritus
of the New York Road Runners Club

"*All in Stride* illustrates the power of perseverance and commitment with a focused target. It makes you feel like you are on a journey with Shadrack and Elvin. They take great pride in serving the country that gave them the opportunity to be the best version of themselves. Their journey is about hope, faith, hard work, and the pursuit of excellence and the American Dream."

—MEB KEFLEZIGHI, four-time Olympian,
silver medalist in the 2004 Athens Olympic Games in the marathon,
and winner of the Boston and New York City Marathons

All in Stride

A Journey in Running, Courage, and the Search for the American Dream

Johanna Garton

ROWMAN & LITTLEFIELD
Lanham • Boulder • New York • London

Published by Rowman & Littlefield
An imprint of The Rowman & Littlefield Publishing Group, Inc.
4501 Forbes Boulevard, Suite 200, Lanham, Maryland 20706
www.rowman.com

86-90 Paul Street, London EC2A 4NE, United Kingdom

British Library Cataloguing in Publication Information Available

Library of Congress Cataloging-in-Publication Data Available

ISBN 978-1-5381-8459-2 (pbk. : alk. paper) | ISBN 978-1-5381-8460-8 (electronic)

∞™ The paper used in this publication meets the minimum requirements of American National Standard for Information Sciences—Permanence of Paper for Printed Library Materials, ANSI/NISO Z39.48-1992.

For Ernie

Contents

Foreword

Kathrine Switzer

Running is a universal language. It instantly conveys shared understanding, allyship, generosity, gratitude, and hope. Where else but in running can 50,000 total strangers speaking fifty different languages run together and feel as if they'd support each other no matter the cost?

This book is about hope, and the unlikely success of hope. At the heart of the story are three talented athletes who represent millions of others similarly striving to achieve athletic success.

The story is also about what it means to be an American and what that looks like today. Almost everyone who lives in the United States has a story that began with an immigrant family. Over time, it's easy to forget those stories, or to recognize that others are just now in the middle of their own journeys to America. For Shadrack and Elvin, navigating the American Dream hasn't been easy, and their story is a beautiful reminder of where each of us started.

How do children growing up amid rural Kenyan poverty find the courage to run, attend school, seek opportunity, and make their way into the American collegiate athletic experience? How do they navigate language, airports, new culture, the United States military, and global sports systems amid daunting expectations? To say nothing of loneliness. What ingenuity, tenacity, belief, and love does it take and where does it come from? Is this the American Dream and is it better than home? And what is, after all, "home"?

As a woman who helped pioneer the inclusion of women in running, as a product of the 1960s feminist movement, and as the daughter of an American Army officer, I find Elvin's journey from Kenya to America particularly compelling. Her story inspires us all to define and reestablish rights for women and people of color that were hard-won and make them secure. We cheer for Elvin to succeed so that the hope of success for all of us remains bright.

I was writing sports and gate-crashing the Boston Marathon while at Syracuse University in the 1960s, which was groundbreaking for women at the time. As a runner herself, Johanna Garton knows this world well. Her own journey included growing up in the brand-new era of Title IX which provided her with the opportunity to run Division One cross country and track. Her alma mater is my own, and as women who proudly ran for Syracuse and studied journalism there, we both know how important it was to pave paths for later generations of women. In sharing this story, Johanna has written a book that is poignant, funny, insightful, and nonjudgmental. It's one that doesn't shy from hard truths as it leads us through the colliding worlds of sports, immigration, the United States military, race, gender, loyalty, and determination.

Athlete, author, and advocate for sports and social causes, Kathrine Switzer is the co-founder of the nonprofit 261 Fearless, whose mission is to empower women through running. Switzer was the first woman to officially register and run the Boston Marathon in 1967, and because she was female, was attacked in the race by an angry official who tried to rip off her bib number (#261). She finished and went on to win the 1974 New York City Marathon, then led the drive to make the women's marathon an official Olympic event at the 1984 Los Angeles Olympics. To celebrate the fiftieth anniversary of her legendary run in Boston, Switzer ran there again in 2017, at age seventy. Kathrine is an Emmy Award–winning TV broadcaster, the author of *Marathon Woman* and *Running and Walking for Women Over 40*, and co-author of *26.2 Marathon Stories*.

Reader's Note

This is a work of creative nonfiction, based on hundreds of hours of interviews and research. All details contained within these pages are true to the best of my knowledge and represent the memories of those I spoke with. Much of the dialogue is reconstructed, meaning that it is accurate as far as the people who said or heard those words could recall when they spoke to me. In some cases, I've edited conversations, added small details, or compressed events for clarity. All persons described are actual individuals, and no names have been changed.

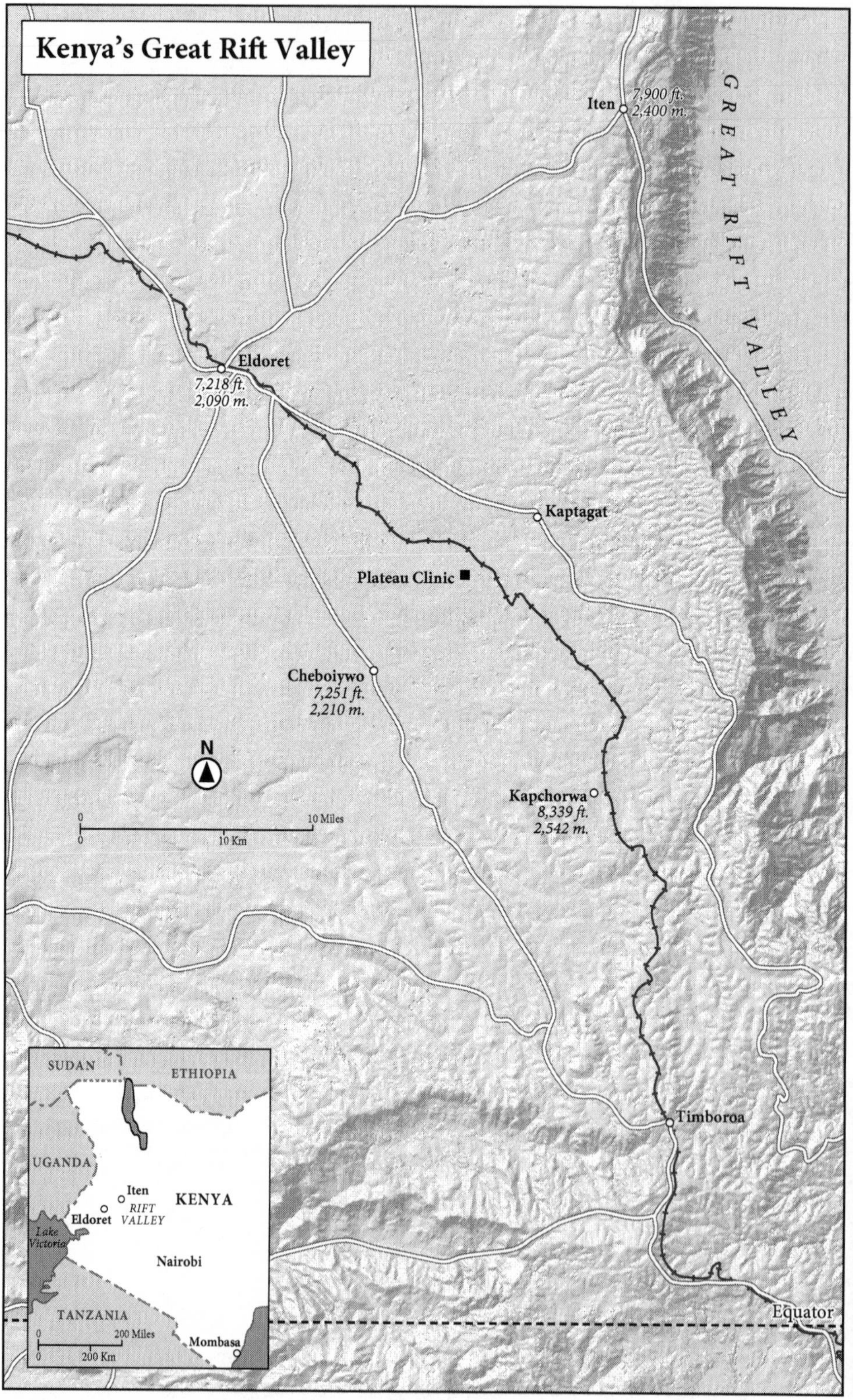

Kenya's Great Rift Valley
Iten
7,900 ft.
2,400 m.
GREAT RIFT VALLEY
Eldoret
7,218 ft.
2,090 m.
Kaptagat
Plateau Clinic
Cheboiywo
7,251 ft.
2,210 m.
N
0
10 Miles
0
10 Km
Kapchorwa
8,339 ft.
2,542 m.
Timboroa
Equator
SUDAN
ETHIOPIA
UGANDA
Iten
KENYA
RIFT VALLEY
Eldoret
Lake Victoria
Nairobi
TANZANIA
0
200 Miles
0
200 Km
Mombasa

Part I

Kenya

Chapter One
Heat

United States Olympic Track and Field Trials
Eugene, Oregon
July 2016

Rising from a chair just inside the entryway, an event volunteer pulled the door closed. It had gotten stuck in the open position, allowing heat from the track to escape into the call room.

"Good green acres, thank you for keeping that baby shut," mumbled another volunteer.

Outside, it was near twilight, but the temperature had risen above eighty degrees. The twenty-seven athletes competing in the men's 10,000-meter final filled the room, each of them trying to stay relaxed. Puffy headphones piped in music for a few and blocked out what little noise there was inside the room. Several men stretched, loosening muscles and trying to ignore their competitors. For others, the only thing to do was close their eyes and visualize the race.

Shadrack Kipchirchir leaned forward, elbows on knees. Looking down at his legs, he took a moment to massage each one. The muscles gave way under his fingers as he kneaded, then shook out each leg and stood to take another lap around the call room. The vibe was intense, like nothing he'd faced competing in college for Oklahoma State. Each of the men in this room deserved to be here, their presence a testament to the years of work it took to achieve this level of athletic success. For most of them, the 2016 United States Olympic Track and Field Trials here in Eugene, Oregon, would be the pinnacle of their professional careers. Only the top three finishers in this race would make the Olympic Team and represent the United States in Rio de Janeiro the following month.

Shadrack intended to be among them.

He'd busted his ass the past two post-collegiate years, not to mention the past four weeks. His coach had taken him up to altitude in Mammoth Lakes, California, with his teammates Paul Chelimo and later, Lenny Korir. They'd suffered through twice-daily workouts in thin, dry air that left them lying on the track gasping, their noses dripping with blood. It was, their coach said, the right kind of training to prepare them for the Trials. The same kind of training that the other top runners were undertaking, including the Nike-sponsored athletes now sitting in the call room with him.

"Just remember, Shaddy," he'd been instructed, "they've got nothing on you and Lenny. Your workouts have been practically identical. The two of you've had the same training that they've had, and the only thing standing in your way now is what's in your head. You've got this. Plus . . . you're wearing the right singlet."

That singlet now hung loose over black shorts with green trim. A camouflage print ran up the lower half where it met the upper, a pale green solid with the word ARMY stretching across the front in bold, black letters. It was a simple top, a contrast to what the other athletes wore, each of them sponsored by big-name shoe companies. Shadrack had once wondered if they'd considered signing him after college. A less than stellar showing at top races almost certainly ruled out a fancy running contract, but the more defining features were his name, the color of his skin and his birthplace, a traditional mud hut in rural Kenya. He presumed he was therefore at the bottom of the sponsorship totem pole.

Instead, he'd found a home in the United States Army, an unlikely but welcoming place for a recent grad with his background. His brother had preceded him, entering after his own college graduation, and now serving as a military vehicle mechanic. It was a decent option, and Shadrack had enlisted in the fall of his senior year of college, hearing only later that he could continue running in the Army if he met the time standard to be assigned to the Army's World Class Athlete Program, also known as WCAP. Though this wasn't what had inspired him to enlist, he'd gone for it, following the same path as any other recruit. Basic training, advanced training and then he'd met the time standard and was assigned to the WCAP unit, with Lenny and Paul not far behind. For eighteen months, they'd been stationed in Oregon, occasionally crossing paths with the Nike professional distance runners training nearby. Running could be a lonely sport, but Shadrack felt a part of something bigger with the Army behind him.

"Hey, brother, you good?" Lenny whispered to him in Kalenjin.

Though the room was quiet, nobody noticed as the two of them stole a quick conversation. With only a couple minutes until the event volunteers led them to the track, talking to Lenny was a needed break in the tension.

"Yeah, I'm good. Just ready to get out there. The heat's intense, man. Eighty-two degrees. Some of these guys are gonna crash."

"No doubt. We'll be okay, but nobody's breaking any records today, that's for damn sure. Hey . . . you know where anyone's sitting?" Lenny asked.

"Nah. I told Paul they could get close if they wanted, but I doubt we'll hear them. There's 20,000 people out there screaming."

"The only spectators that matter to me are those at the Pentagon," Lenny said.

Both knew the importance of the race. If any one of the Army runners qualified for the Olympics in Rio, it would signal a turning point for the World Class Athlete Program. Plenty of American boxers and wrestlers had made prior Olympic teams wearing the Army jersey, but never runners.

Shadrack nodded and looked over at the double doors leading to the track. One of the volunteers had cracked it open, walkie talkie in hand as he got word that it was time. Heat and noise trickled in again. Shadrack could see the edge of the track, red lanes offset with an infield of bright green turf. The low rumble of the massive crowd caught the attention of the other men in the room, and they began to take headphones off, shoving them into backpacks under each chair.

Taking one last sip from his bottle of fuel, Shadrack bent over to give the laces on his racing spikes one last tug. At 5'8" he was far from the tallest man in the race, but easily one of the leanest. Despite packing on the calories the past few weeks, the training had taken a toll and it was hard to keep close to the 120 pounds he needed for the strength to race well. His hair was cut short, buzzed close to his scalp. Deep-brown eyes took in the scene, and he glanced at Lenny one more time, flashing a final smile and offering a fist bump.

"Don't let him go, Shaddy. Just don't let him go," Lenny said in English now, soft enough that nobody heard.

The event volunteer stationed at the door looked up and spoke in a loud voice. "It's time now, men. Let's go. Top six . . . don't forget you're back here for drug testing when you're done."

Swinging wide, the double doors opened and with it the heat, the crowd noise, the smell of the rubber track baking, and the offer of promise and agony for the next half hour.

The stadium announcer's voice broke through the noise as the men stepped from the call room onto the asphalt foyer leading to the track.

"Now entering Hayward Field are your competitors for the final of the men's 10,000 meters. Six point two miles."

Walking into the light, Shadrack looked up at the stadium seating. Somewhere out there was his teammate Paul, most likely talking pre-race strategy a mile a minute to anyone who'd listen, including Shadrack's wife Elvin. It pained Shadrack to think of what she must be going through. Watching him race was stressful, and he knew she could tell that he'd been lying when he told her he'd play it conservative tonight for the first half of the race. There was practically no chance she wouldn't spend the race pacing to and from various points in the stadium.

Elvin Kibet's running accolades nearly matched her husband's. She'd been his biggest cheerleader for years and knew this world just as well as he did. Once the race started, she knew the feeling of settling into a rhythm, listening to both body and legs. She suspected she'd be able to tell once Shadrack started the race how he was feeling and what his game plan was. The two of them could've had entirely different lives in Kenya, but somehow, they'd ended up here in the United States, together. She knew his life and his running better than anyone, no matter what country they were in. The other men on the track surely had faced obstacles to get here tonight, but she believed what she and Shadrack had sacrificed together would count for something.

Elvin heard the call to the start line from the stadium announcer as she was leaving the bathroom. Her former college competitors were swarming the halls of Hayward Field, making things more stressful. If she could just make it to her seat without anyone recognizing her or wanting to talk, all would be well.

Elvin twisted long braids around her fingers as she found her seat. The tank top she wore was already damp from stress and clinging to her 5'0" frame. She caught Paul's eye as she passed his row, several in front of hers.

"You made it," he said, nodding to her.

She paused, noticing how many Army officials had come for the race. They filled up the seats in this small section, eyes glued to the track as the athletes found their lanes. It was a walk Elvin knew from taking it herself many times in college. She could put herself in Shadrack's shoes, a mix of nerves but peace in knowing the hard work was done. Arriving at the starting line uninjured and in top shape signaled he was ready.

"I did make it, which I'm counting as a victory," she said to Paul. "You guys have worked so hard. I just want this to go well."

"He's got this, Elvin. He was born for this. Just watch," Paul replied.

Elvin nudged into her seat. Shielding her eyes from the last of the day's bright sunlight, she wondered if her husband knew exactly where she was sitting.

The athletes were taken to the starting line, one group slightly ahead and further out on the track than the other. Shadrack gave quiet thanks that his group was starting in a shaded section on the track, allowing a few additional minutes of protection from the sun. *I'm not going to let the Army down*, he thought. *They've given me everything*. With the announcer continuing introductions, each runner dusted off jitters, shaking out arms and legs.

"Representing the United States Army, please welcome Leonard Korir and Shadrack Kipchirchir."

Polite claps gave way to bigger cheers as the next runner was introduced.

"He was a silver medalist in the 1,500 meters at the 2004 Athens Olympics, and here to try to make his fifth Olympic team, it's Bernard Lagat!"

Shadrack looked over and smiled at Bernard. They knew each other well. At forty-one, track fans weren't convinced he had enough in the tank to make the top three spots, but Shadrack knew the kind of grit Bernard had.

"Also, please welcome former Oregon Duck and silver medalist in this event at the 2012 London Olympics, Galen Rupp!"

This was Galen's home track, and it was apparent. Everyone in the crowd was pulling for him. Shadrack had studied race videos night after night for months, preparing his strategy and becoming comfortable with the race tactics he knew were about to be unleashed. Galen was at the top of his game, and Shadrack knew if he could just hang onto him, he'd be sitting on the Olympic team. Galen turned around, waving at the 20,000 adoring fans on all sides. The last to be introduced, he toed the line and waited for instructions.

"All right, men, let's have a clean race," the starter yelled.

He stood on the infield, two steps up on a riser. Lifting his right arm, a starting pistol pointed to the sky. A slight pause stilled the crowd, then the command "Set," and with the starting shot, a puff of white smoke dissipated over the infield. The two groups of athletes converged after a hundred meters, settling into an easy pace. Rhythmic clapping greeted the pack as they came around the first lap, followed by more words from the stadium announcer.

"Twenty-five laps around the track for this race," he said.

Shadrack tried to calm his mind as the first few laps passed. Jostling for position, the pack of men watched the race clock with every lap. Sweat covered each of them, and as arms grazed one another, it mixed in slippery patches. *One lap at a time*, Shadrack thought. *You're here to fight*. He imagined himself an hour from now, discussing where to order pizza and sliding into the passenger seat of his coach's yellow Corvette. Breathing from the other men quickened as they finished the first four laps marking a mile. A volunteer stood in the fourth lane, just outside the pack as it came around the bend. She held cups of water, arms outstretched. Shadrack thought about how out of place she looked here, as if it were a turkey trot. Any one of these men running sub-five-minute miles would never have the desire to stop for water at this pace, despite the heat.

Six laps in, Galen picked up the pace. Shadrack hung back, aware of Galen's strategy to create distance on the field but not yet ready to take the bait. He saw Galen's coach behind the blue fencing, shooting Galen a look as he passed. Within seconds, the group was back together as Galen slowed. The men could feel each other grinding, and as they reached the halfway mark, the field began to stretch out. Unrelenting, the sun refused to hide, and several of the runners began to falter. Shadrack tried to channel himself back to the days in Mammoth Lakes—Lenny and Paul grunting on either side, the three of them collapsing on the dirt path at the end of their fifteen-mile runs at noon. Stealing a glance on the turn, he saw Lenny still in the hunt ten yards behind him. *Hallelujah, brother. Don't go anywhere. I need you.*

With twelve laps to go, Galen pulled away again. It was the move Shadrack had prepared for. He was in the big leagues now, and Galen was the best in the business. Shadrack could feel the crowd watching as they tried to see who'd respond. He knew they'd be scrambling if he followed, looking in their race booklets to try to figure out who he was. At the moment, he was just another runner with the phrase "Kenyan-born" forever attached to his profile. Predictably, Bernard Lagat gave chase, passing Shadrack and catching up with Galen. Bernard and Galen were Nike teammates and had likely worked on this plan a hundred times.

Shadrack considered his options, which weren't plentiful. In a matter of seconds, the distance between the Nike duo and the rest of the pack would grow. With it, any chance of hanging on would disappear. His spirit would be crushed. Shadrack looked up, and seeing an American flag flying over Hayward Field, he accelerated, reaching for the unknown.

Chapter Two

Elvin

Kapchorwa, Kenya
February 1990

Warmth tickled Grace Kibet's cheeks as she pushed open the door to the mud hut. Though it was only February, the ice coating the grass outside seemed to be melting earlier than usual. From across the village, she could see two elderly midwives walking briskly in her direction. Inside, Grace's four children began to stir, their bodies packed tightly into a space that would soon have to fit another baby.

"Let's go, woman," one of the midwives whispered, sidling up next to her. "If your water has broken already, there's no telling how fast this baby will be here."

"Thank you for checking on me this morning," Grace responded. "It feels too soon. My girls will have to be ready."

Items on a mental checklist ticked off one by one as she took another deep breath of the Kenyan morning air.

Put the firewood above the stove.

Check the supply of potatoes.

Secure the fence lining the garden.

All tasks the girls would need to attend to the next few days.

Grace's water had broken unexpectedly, the remnants dripping down her leg as she slipped back inside and stepped around the sleeping bodies of her eldest daughters, Hilda and Sylvia. At ages nine and seven, the girls would have to care for their younger siblings until their parents returned with the new baby. Already schooled in the basics of farming and cooking, Grace wasn't worried about the girls carrying the load. This was her fifth delivery in nine years and though it appeared to be an early arrival, she assumed the baby would be well enough that she could come home in a couple days. In the meantime, the children would survive with the help of neighbors and Grace wouldn't be far away, delivering in a mud hut on the other side of the village. Her husband Peter was in the middle of a long stretch working far from home for the military. Without access to a telephone, she'd have to send a messenger to let him know he was a father again. His only means of transportation was a bike. It would take days for him to return home.

"Hilda, darling."

"Mama?" Hilda woke fully as Grace put a hand on her arm.

"The baby's coming early. I must go across the village. Take care of your sisters and brother. Do the chores we talked about last night. I'll send word when the baby is here."

Hilda nodded. Though only nine years old, her memory held strong with the visions of her youngest siblings being born. Her mother's screams at the very end of childbirth from across the village. How the elderly women of the village seemed to know how to handle this terrifying mix of pain and life. With one final hug, her mother was gone, gingerly walking across the village paths while stopping for contractions.

At 8,500 feet, Kapchorwa is a village in the Great Rift Valley in Kenya. The nearest major towns are Eldoret to the northwest and Iten, further north in the Kerio Valley. The valley is ten kilometers wide and eighty kilometers long. The area is a depressed segment of crust, also known as a graben, which is an elongated fault block marked by a series of parallel escarpments that were created when two tectonic plates pulled apart. With its dry climate and clean, thin air, Iten has become a mecca for high-performance runners over the past two decades.

As the valley spreads south, it melts into hilly terrain paved with the territory's signature red dirt. Cows wander the roads; young boys are responsible for their care. On Sundays, families dress in traditional African finery and walk these same dusty roads together to their churches, often miles away. It's a vast and colorful landscape that's remained largely unspoiled by development and technology for decades.

Winding sideways from the main roads are smaller farming communities, each with their own organized town centers. Kapchorwa is one such community. Its main shopping center is a dirt road consisting of butchers, shoe repair shops, and dark but lively teahouses. Each business is equipped with a utilitarian tin roof. Hand painted, wooden signs call out to the locals in English, "Bank" and "Photocopy" to indicate the services provided inside. Women set up blankets on the sides of the road to sell vegetables harvested that morning. The children of Kapchorwa entertain themselves by spinning tops made from plastic bottlecaps in the dirt and kicking soccer balls in the expansive field behind the primary school. It's a community where everyone knows each other, and visitors are warmly welcomed. Indeed, the name Kapchorwa means "place of friends."

Beyond the boundaries of the center of Kapchorwa, deeper still into the hillsides, are even more remote villages. Connected by narrow, rocky bike paths, they are the heart of Kenya. It was in one such village five kilometers away from Kapchorwa Center that Grace took steps to the place she'd birth her fifth child. Only twenty families lived in her village, each in a traditional mud home.

Her husband had labored over their home. Peter Kibet hadn't been satisfied until every layer of the home's walls felt secure. Timber from trees on their property served as the hut's circular framework and it was then filled with layers of red and white clay. A finishing layer of cow dung ensured the home would be protected from heavy rains. Mixing each layer of the clay before applying it provided the most enjoyment of the entire process.

"Harder, Baba, harder!" his children had squealed.

His bare feet had marched up and down on the ground in a pile of red mush, squishy clay running between each toe. It was the only way to ensure the perfect texture before applying it to their walls. Much like the stomping of grapes, it was a moment of delight for the children.

Once the walls had been finished, Peter had collected grass and tree branches to construct the roof. Tightly packed, they covered the home and kept out the intense sun and wind. There was one window situated above the clay stove. Smoke escaped through this window when cooking was going full steam. A ledge above the stove warmed their daily *ugali*, a dense maize porridge.

The family's focus was on the basics . . . enough *ugali* to make it through their days and ample hands to tend to the cattle, sheep, and crops. Privacy wasn't something they knew or even considered, and emotions weren't widely shared. It was enough to have a warm home, insulated from the rainy season. They knew each other's secrets, sleeping patterns, and morning habits intimately. All they owned scattered the floor of the hut. A few tin pots in the kitchen corner, two sets of clothes per child, a durable cow hide for each family member to sleep upon. Only their parents owned shoes, and even those had been repaired twenty times over. Hilda, Sylvia, and Robert had begun going to school, but there was no sign of books or notepads. Like all other kids in remote Kenyan farming villages, they'd been instructed by teachers to practice their multiplication tables without such luxuries. Instead of using pencils and paper, they used sticks and dirt on the floor of their home or outside in the blazing sun.

Grace's labor persisted for hours. "It's almost time, Grace. It's almost time to push."

"I cannot. It's too many mouths to feed. How will I care for another?"

"You will, woman. You will like we all do. You're a strong Kalenjin woman and you'll birth this baby and many more."

Her pain intensified, the muscles of her inner thighs straining and her lower back on fire. The herbs and oils that the midwives had used to help with discomfort were long rendered useless. Deeply breathing, she focused her thoughts on more peaceful places and happier times.

All her life, Grace had been a daddy's girl. His unfulfilled dreams of travel and adventure for himself had seeped into her. The two were constant companions, and he encouraged her love of travel, taking her to Nairobi which felt worlds away from their village. The city and its nightlife were full of promise to her as a teenager, but now the travels she'd dreamed of slowly slipped away with each birth. Her husband's constant absences didn't help. With fields to tend and animals to care for, Grace needed each child to sustain the family. Love for each of her children was a given, but the hugs that used to infuse her mothering seemed less frequent. She relied heavily on her mother-in-law for all jobs she used to do herself, including the provision of tenderness.

"Baby is coming, Grace!"

The midwife gripped her forearm.

As Grace gave one final push, she sensed hands reaching down to gently guide the baby out.

"It's a girl!"

The infant was placed on Grace's chest, face down and covered with a cloth. The baby screamed for a moment, then quieted as her cord was snipped. Grace's hand rested on top of her new daughter, her fourth girl. Grace's body was weak with exhaustion, yet she was overcome with an unfamiliar sensation. Her insides still felt full, and her pain hadn't disappeared. Looking down she saw one of the midwives sopping up blood. It was pouring from her at an alarming rate. This was more blood than Grace remembered from the other babies. A hand slipped inside her, feeling for clues. The midwives looked at each other with concern and one reached over, taking Grace's hand, and bringing it to her breast. She was sick with realization, knowing that she was being asked to massage her nipples, a method of inducing yet more labor.

"Glory be to God, there's another one, Grace," one of the midwives called out. "We can't wait longer. More pushing! Strong pushing, Grace!"

There was no time to think. Everything froze. Five mouths to feed would've been a struggle, but six would surely kill her. The first twin would have to sacrifice breast milk for the second, which would be lighter and might not make it through the night. Daring to think this might be a blessing, Grace lifted onto her elbows.

Howls pierced the walls of the mud hut. By now it was late afternoon, the labor having lasted many hours. Children walked past the mud hut, knowing from experience that the screams meant another member of the tribe was being born.

There were two. The second indeed smaller than the first.

"Another girl!"

Grace closed her eyes while the midwives cleaned the baby. A part of her lifted away, far from the mud hut, drifting into the places she dreamed of returning to. Far from motherhood. Far from the responsibilities of caring for their home and tending cattle. And so far from pregnancy and childbirth.

A moment later she had a light bundle placed on her chest next to the first. Her second baby was so tiny that Grace imagined she'd fit into a coat pocket. It was possible she wouldn't make it to daybreak.

"Tomorrow. We must go to the clinic tomorrow," she heard one of the elders say. "The babies are underweight and need attention. It's the only chance to keep them both alive."

"She cannot make the trip alone. We'll have to go with her, and the children will need to take care of themselves," the other replied.

"They can do it. Hilda is nine years old. Plenty old to watch after the others until their father returns."

Grace listened, secretly looking forward to nights in a fancy bed instead of on the cow hides they currently shared. Going to the clinic with such tiny babies would mean being taken care of for weeks. They'd need her to nurse, which meant they'd feed her well. She'd rest and be free from housework, caring for the animals and cooking. With any luck she'd be able to stay for a couple months, until the time of her original due date. For the moment, she'd need to find a way to keep the babies alive until tomorrow.

"Oh, sweet girls," Grace whispered, pulling back the blankets. "You've come into such a cruel world."

The firstborn was already nursing, eyes still shut. The second lay silent and so terribly small. Gently pulling her first away from her breast, she brought the second over, milk dribbling onto her lips. *This one is my priority*, Grace thought. *We all must make sacrifices. My first will be strong. She will survive.*

Elvin Kibet's tiny mouth twitched as she was pulled away from her mother's breast, and her eyes opened. Denied milk to save her twin, she looked at the world for the first time.

As sun rays cracked though the window the next morning, Grace overhead the elders whispering.

"1,100 grams for the first. 900 grams for the second," said one of the elders. She'd placed each baby on a makeshift scale weighted with rocks and pebbles.

"We must go now, Grace. Time is not on your side."

Willing herself with visions of warm meals and a comfortable bed, Grace walked slowly behind the elders. Each twin was carried by one of the old women. The trio and the two babies were headed to the main road, five kilometers away from the village. Once there, the van that stopped once a day would take them to the nearest clinic in a neighboring village. Plateau Clinic Hospital provided the best health care in the area. Newly opened and funded by foreigners, Grace had even heard that white doctors worked there.

"Peter will be so angry," Grace muttered as she walked. "These babies came early, and he only expected one."

"He will manage, and once they're older he'll be happy for the help," one of the elders replied.

She glanced down to see that the baby she was carrying, the tiny one, had woken from a nap. Grace had named this one Ivy, and like her sister Elvin, she came out without hair and only the faintest of fingernails. She'd need weeks of oxygen and special hand feedings to survive.

An hour later, Grace settled into a seat in the van, pulling back her shirt and bringing Ivy to her breast. Elvin remained wrapped up, practicing patience.

Peter Kibet received word about the birth of the twins several days later. As expected, his reaction was muted rather than joyful. It was an excuse to leave his military work until his wife was able to return to the family, but equally exhausting to make the trek back and forth between their home in the village and the clinic. The thick wheels on his bike could only handle so many kilometers, so he often resorted to walking. This was an effort he could only undertake once a week. Leaving the village at 1:00 a.m., he'd walk eight hours, stay with Grace and the babies for a meal, catch her up on the happenings at home, then walk back to the village. He'd arrive late at night, only to be back to work in his fields the next day. His drinking made everything easier for him, at least for a few hours.

After many weeks of this routine, Hilda insisted on joining her father for a visit to the clinic. The absence of her mother had been stressful, and she couldn't believe her father's claims that there were two babies, and not just one. Not until she laid eyes on her sisters at Plateau Clinic did it sink in. Her father was right . . . times would be difficult.

Stealing a swig from a bottle shoved in his shirt pocket, Peter left the clinic one afternoon following a visit. The babies had made it through the first few weeks with regular feedings through tubes and syringes. Elvin and Ivy were growing, with Ivy catching up in weight to Elvin quickly. Ivy cried constantly and barely slept, while Elvin always appeared quiet and content. Only a few more weeks and he'd be free to return to his military job, escaping the village and family responsibilities.

Red dirt coated his shoes as he pedaled. He'd taken his bike this time and he turned off the main road and onto one leading to their home. Evening light mixed with dust kicking up from his tracks, but through the haze he thought he saw plumes of smoke. He pedaled faster.

When he heard the wails, his heart sank. One of the mud huts in the village was burning down. This wasn't uncommon, as each hut was topped with a grass roof and inside, fires burned for meals. Still, he hoped it was being contained.

As he got closer, Peter saw the unthinkable. The girls, Hilda and Sylvia, running toward him.

"Baba . . . the house is burning!" they screamed.

"My god, what happened?" he shouted, pedaling past them. His legs pushed hard, burning from the effort. The girls shouted something he only heard as "cat."

By the time he arrived at the house, it was clear the loss was catastrophic. Neighbors were desperately running with buckets of water from the river, but each one seemed fruitless. Accounting for his other two children, Peter could do nothing but watch as their home burned, holding his sobbing children. What had once been a magnificent home of mud and straw was now a soaking wet pile. His own hands had made it the perfect dwelling for their family. He'd built it himself and suddenly he realized he'd need to do so again. With the babies coming home soon and the rainy season ahead, he would have to act fast. The kids could go to their aunt's house in a neighboring village, and he'd recruit a few friends to help him put together a new home. Bigger, this time.

"I didn't mean it, Baba," his son Robert said. He'd inched over to his father as they watched neighbors wander away with empty buckets.

"Son, it's not your fault."

"But it IS! Baba, it IS his fault," Hilda cried.

"Child, what happened?" he asked.

Robert looked down, unable to make eye contact as his three sisters clung to each other, crying.

"I told you, Baba . . . it was the cat. Robert set the cat's tail on fire, and she ran up the walls. The roof caught on fire."

Beyond the ruins of the home, Peter saw the cat, lying in a soft pile of maroon dirt, gently cleaning what was left of its charred tail.

Indigenous to East Africa, the Kalenjin are a collection of 200-year-old tribes, each linked through culture and language. Though there are small populations of Kalenjin in Uganda and Tanzania, its present-day roots are primarily in the Western Rift Valley area of Kenya. The Kalenjin of today has political and territorial units imposed by the British colonial structure, and the group's tight-knit society was impacted further by British domination. Villages generally have elders who oversee minor disputes and handle affairs with neighboring communities. Daily life tends to revolve around caring for cattle and crops, with formal education becoming more critical in recent decades.

Among the people, a unique social order has until recently determined much of how individuals will move through life. This distinction is known as age sets, and as the name suggests, age sets are a collection of individuals who pass through stages of growth together. This provides a way to bond members of individual tribes and foster an alternate support system to the family, much the same way religion forms similar bonds. Though families today are largely Christian, traditional Kalenjin religion is based on the concept of a supreme god, Asis, who is represented in the form of the sun. Each village has an elder who serves as an expert in rituals, both religious and cultural.

Today, six million Kalenjin are divided into sub-tribes, each with its own culture and slightly different version of the Kalenjin language. The linguistic differences are subtle, allowing ease of communication among tribes. In addition to Kalenjin, most people today speak Swahili and English since they are official languages and taught in school. The focus placed on the teaching of both Swahili and English differs, with rural communities offering less instruction than bustling city centers.

In 1990, Elvin and Ivy Kibet had entered a world of contrasts. Everyday rules of their village were clear, but the goal of many villagers was to leave Kapchorwa for bigger cities in Kenya, which seemed complex. Simplicity bred joy, but also patterns of poverty that deepened over time. In all of this, their fates were tied not only to each other, but also to the dreams already living inside their tiny bodies as they made their way back to the safety of home in the village.

Chapter Three

Shadrack

Cheboiywo, Kenya
February 1989–2001

Stretching the fabric of her sling, Rose Tirop slipped another piece of firewood onto her back. The load she'd collected would be plenty for another week. Enough to fuel the stove and keep the family warm at night. Located just outside the Kerio Valley, the nights in Cheboiywo were chilly, but not as cold as those higher in the hills. Rose had heard sometimes villagers in the mountains nearby awoke to icy patches of grass. Her four children would love nothing more than to see ice, she thought.

Beginning the walk back to the village, Rose calculated the effort she'd need to put in to return for another load after lunch. It would be a delicate balance between serving her family's needs and making sure this baby didn't arrive early. Waking up in the morning, she knew she was close to delivery time. Reaching the village, she saw her oldest son Titus jogging up the dirt path leading to their home. The eight-year-old was arriving home for lunch from school with his younger sister. It was a three-kilometer barefoot run they knew by heart and managed to avoid only when it was time to harvest their crops of maize, beans, and potatoes.

"Titus, fetch some water from the well, dear one," Rose said.

"Momma, you've been in the forest. Baibai told you not to go out anymore," Titus answered.

"Never mind him. Your father is full of big ideas on when this baby will arrive. I think another week. Now water . . . quickly, please."

She ducked inside the hut, finding her youngest two children asleep. The baby was curled up next to his sister, and he shifted as Rose unloaded the firewood. Sitting down, she gathered him closer, offering her full breast.

Their home consisted of three huts, all constructed with mud and grass. John Tirop was a local politician with a strong work ethic and a big laugh. His wife Rose balanced her babies with a desire to work outside the home, a rarity for Kalenjin women. She'd opened a local shop which sold simple groceries and household goods. Only when she had time was it open, but she longed for the days when she'd be there all day and expand her offerings.

Rose shifted, trying to get comfortable. Her back was beginning to cramp. Underneath her, she felt a cool wetness. The lining of her skirt darkened as she spread her legs, making sure the children couldn't see. There was no need to upset them.

"Well, imagine that . . . the man was right," she whispered to herself.

An hour later, three of them had made it onto a local bus headed to the nearest clinic. Rose, John, and a midwife. Her contractions were arriving fiercely as the bus pulled up in front of the clinic, its sign still freshly painted blue and white from an infusion of foreign money: "Plateau Clinic Hospital."

"You'll be well taken care of, Rose," John said as they unloaded themselves. "I'll be back in three days. Think about a name."

"This baby will be a boy. He's been feeling like a boy all these months," she replied.

John chuckled, his bright smile showing. "If you say so, love."

He kissed her on the cheek as she walked away, her hand cradling her low-slung tummy. Rose offered last words to him as he left.

"He's a boy, so prepare for more hands to help carry the load. And I've already thought of a name. He'll be Kipchirchir."

It was a name that meant "fast labor" in Kalenjin which suited her new baby perfectly, she thought. The child would hold this for his middle name, keeping the family's last name of Tirop, at least for the time being.

"And his first name?" John shouted back.

"You remember the story I love? The one that about the boys in Babylon. They were true to their beliefs and refused to obey the king's silly rules. He'll be just like those boys. This child will be strong and independent and willing to stand up for himself. He will be Shadrack."

The pattern of naming Baby Shadrack Kipchirchir Tirop after what was happening at the time of his birth is in keeping with Kalenjin tradition. The weather, the time of day, or a special occasion often determines how a child is named. Pairing this name with a Christian first name has become common, as is assigning a father's surname to children. This results in many Kalenjin having three names at birth. It's only when children become independent that a twist enters the equation.

In adolescence, many Kalenjin youth opt to change their names. This could involve dropping and/or changing part of their name. It's a move that some make to signal greater independence and forge new identities. Baby Shadrack would be nicknamed Tata and Shaddy, and he'd eventually grow up and drop the Tirop when he was a teenager. On February 22, 1989, however, he was just another newborn baby from a local village, swaddled and healthy at Plateau Clinic.

The land where the Tirop family lived was a vast swath of land located thirty-eight kilometers from Eldoret. Nestled between farming communities, Shadrack's grandfather had claimed rights to the land after it had been deserted by British colonists in the 1960s. Because it was land that he'd previously been enslaved upon, it felt a familiar and natural transition to now grow it as his own. Fertile and ideal for harvesting maize, the wealth from the land had allowed Grandfather to take a second wife. Polygamy was a common feature of the Kalenjin sub-tribe to which the family belonged, the Nandi. Eventually, Grandfather's two families merged children and grandchildren who supported one another through their shared paternal bond.

Shadrack's father John had been born to the first wife, a traditional Nandi woman strong in character and wisdom. Her earlobes had been pierced and stretched when she was young, creating an oval-shaped flap of loose earlobe skin that hung nearly to her shoulders. Her grandchildren grew fond of playing with her earlobes as she cooked and told stories. With property adjacent to Rose and John, the children saw their grandmother daily.

John Tirop's touch with his children was gentle but firm and led by an extraordinary belief in the importance of education. His career as a politician took him away from home frequently, but when present, the children were on their best behavior. The slightest bit of distraction from studying meant a caning on their bottoms. Each child was expected to graduate their first eight years in school at the top of their class. Extra money was poured into supplemental curriculum. When he was present, Monday through Saturdays were John's domain, while Rose held onto Sundays. The huge, drooping, leafy tree in the family's front yard provided shade for forty children who'd pull up seats on wooden benches and listen to her Sunday school lectures.

"Pretend you have a dress on, Shaddy!" squealed his little sister Sheilah.

He couldn't believe he was being forced to play make believe again. The game with his younger sisters took endless turns after school each day. One day he'd be forced to play teacher, another he was the old lady who sold mangoes down the road. Shadrack grumbled at the role he was being instructed to play today, a farmer's wife. Still, he relished the time with his sisters rather than the hours of work in the fields his brothers were doing. There were nine of them now, and Momma swore she was finished.

At age twelve, Shadrack had become a de facto mother so that their own mother could now grow her business. He was doing it all. Washing clothes, cooking, cleaning the home, helping his siblings with homework.

Rose's transition to work outside the home hadn't been easy. To sustain the family's school fees and her shop inventory, their father John had taken a loan to buy supplies. When the loan couldn't be paid, loan collectors had arrived, taking all their possessions. Everything they owned, including their furniture and the family's cows, had been loaded onto trucks. The vision of his pregnant, sobbing mother holding onto his older brother Titus had faded, but he'd heard Titus talk about the incident, and how it had changed him.

"It's our job to care for the younger ones, Tata," Titus said, using Shadrack's nickname.

"We can help make things easier for Baibai and Momma if we do what we can to let them earn money outside the home. Better yet, we all need to strive to leave the village someday."

His brother's motivation worked its way into Shadrack's consciousness, and in little ways, he, too, began to support his younger siblings. He'd saved his shillings for months working odd jobs in local fields when he could, with hopes of buying his first pair of shoes. When the day finally came, it was a monumental purchase. He had been ten years old and the shoes he bought allowed him to run to school without injuries to his feet. Each night he'd carefully clean them, proudly slipping them next to his school clothes.

Predictably, his younger brother Nicholas began to beg for the shoes. Just once, he'd ask. Just once could he wear them to school? Or perhaps for a week? Shadrack's resolve withered, and after only a few weeks, he handed the shoes to Nicholas permanently and returned to running barefoot to school full time.

Now, two years later, he maintained his vigilance in caring for his little sisters. If that meant playing a farmer's wife, bring it on.

"I've been taking care of you since you were three weeks old, and this is my payback?" he asked.

"Please, Shaddy. You have those skinny, long legs that look so funny in a dress."

The four-year-old looked up at him, her eyes wide. She had the same look as him, her perfect oval face marked with full cheeks. Both of their hairlines started from a place halfway up their heads. Tight curls shaved close. They'd seen photos of Kenyans in Nairobi, both men and women, who wore long dreadlocks or braids, but like most other villagers, keeping hair short for both boys and girls was easiest and less expensive. Shadrack's forehead was marked with a crescent-shaped scar which he'd received at the hands of a neighbor boy who'd taken aim at him with a slingshot and a rock the previous year.

Shadrack lifted his voice into a falsetto, "Time for me to milk Cheboit," he said.

Sheilah roared with laughter, running to get a bucket. Shadrack figured if he had to play a farmer's wife, he might as well knock out chores in the same breath.

"Here you go, Mrs. Farmer," she said, handing him a yellow milking bucket.

"I must say, Cheboit, you sure have enough milk today to make a kilo of cheese," Shadrack said as he squeezed her udders and released the liquid into the bucket.

His sisters sat watching, forgetting their own roles in the game of make believe. He'd miss the time with them. Though caring for his sisters was his main job at home, he needed to balance his own studies. His parents never let them miss school, and in a couple years he'd have to go to boarding school just like his older siblings. His first choice was Kipkabus Boys' High School. To get in, he'd need good grades. While other kids in school fooled around and were caned as a result, Shadrack had maintained a decent average and tried to remain invisible.

His time to shine would come someday.

Chapter Four

Struggle

Kapchorwa, Kenya
1996–2004

"Ivy, you're too loud. You made her fall into the mud!" Elvin barked. "She's my favorite cow and your screaming scared her."

She ran her hands through her cropped hair. Her sister had grown much larger than Elvin, making the girls unrecognizable as twins. A new mud hut had been built before they'd arrived home from Plateau Clinic as infants, similar but bigger than the first.

The six-year-olds tromped up the hill following Cheptelit, Elvin's pride and joy. The heifer she milked every day was covered in mud and weeds after a harrowing plunge into the river and muck at the bottom of the family's field. It had taken eight men to lift her out, but she'd recover and be ready for a milking the next morning as usual.

"It suits her. She trampled the fence last week and ate our vegetables," Ivy replied.

At the top of the hill, the girls could see Gogo, hands on hips. Their grandmother, Baba's mother, had recently moved to their property, living in her own hut near theirs. Their grandfather, Guga, had another home in a far corner of the property and it was his job to take care of the cattle. Baba was still gone doing military work far away and since the twins' arrival there had been three more babies, two boys and a girl. That made nine. After the last one, Mama had disappeared, leaving the eight children alone and taking only the baby with her. It wasn't uncommon for women in Kenya to abandon their families when they grew too large. Often men found second wives or lovers, driving first wives to alcoholism and sometimes they'd leave home. It stung that it was the fate of Elvin's own family. Soon, her older sisters would be heading to boarding school in Iten. It would fall to the middle children to keep the younger ones alive.

Gogo made everything better. Her grandmother kept them together. She always managed to have food in her house when their stove was empty. Somehow her kitchen always brewed with a meal, even after a full day of milking cows and fetching firewood and water from the river. Her work ethic inspired her grandchildren, but even better were the stories she told.

Elvin wandered inside, settling into her usual seat next to Gogo as she stirred a pot. It had been another long day at school. The journey of five kilometers each way was one Elvin could undertake with her eyes closed. Coming home for lunch meant doing it four times each day, for a total of twenty kilometers per day. Like most of the other village children, she covered the distance in the most efficient way possible. By running. Without shoes.

Elvin and Ivy enjoyed the routine of school, though occasionally Elvin was bullied for her small size. Ivy tried to stand up for her sister, and from time to time, the two of them would march to the middle school building and find Hilda. Their sister was just about to leave for boarding school, but as the oldest girl, she cared for her younger siblings and took them home when they needed escape from the school bullies.

"School is important, my sweet child," Gogo said. "There's so much about the world you need to learn."

Gogo's bright blue eyes matched her father's and Elvin wished they'd been passed down to her. None of her brothers and sisters had these eyes. She'd heard that in other parts of the world blue eyes were common. Maybe this was part of what Gogo meant when she told her grandchildren to learn about the world.

"I love school so far, Gogo. The other children like to fool around but I think it's fun to listen to what the teacher has to say."

"You're like me. A strong head on your shoulders. You must keep it there and not let anyone else tell you what to do."

"I want to find a boy I like, and make that my own choice, too."

Gogo laughed, "Well, I certainly hope that's the case for you. You know it wasn't my choice to marry your grandfather, but perhaps times will be changed by the time you marry."

"But are you happy?" Elvin asked.

"It was scary at first to marry someone I didn't know, but I got used to it. I didn't have the luxury of not listening to my parents back then. But I learned to stand up to your grandfather when he hit me and that made me stronger."

Elvin squirmed, imagining her grandmother as a young woman being smacked by a new husband. It seemed unfathomable compared to the woman who sat before her.

"You know I went away just like your mother has. I took my children and left for a few years before I returned to your grandfather. When I came back, I found us this land in the village, and I made it mine."

Gogo scraped the sweet crusty sides of the pot and put them into a silver bowl, handing it to Elvin.

"Guga didn't want the land?"

"Well perhaps he did, but he was too drunk to know any better, so I registered the land in my name. It's not something that happens in Kenya, but I did it all on my own."

"And what happened when the British came?"

"They certainly didn't know I was a landowner, and they didn't try to take my land, but they forced me to work on their plantations. The time of the colonists wasn't a happy time, child. Many people lost their lives and our country lost much of its culture. Don't ever forget where you come from, Elvin. No matter where you go in this world."

"But did you? Did you work for them?"

"Sometimes. Sometimes I'd take your father. He was a baby and I'd have to strap him onto my back and work in their fields. Other times I'd refuse. They'd beat me, but I wouldn't go. It's important to have principles, sweet child."

Elvin let the words sink in, her fingers sweeping up the last bits of crust from the bowl.

Chapter Four

Under the shadow of their property, a river stretched through the village. Down a hill, it provided both drinking and bathing water. Without a well, every day's main task was to ensure enough buckets were brought from the river up the hill and dumped into a larger tank. On days when they'd bathe, Elvin and her siblings would carry down slivers of soap. Stripping naked, they'd diligently wash their clothes, laying them on rocks to dry while they washed their bodies. Once the clothes were dry enough to put back on, they'd trudge up the hill carrying water.

Christmas arrived and with it, some joy. The family had Mama back, at least temporarily. Elvin and her siblings loved this time of year. It always meant a little more food and time spent decorating their mud hut with thicker layers of clay.

Standing on the side of the river, Elvin gnawed on the remnants of an ear of corn. Her older sister Valentine held a bucket, dipping it into the river.

"You're just standing there, silly girl. Help me," said Valentine.

Elvin took a step closer to the river, kernels of corn falling at her feet. The ground seemed unsteady, and she looked down, slipping as she tried to regain her footing. A sharp pain radiated from her ankle, but it wasn't until Valentine's scream that she realized.

"Snake!" her sister yelled.

The sound of her sister's voice rocketed through Elvin's body as she looked down. In the grass lining the river, a yellow snake with black dots slithered away into the bushes. Elvin felt sick, more from Valentine's screaming than the pain. Her brother Robert had heard the sounds, and along with a pile of villagers, was racing down the hill to the river.

"Oh my God, Elvin you've been bitten," Robert cried.

Valentine was still screaming, her arms wrapped around herself as some of the elders tried to calm her. The scene was more terrifying than the pain, though Elvin was beginning to realize the gravity of the bite.

"I can't feel my leg," she said.

The pain was kicking in, making her dizzy. A crowd had gathered and one of the elders took Elvin in his arms and carried her away from the river and up the hill. As he laid her on a patch of grass, Robert undid his belt and pulled it from around his waist. He was only ten years old, but seemed to know what he was doing. *How does he know what he's doing?* Elvin wondered.

"Sister, this will hurt, but it's going to stop the poison from going to your heart."

Robert wrapped the belt around her upper thigh and yanked. The grip stung, and she cried out loudly, with a scream now matching her sister's. Again, Robert pulled at the belt, tightening it so firmly that she knew the circulation in her leg was fading. Things were becoming fuzzy as she lay on her back. More villagers arrived, their chatter becoming louder as they hovered over her, planning.

"The child will die if she doesn't get help right away!" one of the villagers shouted.

"But what about Christmas?" Elvin mumbled.

Then she passed out.

She woke later in the arms of five of her neighbors and Robert. They held her in a prone position as they walked swiftly, allowing her to look up at the trees.

I've spent so much time looking down so I don't trip over rocks when I run to school, she thought. *I've never noticed the beauty of the treetops.* The wind blew as the leaves glistened, each one a slightly different shape.

It was the first time she'd left the village by anything other than the weight of her own two feet, and it felt odd.

"Where are we going?" she asked.

"We stopped in Kapchorwa to see if the local nurse could help, but she was in Eldoret," Robert said.

"So, we're taking you to Mama Koko."

"But . . . she's a witch!" Elvin responded.

Elvin remembered the whispers in school about Mama Koko. She was the last resort for elders in the village who were dying. A witch doctor.

Her mother had joined the caravan and put a hand on Elvin's shoulder. "She's all we have now, Elvin. You need help immediately."

The group walked on, at least a dozen of them, taking turns carrying her in shifts. Along the way, someone handed her a piece of bread. *How lucky am I today, to be eating bread*, she thought.

An hour melted into two as they crossed the river on the other side of town and into a forest that Elvin had never seen. Robert kept pace the entire way; his pants legs were covered with dirt. She made a mental note to thank him for saving her life, assuming that was the outcome. As they approached a simple mud hut, Mama Koko opened her door.

The woman looked about seventy years old and had short hair that was speckled gray and white. In her ears she wore big loops of red and gold. Elvin had never seen earrings that big, not even on Sundays when they made the journey to church. Billows of fabric swept the ground from her dress. Her skin was dark, with long arms ending in slender wrists and fingers.

"My daughter has been bitten by a snake," Elvin's mother said.

"What did it look like?" the old woman asked.

"Yellow. Yellow with black dots," Elvin whispered, her voice weak.

The pain from both the bite and the belt were intense.

"Yellow with black dots is serious. Come, come, and lay her on my table."

Stepping inside, the men rested Elvin cautiously on a table in the center of the hut, then scurried back outside. Mama Koko mixed several vials of powder and liquid together and got out a scalpel.

At six years old, curiosity was getting the best of Elvin.

"Are you a witch?" Elvin asked.

"Little girl, I am not a witch. I am a traditional medicine doctor, and I help more people in this village than regular doctors. Trust me. I will take care of you, but it will hurt, and you will not feel your leg for a long time."

"Will I heal?"

"Your mother will help you heal."

"My grandmother," Elvin replied under her breath, hoping her mother hadn't heard.

"Your grandmother, yes. She will need to clean this wound every day."

"But school . . . will I still be able to run to school?"

"With time, my child, with time. In three or four months you can return to school. Until then, your sisters and brothers can teach you."

"My sister Ivy will teach me. She knows I hate missing school. I'll make her give me lessons every night. I still want to be first in my class."

"I have no doubt you will, my child. You seem very strong. You've survived the long journey here today and you'll survive much more."

Taking Elvin's hands, she placed one in Robert's and one in her mother's. As far away as a kilometer, Elvin's screams could be heard as Mama Koko sliced deep into her leg at the bite mark, then poured the concoction into the wound.

Being bitten by the snake only strengthened Elvin's character. Ivy faithfully brought home lessons from school each night and Gogo attended to Elvin's wound. True to her word, she'd ended up first in her class at the end of the year, and again the following five years after that. At Kapchorwa Primary School, her teachers marveled at how advanced she was for a sixth grader.

The two trees that Peter had planted in the yard when he began his military service provided shelter from the rain. It was March and the rainy season meant crops would begin to flourish, turning the hillsides green. Mango trees and cabbage had sustained local farmers for a few months, but the rain would bring the promise of more food for Elvin's family. The fields that her grandfather had once maintained were falling into disrepair, leaving their plots of land uncultivated. Only through the generosity of neighbors and their donations of maize and vegetables could the family survive. Gogo did her best to pull together meals, but she was aging rapidly.

Meanwhile, it was getting more difficult to juggle the responsibilities of school and caring for her younger siblings.

Guga was now gone, his death the result of a tragic fall into a fire he'd built inside his hut. Baba had been around at the time, running to Kapchorwa for food and bringing the older children with him. He'd told

Elvin and Ivy not to let Guga make a fire inside, but the old man was now senile and didn't obey.

His leg had been badly burned and without money to pay for medicine or a doctor, Guga suffered for two weeks at home until he died. At eight years old, Elvin blamed herself, asking out loud at the funeral, "But who will take care of Guga's cows?"

One by one, the cows were sold.

Elvin was now eleven years old and there had been one final baby, her sister Daisy. Ten children in total. Her mother's visits home were rare. When she came, she often smelled of alcohol and Ivy would pick fights with her about her poor parenting. Sometimes her mother would take the younger children, disappearing for long periods to unknown places and then returning them, haggard-looking and unfed. Daisy's two-year-old stomach looked as if it contained a beach ball, and her hair was falling out in clumps.

"Collins, come with me!" Elvin called to her younger brother.

Ivy walked beside her, dressed in a torn school uniform that had been handed down four times. She and her sister had begun taking turns going to school on alternate days, then teaching each other the lessons they'd missed at night. When they weren't in school, they were working in the neighbor's fields.

"I'm going up the hill to the neighbor's house to work this morning. Come with me on your way to school, little man."

She suspected her effort to get Collins to school would be fruitless. Their mother had left this morning, with promises of coming home at lunch with milk. It was a vow she'd made before and never kept, but at age five, her younger brother held onto hope.

"She's not coming back, Collins, and school is important. I must work the fields today to earn a little money for our meat, but you should go to school. You know Baba was the very first one to graduate from primary school in 1974. If he was here, he'd want you to go. He'd want you to go to school as long as you could, like he did. Even high school."

Her brother shook his head, and Elvin could see his eyes welling.

"Okay, then stay here. I'll be back in a couple hours."

She watched her brother duck back inside the mud hut where he'd tend to his even younger siblings until Gogo came.

"I hate leaving them," Elvin said as they climbed the hill leading out of the village.

"Almost as much as you hate missing school, right?" replied Ivy.

"Exactly. You know my greatest fear is that I'll come home one day and find them gone or sick or even worse."

"Me, too. Mama is terrible for leading them on about returning."

Though the fields were dry, enough green remained on the trees that the village sparkled from the top of the hill. Terraced plots of red were connected by paths. Along the paths which connected families in the village were handsome fences made of twigs and vines. Many of the vines bore thorns to keep cattle at bay. Morning hours in the village were the most brilliant, with the hope of a new day.

"Go go go, Sissy. You're late. We'll be fine this morning. See you at lunch. Take good notes!" Elvin requested.

Ivy skipped into a run, her pace quickening as she floated down the crest of the hill toward Kapchorwa.

As Elvin was entering her middle school years, distance running was becoming popular seventy-five kilometers north in Eldoret and Iten. A team of young men from the area had been pulled together for the first global track and field competition for youth, the World Junior Championships, bringing home fourth place, just behind the United States and ahead of Great Britain. Athletes began to travel to Iten, enjoying its climate and altitude, along with success at the international level. By the late 1990s, a running mecca was born.

Escaping Kapchorwa for what Elvin knew would be a better life seemed light years away. Though the village had no phones or electricity, she'd started to hear stories of young Kenyans leaving the country to run competitively in places around the world. Robert said that their Auntie

Lornah was running in The Netherlands and would open a center in Iten to help train other young Kenyan athletes. Athletes were apparently running in packs around Iten to build their speed fast enough to be noticed by coaches from other countries.

The image baffled Elvin. *Running was a means of transport, not a sport or something you did for enjoyment*, she mused.

Meanwhile, with Gogo's encouragement, Hilda and Sylvia had gone to boarding school, studied hard, and managed to finish their high school years in Iten. The money Baba earned from the military was enough to cover their costs before it ran out every month. Traveling back and forth to the village was a near impossibility, so long stretches would pass between their visits to the village. Instead, Elvin relied on word of mouth to hear about their progress. To her amazement, both girls had started discussing running as a career after high school, and Hilda had recently left for The Netherlands to take a crack at college and running. Lornah had taken Hilda under her wing, and Elvin had heard that she even had a Dutch runner boyfriend.

Incomprehensible, she thought.

"Elvin, your work is excellent, but I'd like to see you more than two days a week," Teacher Kosgei said.

Her middle school math teacher at Kapchorwa Primary School had pulled Elvin aside to discuss the eighth grader's work. She was a star pupil, scoring at the top of the class even though she attended school less than half the week.

Wooden desks bumped together in the classroom. Elvin sat at one, stirring the dirt floor with her toe. On Fridays, the children would bring in cow dung, mix it with water and spread it all over the dirt floors, making it smooth and resistant to dust until Monday morning.

Windows lined one side of the classroom, with each pane of the lowest row painted blue to keep the children from staring outside during lessons. The paint had been chipped at over the years, likely starting with her father's fingernails. He'd been the "founder" of this school; the very first graduate and the only one in the family to go on to high school.

"I know things at home are hard. Your father was a great friend of mine in primary school, and I've tried to look after your family. He was kind to me, and I always like to repay kindness, no matter how many years have passed."

"I can try to come more often, but the little ones are alone," Elvin answered.

She liked Teacher Kosgei. She was one of the few who didn't beat students and had a tender voice and friendly eyes.

"I know your father is away working and your mother is not around, is she?"

Elvin shook her head.

"And food?"

Without a response, Teacher Kosgei continued.

"Elvin, if food is the barrier, I can help with that. Will you come to school if I provide you with food?"

"Not just food for me. Not just my lunch, but food for my brothers and sisters?" Elvin inquired.

"Yes, all of you. Your potential is enormous. I know you hate making mistakes, which is the mark of a good student. I can tell you won't believe me, but I have faith you could get into Moi Girls' High School in Eldoret if you were here five days a week, my child."

Moi was the best girls' high school in the country. The thought of being offered a spot there felt like a fantasy. Still, if Teacher Kosgei believed in her and would help her family, Elvin owed it a shot.

"If you feed my family, then yes, I'll come every day."

Teacher Kosgei crossed the room, opening the door to a little closet. Reaching inside, she pulled out a bag of potatoes and an armful of corn. It wasn't a lot, but it would sustain the family for a week.

Relief pulsed through Elvin, knowing that neither she nor Ivy would have to work in the fields next week.

"Every Friday. If you come to school all week long, I'll give you potatoes and corn every Friday. Deal?"

"Deal," Elvin said.

Gogo won't believe it, she thought, walking home with the bounty. *Potatoes for classes. Life doesn't get better than this.*

Chapter Five

Kipkabus

Kipkabus Boys' High School, Kenya
2003–2008

SHADRACK HEARD THE SCHOOL BELL RING AND FELT FOR CHANGE IN HIS pocket. Five shillings. Enough for a snack. If he had enough speed, that is.

Teacher Tallam put his physics textbook on the desk. He knew it was fruitless to spend another moment teaching a group of restless seventeen-year-old boys who'd just heard the bell.

"Okay let's start again tomorrow. In the meantime, don't forget chapter seventeen."

The boys rushed the door, lanky limbs flying. Across the yard, the snack house had opened, and all the boys knew the number of treats was limited. You'd need not only shillings, but also luck to get to the front of the line before all of them were gone.

With hard work, Shadrack had arrived at Kipkabus Boys' High School for his last four years of school. The boarding school took him away from his younger siblings whom he missed, but he'd still loved every moment of his time at Kipkabus. There was absolutely nothing fancy about the place, and it suited him. The perfect mix of order and companionship. His 195 classmates came from all over Kenya, and together the boys formed a tight community.

The distance from home was only fourteen miles and his parents lacked a car. Each trip home for school holidays meant walking down the long hill outside the grounds of school and covering the distance by foot. With a combination of walking and running, he could leave school at 8:00 a.m. and make it home by 1:00 p.m.

The routine at school was simple.

Up at 7:00 a.m.

Dressing in their signature white shirt, dark tie, green sweater, and gray pants.

Breakfast of coffee and porridge, always served in the dining hall with its metal benches and echoey walls.

Time for washing clothes in the buckets outside their dorm. No plumbing. Only outhouses and a well where the boys went to haul water for the kitchen staff. A hole in the ground behind the dining hall to burn their trash.

Classes.

Sports in the afternoon. Shadrack picked soccer, though his friends nagged him for not running. He was built for it, they said. And not very good at soccer anyway.

Lunch and dinner, the same menu every day. Rice and beans for lunch. Ugali and cabbage for dinner. Meat served twice a week. Never second helpings, but unlike home, always enough for one complete and fulfilling meal.

At night, back to the dorms. His was Njiru Dorm. The room he shared contained bunk beds and he'd finally moved to the top of one bunk as a benefit of senior year.

"Gideon, you loser, I saw you cut the line," Shadrack yelled as he reached the crowd of boys in front of the snack house. As usual, he'd made it faster than the rest of his classmates.

"Come on, bro, you get here every day with zero effort. Give the rest of us a break," Gideon laughed.

Shadrack inched back in line. He'd let it slide this time.

"Meet on the soccer field after school?" he asked Gideon as his friend walked away, snack in hand.

"Yea, just for a bit. I've gotta put in some extra time tonight. These exams coming up are stressing me out."

"I'm not sure how they expect us to know who we are and what we want to do yet. We're only seventeen," Shadrack added.

"All I know is that I don't wanna go back to my village, brother," said Gideon.

Shadrack knew where his friend came from, and his growing-up experience mirrored Shadrack's own. Both boys had parents pushing them to find an escape path to bigger, brighter futures.

"You should think more about running. You've got real athletic talent, and didn't you say your brother-in-law is doing well in running?" Gideon asked.

"I think so. I'll see him in a few weeks. I think he's made the Kenyan national team. He's on leave from training in the United States now. He's been working with a team from Nike," Shadrack replied, moving closer to the snack bar.

"Bro, that's cool. Use your lifelines. Running could be a ticket out of here if you've got the talent. I know you don't love it, but you'd probably be good at it."

"I know, I know. I'll think about it. My brother Titus is in the States now, and he wants me to come," Shadrack added.

"There you go. I'm telling you . . . it's worth a shot. The running scenes in Iten and Eldoret are crazy. College recruiters coming from overseas to do time trials. Insane stuff."

Making it to the front of the line, Shadrack plunked down his five shillings. Success. He knew he was being pushed to find a future outside Kenya, but it was hard to imagine life could be sweeter than it was right now.

It was nearly May, and the time for final exams was drawing closer. The exams were a huge part of a graduating senior's portfolio in Kenya. Once completed, students needed to wait months for results. The period was a state of limbo that offered the opportunity for young people to explore their options for work or further studies.

In preparation for the exams, Kipkabus Boys' High School saw its usual influx of families. They'd quietly come to visit the boys, offering prayers and perhaps an extra bit of food or advice.

Chapter Five

Alfred Yego and his wife Irene brushed themselves off as they got out of their car. It had taken three hours on a Sunday morning to make the drive from their home in Eldoret. The rainy season had arrived, bringing a torrent every morning and roads full of slick mud that made the drive challenging. They'd brought a pile of goodies for Shadrack, having stopped at his village on the way here. Irene, Shadrack's older sister, had made a life for herself as a hospital administrator. Along the way, she'd met and married Alfred.

"There he is!" Irene called out as Shadrack came to them from the school yard. "The next Tirop to make his way in the world!"

Shadrack shook Alfred's hand and gave his sister a hug.

"Sissy, you should know that I'm dropping Tirop," Shadrack said.

"Really? Well, Momma always loved the Kipchirchir in you," she said. "Shadrack Kipchirchir, it is."

The three walked out to the track behind the classrooms.

"So young man, what are you thinking about after graduation?" asked Alfred.

Alfred and Irene had been told there might be a buzz among the boys when they arrived, as word had spread that Shadrack's brother-in-law was doing well on the international running circuit. Adorned with fancy Nike gear head to toe, he'd be a contrast to the pile of boys in drab uniforms, and a potential distraction.

"Not totally sure. Obviously, I know I should try running, but it's not really my passion. I love soccer," Shadrack answered.

"I get it," said Alfred. "I wasn't certain it was my thing, either. But look . . . you're not big. You're built like most of the very successful Kenyan runners. Your brother Titus is making a real life for himself in the United States now. I think you could do the same with some practice."

Shadrack listened, kicking the sand lining the steeplechase pit. The track's dirt lanes were marked with black paint.

"I know it feels like a long shot, but I'm telling you it's a billion miles between this track and the ones I run on in the States. You wouldn't believe them. State of the art. The Nike facilities near Portland are unbelievable of course, but even the top colleges in the country have excellent places to train."

"That's great, but I'm more interested in getting there because of my education. Running could be a side gig, right?" Shadrack asked.

"Of course. Whatever you wanted it to be. I'm just saying, give it a shot. I thought I wouldn't like it either, but now, to be racing fast and feeling my body live up to its potential feels amazing."

"I don't know where I'd even start. I don't even have shoes, Alfred."

Irene smiled, saying, "Oh Shaddy, Alfred has enough shoes to keep you running for years."

"That's true. And you could live with us. In Eldoret. The training groups are all in Eldoret or Iten now," said Alfred.

Climbing from Eldoret to Iten by road is a straight shot by two lane highway. Along the way, fruit and vegetable vendors sell from roadside stands. Crops are interrupted by cell phone towers. The drive itself can be a maddening experience with speed bumps inserted every few kilometers to discourage speeding and drunk driving. Hardly noticeable is the ascent in altitude which brings you just shy of 2,500 meters. A burnt red sign spans the highway, marking the entrance to Iten, which has become a training destination for distance runners from around the world.

"Welcome to Iten, Home of Champions" it reads in white lettering. On either side, a Kenyan flag is painted, a tricolor of black, red, and green. In the middle, a Maasai shield and two crossed spears.

What began quietly in the late 1990s has only continued to grow over the past several decades. High altitude training centers ring the city, their grounds covered with lodging, dining accommodations, and often a dirt track. Runners from Kenya and other parts of the globe congregate here. Some are recreational runners coming to test personal goals. Others are professionals brought here by shoe sponsors. In all cases, their days are similar and designed to maximize the effects of both the altitude and the culture that has made Kenya a powerhouse in distance running.

Mornings start early, often before sunrise. Though training facilities organize runs, it's not uncommon for groups to form on a more informal basis on the outskirts of town. Peeling off layers of clothes, packs of athletes set off in the darkness. With each step, the oxygen deprivation works its magic to build the glorious supply of red blood cells that will make the athletes stronger once they return to sea level. These morning runs can be on roads, rocky trails, or through nearby forests. Local children with backpacks going to school often intersect with the runners, even in these early morning hours. The contrast is sweet and as the kids cheer the runners in the darkness, it's not lost that the art of running has been elevated here. Kenyans of all income levels and status respect and encourage distance running the way that other countries champion basketball or soccer.

When groups have returned and refueled, the day turns to rest. Rest is an integral part of the plan, and it's often overlooked in other countries. Sleep and massage are as important to recovery as a cool down run or a bottle of electrolytes. In the afternoon comes a speed workout and sometimes a slow run in the early evening. Then it's on to more food, all of it unprocessed and simple. Potatoes, ugali, a flat bread called chapati, meat, cabbage, beans, eggs, chai tea with milk and sugar. Protein powders and Gatorade aren't a thing here. In their place is real food from local farms, fields, and gardens.

Every Saturday on the edge of town a huge market sells goods of all sorts. Anything from produce to dinnerware to swimming suits, all laid out on a dusty field. Without fail, there's a disproportionate number of vendors selling running shoes and apparel. Some of it in cheap counterfeit versions, and some of it used and handed down from local training groups.

For athletes who train in Iten or Eldoret, running and its adjacent activities are enough to fill the day. Those who are lucky enough to observe the storied packs of Kalenjin runners on long, early morning workouts will witness a mesmerizing scene. In packs of twenty or thirty, footsteps on asphalt, runners head toward sunrise. Long, slender limbs with a leg turnover that seems breathtakingly efficient. For each pack of thirty, another five cars trail behind or alongside to provide fuel and water. Coaches open car windows, shout out the pace times, and receive hats and sweatshirts thrown into the backseats as runners heat up.

Eventually the pace quickens, signaling the final kilometers. The tight pack separates, and it's only now, some thirty-five kilometers into the run, that you can witness the slightest strain on a face or the tightness of an arm carriage. And then it's complete. Runners scatter to the sides of dirt roads, laying and stretching as their coaches debrief. Was the pace too fast or too slow? Was that surge in the middle important or misguided? How will this translate to the hills of the Boston Marathon or the flatness of the Berlin Marathon? All of it will be discussed and deciphered and used for the next run. Until then, the runners unwind their dust-covered legs and cram into the pace cars, driving back to Iten or Eldoret where a meal and a nap awaits.

"You've got nothing to lose, Shaddy. Come live with us. Try running. If you hate it, you can explore other options, right?" Irene persisted.

"I'll think about it. I promise. Until then, studying. I didn't come all this way to fail my last big tests," he replied.

"Fair enough," said Alfred. "We'll talk after you're done."

The Sunday sun had risen, drying the roads. Alfred and Irene walked back to the car to collect the goodies they'd brought. Making his way briefly toward the fence lining the school property, Shadrack looked out to the road. A line of girls in school uniforms was walking toward the primary school down the road, no doubt to one of the essay competitions held there on the weekends. He knew they'd probably walked miles that morning.

Jumping puddles, the girls squealed. Shadrack smiled, then turned back to Kipkabus.

Chapter Six

Opportunity

Kapchorwa and Eldoret, Kenya
2004–2009

Elvin shouted back to her sister as they turned onto the road toward the primary school. "Ivy, you're slower than a turtle!"

The girls and their classmates had gotten caught in the rain on the way to the interschool essay competition earlier that morning. Though they'd ducked under a tree and escaped the worst of it, the group was now running late.

"They'll never start without you, fancy pants," said Ivy. "You win every single one of these things. I can't believe I let you drag me along every time."

"Isn't it better than sitting through seven hours of church?" Elvin posed.

The girls had left the village at 6:00 a.m. that Sunday morning, walking six hours to get to the school where the competition would be held. They'd be there for two hours, then walk back another six hours, arriving at the village at 8:00 p.m. Ivy complained, but her sister knew she loved these Sundays.

"Yes, it's better, but it's even better to do *this*!"

Ivy raced past Elvin, jumping over a puddle, and screaming as her heel grazed the edge of it and splashed water back onto her sister.

"Hey, Princess! You got my uniform wet!" Elvin laughed, taking two skips to catch up.

Mud oozed between her bare toes.

Peeking through the clouds, the sun glinted off the puddles. Ahead, the girls saw a large field with a dirt track. Kipkabus Boys' High School marked the spot where the group took their final turn. They were close to the primary school, and surely another blue ribbon for Elvin.

"If you get first prize again, I think we should tell Gogo it's mine," Ivy said.

"You're so cruel, wanting to trick an old woman," Elvin replied.

"She's not that old. Or maybe she is, but she doesn't *feel* old."

"Did you hear her last night telling me how she wants to come to school and reprimand our teachers if they whip us?"

"No, I didn't! Tell me," Ivy asked.

Putting her hands on her hips like Gogo, Elvin dropped her voice an octave, imitating her grandmother.

"Did you say that your teacher hit your classmates, Elvin? I wish I had enough energy in these old bones to walk to town. I'd come down to Kapchorwa Primary School and beat her up myself!"

Ivy's laughter carried to the front of the pack of girls. Each one of their classmates understood the bond the twins shared. Though it was clear they were on different paths, the connection they'd forged since birth was unlike any other in their lives.

Accolades continued to pile up for Elvin at Kapchorwa. She'd approached the end of her studies and taken the country's national high school entrance exams. True to the prediction of Teacher Kosgei, Elvin's score was one of the best the school had seen in years. An offer to a quality boarding school in Eldoret was beyond anything she could've imagined a few years ago, but now it was a reality. When the offer came, a special announcement was made in class. Teachers cheered and hugged her, each one assuming it was the last they'd see of the girl from the outskirts of the community who'd traded potatoes for school attendance.

But the decision weighed on Elvin, and for her there seemed little doubt of the outcome. The family still had no money. There was no way

Elvin could leave the village, nor her younger siblings. The money that Baba made and sent home was exhausted once the boarding school fees for her older siblings in Eldoret had been paid.

Sylvia and Hilda had both gone overseas to run. What this meant and whether the family would ever see them again was unclear. There were no phones in the village, and no way to know if their dreams of earning money from running were coming true.

Elvin's little brother held a stick up to the sun late one weekend morning.

"Collins, you silly boy, it's not time for lunch. The shadow needs to be shorter," Elvin said.

"But Gogo said it was time for lunch when I held a stick to the sun," he replied.

Collins was now eleven years old and still learning the tricks his grandmother had taught him.

"It's not about just putting it up to the sun, but about looking at the shadow. Look how long that shadow is," Elvin said, pointing to the darkness that swept the ground toward the garden.

"But I'm hungry," Collins said.

"I know, sweet one, but it's early. When it's midday, the shadow from your stick will be shorter and then we can have our lunch."

Collins tossed the stick on the ground, dejected. He wandered toward Gogo's hut, in time to see her step outside.

"Come, come, Collins. Go inside and get yourself a cup of tea. That'll fill up your tummy until lunch," said Gogo sweetly.

Collins ducked inside and Gogo motioned for Elvin to come over and sit down next to her in the grass. Her grandmother had been in a poor mood since the news about the boarding school offer and Elvin's certainty that she couldn't go.

"I know you're going to try to convince me to take the spot, Gogo. Again. But I just can't. I can't leave them."

"My child, we will be fine. Ivy failed her grade this year, so she will be home again, repeating the year."

"Ivy isn't responsible enough to work the fields and still work hard in school, Gogo. There won't be enough money for food. And plus, I don't know how I'd pay the school fees."

Elvin twisted blades of grass around her fingertips. It had grown long over the past month, and she made a mental note to work on thinning the yard when she had time.

"You're resourceful. You'd find a way. A small job in Eldoret, perhaps. I think your sister Sylvia will be back from Europe soon and maybe she'll be there to help you."

"I don't have enough money for shoes, Gogo, much less books or a bus ticket. And my English isn't strong enough. Plus, I like my life here in the village."

"It sounds to me like you're trying to justify your decision, child. Remember how often I've talked to you about your education. Come back here someday if you want, but now it's time to go see the world, like your sisters are. Listen to me. I'm an old woman now, and I wish I'd had the opportunities you have now."

Gogo could always see right through her. It was a blessing and a curse.

"Next year. This time, next year. I'll try hard again all over, Gogo. I'll repeat the grade. I'll take the test again and score just as high, if not higher. This time, I'll get into Moi Girls' High School. The best of the best. And by then maybe we'll have the money to pay the school fees."

Gogo's sight was failing, her eyes cloudy. But beyond the soft blueness of each one, Elvin was sure she saw a spark.

Rural Kalenjin women are still largely responsible for most tasks related to keeping their families afloat. In addition to caring for children, they're often expected to work in the fields, cook, and oversee the collection of firewood and water. Such burdens often become prohibitive for girls who might otherwise have promising athletic careers. Indeed, it's only on a family-by-family basis that the status quo is being altered for girls. Families with relatives who've had success outside the villages are slowly beginning to see opportunities for girls.

One of Kenya's first distance running superstars, Lornah Kiplagat, climbed from a rural farm to the international stage. A three-time Olympian, Lornah competed for Kenya, then found a home in The Netherlands. In the early 2000s, Kenyan women racing at such elite levels was a novelty, and it was one that she strived to change. Funneling her prize winnings back into Kenya became a passion, and Lornah opened the first training program initially targeting girls and women, the High Altitude Training Center in Iten.

In the twenty-plus years since the training center opened its doors, Kenyan female athletes have seen a growth in opportunities, though long-standing perceptions about the role of women in Kenyan society persist.

Once the stigma of women participating in running is cracked a bit, the next challenge comes in the form of their success. Women who achieve notable victories and return home with prize money are often manipulated into violent or unhealthy relationships, sometimes giving up earnings due to the greed of their husbands, other family members, agents, or coaches.

Upending the way women have always lived in the Rift Valley, the resources in Iten at programs like Lornah's camp provide safe and encouraging environments for women to develop their talents. Some camps today serve girls as young as high school and include formal education in addition to athletic training. In the past several years, this education has started to include lessons on domestic abuse, gender-based violence, and consent.

Training under the watchful eye of her Aunt Lornah in Iten, Hilda Kibet had made the leap from Kenya to the international scene. By 2008 both Hilda and her sister Sylvia were winning titles in Europe, and with it, prize money. Running had given them both lifelines out of the village and into new experiences and relationships outside of Kenya. Travel was nonstop, and visits to Kenya were rare. Still, their hearts remained at home, off the winding red dirt roads that led them home to their village.

Chapter Six

A full four seasons passed. Heat melting into rain and then frozen ground until the warmth returned. The sisters continued their studies, with Elvin desperate to keep her promise to Gogo. She had no clue how she'd pay for boarding school, but step one was scoring well on the high school entrance exams again.

Word had come to the village that Hilda had married her Dutch runner boyfriend, named Hugo. The family celebrated from afar, but to Elvin it seemed a recipe never to return to the village.

On the day invitations arrived from boarding schools at Kapchorwa Primary School, Elvin got there early. She'd scored high on exams. This meant another invitation from a top boarding school was imminent. Which school it might be was the only mystery. Teacher Kosgei sat correcting papers at her desk as Elvin stepped into the classroom.

"Elvin, come, come."

She set her papers aside and motioned to the seat next to her.

"I know you're anxious. You've worked hard. Harder than any student I've ever had. Your father would be proud. He'd like to be here, no matter the news today."

The family hadn't seen Baba in months, and Mama continued to make only brief appearances in the village before disappearing again. She'd long since stopped trying to take the younger children with her and they were big enough now to help with household tasks.

"I've got no idea how I will attend boarding school if I'm invited," Elvin mumbled.

"Let's just see what the day brings, child."

Six hours later, all the kindergarten through eighth grade classes crammed into the main outdoor school yard for the announcements. One by one, the teachers streamed into seats in the front of the yard. Each teacher held a pile of letters with invitations from various boarding schools around the country that they'd reviewed earlier in the day. Teacher Kosgei's wide yellow skirt splayed around the edges of her metal chair. She looked out across the hundreds of students sitting on the grass awaiting news. Holding her hand up to her forehead to shield her eyes from the sun, she scanned the eager faces.

There was only one student she was looking for.

Their eyes met and, in her teacher's broad, knowing smile, Elvin felt relief first, and pride a distant second. The smile could only be that of an invitation from Moi Girls' High School.

Two months later the river swelled. Elvin and Ivy lay near the riverbank. With only a month to go until school began, Elvin still hadn't accepted nor declined the offer from Moi Girls' High School. She was stuck. Baba's paycheck hadn't increased, and the younger kids wouldn't have a means to earn money for food if Elvin left. Declining the invitation was unthinkable, but she couldn't see another alternative. Nobody talked about the inevitable, especially Gogo.

Up the hill, the girls thought they heard shouts. Usually, the shouts from villagers indicated trouble. And because one family's trouble impacted the next, it was always an occasion to spring into action. But these shouts sounded different. Lighter and more like a song. Ivy and Elvin looked at each other with recognition and amazement.

"It can't be, can it?" Ivy asked.

"I mean . . . it *could* be," Elvin responded. "You were only 900 grams when you were born, but now, I'm 5'0" and you can break me in half. So, *anything* could be."

Blending into the sounds of gleeful shouts, the girls heard the unmistakable sound of a car horn beeping with celebration. A vehicle of any sort coming down the narrow path to the village had happened on only a couple of occasions. It provided enough certainty.

The sisters jumped up, racing up the hill to the mud hut.

A crowd of thirty villagers had gathered outside the hut, including Gogo, who was weeping. Joyful chatter and commotion consumed every inch of the small area. Layers of villagers peeled back until Elvin saw a flash of white. He was wearing shorts and his leg muscles were defined from hundreds of miles of running. Children from the village touched his arm, outstretched to receive handshakes from the elders. With a wide grin, his eyes almost disappeared into his cheeks, but Elvin could see that they were blue like Gogo's. She strained to see beyond the white man, her eyes following his free arm. It was connected to hands clasping it at the wrist. She knew those hands.

"Elvin and Ivy, what took you so long? Always off adventuring, aren't you?" Hilda said, scooping them both into her arms.

Hugo and Hilda's arrival in the village kicked off a forty-eight-hour celebration. Meals, music, dancing, and games carried on late into the nights. It wasn't until after midnight that Hilda and Elvin had time alone. By only the light of the fire in the stove, they sat side by side.

Hilda was dressed in jeans and a clean, pressed blouse that looked as if it had been bought that day. Her nails were clean and painted pink. Several fingers had rings, including a gold band on her left ring finger. Instead of the rubber slippers she used to wear in the village, she had on fancy white running shoes. Elvin could see that she'd let her hair grow and it was piled in tight braids on the top of her head.

"I've become successful, Elvin. There's a whole world out there and I owe my ability to explore it to one thing. The sport of running."

"I'm happy for you, Sissy," Elvin said.

Hilda pulled over her purse and opened it. Inside, Elvin could see wads of money in rubber bands.

"I have the money to pay your school fees, Elvin. When I heard the news today about your acceptance at Moi Girls' High School, it blew my socks off. You must go. The opportunity is too incredible to pass up. It's the best high school in the country."

"Oh, Hilda. I don't know what to say. I'm so desperate to go, but I don't want to leave the kids."

"This isn't your concern anymore, Sissy. You've spent years and years caring for them. I have money now, and it'll pay for their food and then some. It's more than enough."

"Is it enough for everything? There's so much we need. We all need shoes and clothes. The house needs repairs. Gogo needs to see a doctor and get proper care."

"All of it is taken care of, Elvin. It's your job now to focus on your studies. These years you've been stuck here without Baba and Mama . . . it's too much. I wish I'd been able to come sooner and provide more."

"Leaving Ivy isn't my first choice."

"I understand. But Ivy will be just fine. We'll find a way to get her out of the village. It'll just take a little bit longer."

Darkness had taken over the inside of their home. The stove had worked a full day, feeding many people, and now was left with only embers. They crackled as Hilda and Elvin whispered final thoughts. In the corner of the room near the front door, Hilda's bright white running shoes reflected the moonlight. They looked totally out of place here, Elvin thought, and yet represented everything.

Eldoret, Kenya, is the country's fifth biggest city. With a population of a half million, it's surrounded by agricultural lands which support its economy. Opened in 1995, Eldoret's airport has a single, asphalt runway that's been instrumental in welcoming athletes from around the world who seek to train in the Great Rift Valley.

On the edge of town sits the campus of Moi Girls' High School. Its grounds span a dozen acres and hold a series of elegant buildings, each white with dark red pillars. Tree-lined paths take visitors from one part of campus to the next. Staff work hard to maintain the gardens inside so that it's a quiet oasis for learning. Elvin had only heard about it from others and couldn't believe she was about to set foot inside the compound, much less be a student there. As Hilda's car eased its way toward the main gate, she noticed Elvin biting her nails.

"It's gonna be just fine, Elvin. These girls are all scared like you."

"Maybe, but at least they know how to speak decent English. The British version. Kalenjin isn't going to help me here, nor Swahili."

"Perhaps not, but you're smart. You'll pick it up in no time. This is your home, now. Just soak it in and know that Sylvia and I aren't far away."

Hilda and Sylvia had started going back and forth between Europe and Kenya. The prize money they'd won was enough for them to think about purchasing homes in Iten, forty miles to the north. The city's running community was booming, and Hugo thought it would be wise to invest in the country, perhaps opening a guest house and training camp for aspiring professional runners.

"You and Sylvia are not far away. I hear you and I'm not going to forget that," Elvin responded.

The gates to Moi Girls' High School swung open, a guard waving them through.

Elvin's years at boarding school sailed by. Money from Hilda, Hugo, and Sylvia was sustaining her in school and the rest of her family left in the village. She dived into her studies and adjusted to life in the city bit by bit. Whenever she could, she'd take a public bus north to Iten, where her sisters now had bustling homes. Hugo and Hilda had opened a guesthouse, complete with a stream of foreign visitors.

One weekend she arrived to a crowd in the living room watching television. Television itself was a new experience for her, and the images on the screen were beyond what she could comprehend. Nudging closer to Hugo, Elvin peppered him with questions.

"Is that boy real?"

"Can you tell me what that flying stick is? And how does he do that flying thing?"

"How did he get powers like that and where does he live in real life?"

"Elvin, you've got as many questions as you did the first time I came to the village," Hugo chuckled. "And you need to start getting used to these things . . . this is called a movie. It's made up. None of it is real and neither is that boy on the screen—named Harry."

While Hugo and Hilda's guesthouse served as a hub for foreigners, Sylvia lived across town, launching a guesthouse of her own. She'd begun charging athletes tiny amounts of money in exchange for help with training and navigating local trails. Both older sisters were still running competitively and Iten's constant influx of runners needed places to stay and food to eat. To stay with world-class runners was appealing, and soon Sylvia's guesthouse was thriving just as Hilda's was. It fell to the staff to make sure both foreign and Kenyan runners alike were well taken care of during their rotations training in the hills around Iten. Like Hilda, Sylvia had done her best to employ as many local young people as possible to run the guesthouse.

Elvin carried in a basket of cabbage from the market and plopped it down next to her favorite cook at Sylvia's guesthouse. He was several years older than her and felt like a big brother. He made a delicious ugali and she enjoyed trying to make him laugh. His work ethic was impressive. Like the other employees at the guesthouse, he was both working to earn a living and going on training runs. How he did both and where he hoped to go with his running intrigued Elvin.

Walking in, she saw that he had a thick book sitting next to the cooking table, a page marked where he'd left off.

"Hey, mini-Sylvia, wanna help me make the soup?" he asked.

"Sure. Hey, what's that huge book you're reading? Goodness, I've never seen anything so enormous!" Elvin inquired.

"It's an SAT book. I'm studying to get to the United States."

He sliced a head of cabbage and handed half to Elvin, who began to tear it apart with her fingers and put it in a bowl. She noticed his legs, lean and muscular from hours spent running on the roads around Iten.

"Going for running or studying?" she asked.

"Well, both. I'm training to get a running scholarship, but you need good grades to get there. America is where I'm hoping to go, though there are opportunities in a lot of countries, you know?"

"My sisters did that. They both ran after high school."

"Duh, silly. Why do you think I'm here? Your sisters are amazing. Look what they've done with their lives. Everyone here in Iten is running like crazy to try to get the attention of colleges in other countries. I tried college here in Kenya but figured I'd give this a shot."

"My sisters didn't run in high school. Hilda just got a pair of shoes when she graduated, and then she gave one to Sylvia when *she* was done with high school and Sylvia gave a pair of shoes to my sister Valentine when *she* graduated."

"So, it's what all the sisters do in your family, then?" he asked.

"I suppose. Running isn't really *my* thing, but I'm glad it's worked out for them."

"Never say never," he said.

"Perhaps. We'll see. If you make it to America, don't forget me."

"I won't. Between now and then, you're gonna need to add some meat onto those bones if you want to run. Double serving of dinner for you tonight."

Peppering the rosters of many American Division One cross-country and track teams are gifted Kenyan-born athletes. It's a number that's increased over recent decades. How the trend started and how it works in practice isn't something most people consider. Instead, most assume that these runners are in the United States solely for their athletic ability, and somehow manage to squeak by academically on the side. The perception could not be further from the truth.

NCAA rules allow scholarships to be provided at the Division One and Two levels, with the stipulation that students be academically qualified as well. Scholarships can also be given at the junior college level, an option some international students take to get a foot into the United States and improve their academic and athletic standings which they leverage to later transfer to more lucrative programs. For international students, and specifically those from East Africa, it's a high bar requiring a convergence of factors.

First, the desire and resources to leave their families at a young age to train in cities like Iten or Eldoret. Next, the ability to excel at running. In addition, exceptional academic ability. Lastly, a willingness to leave their home country and families for an undetermined amount of time. The benefits they will reap by coming to the United States are many, but those sacrifices they make are largely overlooked.

For American universities, the opportunity to recruit distance runners from Kenya began to catch on in the early 2000s. While many top-tier universities were busy recruiting talented American high schoolers, other programs didn't have the name-recognition to bring on quality talent. To stay competitive while at the same time offer opportunities to young people abroad, the Kenyan distance-running pipeline began.

"The reality is that those who can attract the top Americans do and those who cannot look in other parts of the world," says one big-time college coach.

Visiting Kenya in person is often the most important factor in a coach's decision on whether to extend a scholarship to an athlete. Coaches may watch workouts, their stopwatches in hand, verifying the times that athletes are able to run. Conversations may take place, enlightening coaches on potential recruits and allowing them to share their training philosophies and expectations with one another. As with domestic recruits, finding the right fit between athlete and coach takes time and patience, and the cultural barriers often make the task daunting.

Unlike other college sports, distance runners are expected to participate year-round, with only short breaks. Their sport consists of three seasons: cross-country season, indoor track, and outdoor track. After four solid years of competition and with a college degree in hand, international student-athletes have a short period of time to make a choice. Return to their home countries or find a way to stay in the United States. This might involve further schooling, finding employment, or in some rare cases, joining the military. For some the choice is easy.

"I went straight from graduation to the airport and got on the first plane back to Kenya," one former student-athlete reports. "I'd had enough of the United States for a lifetime."

For others, the choice is just as clear, but reversed. America is now home.

Chapter Seven

Departure

Eldoret, Kenya, and the United States
2009–2010

"He's doing well, but I think he needs a few more weeks," Alfred said, wandering his house in Eldoret with a phone to his ear.

Shadrack's brother Titus was on the other end, watching snow come down in Kentucky. Titus and Alfred had been talking regularly since Shadrack had agreed to give running a try. He'd been in Eldoret living with his sister Irene and brother-in-law Alfred. Their time together had been a crash course in how to perform well and treat the body properly. Everything from nutrition to sleep to the proper clothing to wear. Shadrack was a blank slate, and Alfred was fresh from four years of training with Nike in the United States. His closet overflowed with apparel, and he outfitted his protégé with technical gear and shoes which cost a hundred times more than the pair Shadrack had saved for in primary school.

"So, he seems at least mildly interested in the option of trying to get a running scholarship?" Titus asked.

"Mildly, yes. He said he'd do it because he was waiting for his exam scores and had nothing better to do, but he's taken to running. I mean, he's got incredible talent, Titus. We both know it. I think I should send him to Kaptagat."

"Not a bad plan. Getting him into a training camp might light a fire in him. I realize he comes across as mild-mannered, but he's got a competitive streak," Titus replied.

"I can see that. He's focused and determined. It shows. I'll try to get him into the camp at Kaptagat and meanwhile, I think you should start looking for scholarships."

"I don't think I'll have to look very far. Western Kentucky has been good to me, and I know the coach would love him here."

"What about Oklahoma State? You know Coach Smith, don't you?" Alfred asked.

Titus had met Oklahoma State's cross-country and track coach years prior, when he visited Kenya and it fell to Titus to drive him around the country looking at different athletes. Though his own grades fell short and Titus's hopes to attend OSU had died, he and Coach Dave Smith had remained in contact.

"I do, and I mentioned years ago that I had a little brother who was going to be a natural. He was interested at the time, but OSU is the big leagues now. He only takes top-notch talent. Shadrack's not quite ready. He could always transfer there if he does well, right?" Titus inquired.

"Of course. The goal now is just to get him an offer at a decent school."

"You know it. I'm not resting until I get at least a couple of my siblings over here."

Titus had made it his mission to help his younger siblings leave Kenya. Their life in the village had been marvelous, but he wanted a different ending for his siblings than those in previous generations. Their father John agreed. He'd pushed for Titus to think about running from an early age. When Titus was offered a scholarship to college in the United States, the only thing standing in the way was the cost of the plane ticket. But in no more than a few days, John had sold a parcel of land to pay for Titus's airfare.

Titus's three previous attempts to bring siblings to the United States had failed. His oldest sister Florence wasn't interested in running. Irene had married Albert and begun having children and another brother was so wildly skilled at running that he was offered a plum position in the Kenyan Army to run on their national team.

Shadrack was next.

Two months later, with a burst of training and several good track workouts, Shadrack held an offer from Western Kentucky University. With his brother and brother-in-law carving a path, Shadrack had found enough speed in his legs and high-enough grades to gain a full ride to an American university.

For a second time, their father toiled over how to pay for the airfare.

On a cool November morning, Alfred and Irene pulled into the family's property in the village. The drive from Eldoret was only an hour, though the distance from the city seemed vast. Alfred's fancy car attracted the usual attention as they pulled through the dirt roads to get to John and Rose Tirop's land.

His father-in-law came out to greet him, a shovel still in hand from morning chores.

He gave his daughter a hug and shook Alfred's hand.

"I know why you're here and I can't let you do it. I'll sell more land. I'll sell the cows if I must," John said.

"We won't let you do it, Baibai. I want my little brother to get to America without my father going into debt," Irene said.

John looked unconvinced, but suspected this was a losing battle.

"John, the boy is living in my house. I'm a world champion and have the resources. I will take care of this," Alfred said.

John eyed Alfred. His son-in-law wore red running shoes and jogging pants that gathered at the ankle, while his own legs were covered in old black trousers and on his feet, flip-flops.

"Here," John said, handing Alfred the shovel. "There's work to do clearing wood on the edge of the property. We can talk about the details."

Though intended as a gift, the cost of the air ticket would be repaid years later to Alfred in Kenyan shillings not by John, but by the boy who'd worked hard to buy his first pair of shoes and was now on his way.

Chapter Seven

The theories on what makes Kenyan athletes such superior distance runners have filled the pages of many books. Among the countless writings that have covered this topic, the concept of genetic superiority is always front and center. Most Kenyan dominance stems from the Kalenjin, a group of tribes which is a minority in the country. With laser precision, scientists and journalists have tackled the issue from every angle, trying to decipher the answer as to whether there's some specific sequencing in the genetic code which influences performance in the Kalenjin.

The answer for now is unclear. While there might be a slightly beneficial gene variation, it's the combination of many factors, including those both socioeconomic and cultural, which breeds superiority. To lean into genetics entirely is thus a diminishment of the accomplishments of Kalenjin athletes based merely on one factor. With more genetic variability in the Great Rift Valley than in other parts of the world, the differences are likely too subtle to identify. The science conducted so far shows mixed results in anatomical, biomechanical, and physiological differences between Kalenjin runners and those from other parts of the world. Instead, it's a combination of factors which point to Kalenjin dominance.

Like the Sherpa of the Nepalese Himalayan region, the altitude at which runners live and train in the Rift Valley is certainly a factor. Running above 7,000 feet has been shown to develop stronger pulmonary systems through the increase in red blood cells used to transport oxygen to muscles at work. The reason legions of Sherpa haven't joined the ranks of world-class distance runners is a fascinating case study in the body's adaptability to altitude. Some data has indicated that this may be due to the length of time a population has lived at altitude. While Himalayan Sherpa have lived at altitude for possibly tens of thousands of years, the Kalenjin in Kenya are somewhat new to the altitude, having only settled in the past two thousand years. Scientists say that the difference in ancestral time frames may mean those populations who are benefiting the most are those who are not yet fully adapted to the altitude. Best, they say, would be those with sea-level ancestry but who are born at altitude to develop maximum lung surface area. The Kalenjin certainly fit this bill. Not only are they perhaps best suited to reap the benefits of the altitude, but from a very early age, many (but not all, and in fact fewer as time passes and villages are modernized) of them run as a form of transportation. By clocking hundreds of miles by the time they reach high school, the practice of running has become part of daily life.

Finding anything processed in the kitchens of Eldoret and Iten distance runners can be a challenge. For this reason, their diet of simple carbohydrates, meat, milk, tea, eggs, and vegetables has also been considered a factor in athletic success. It's a case of less is more which propels their daily workouts. Kidney beans and maize in the form of ugali provide an excellent balance of the carbs and protein needed for distance runners. No supplements, no protein powders, and no vitamins are found in the Rift Valley. Instead, it's only locally sourced foods eaten throughout the day and especially post-workout which undoubtedly leads to stronger recoveries between runs.

Another oft-mentioned contributor to Kalenjin running success is probably best described as force of will. While not a contributor in all cases, there are enough examples of modern-day champions to see a thread. Eliud Kipchoge is most notable, and his story is well documented. The son of a single mother, Kipchoge collected milk from farmers and delivered it to the local market to earn his family extra money. Eventually he convinced a national coach to develop training programs for him. The two would stay together for decades, mastering the art of the marathon and taking Kipchoge across the finish line in the first sub-two-hour marathon in history in 2019.

While Kipchoge's achievements are unique, his upbringing in rural Kenya was not. Mental toughness is often bred in times of poverty and pain, and when economic motivation is at play, the force of will likewise increases.

For young Kalenjin men, there's yet another factor tied to pain which some say increases their ability to tolerate the discomfort of competitive distance running. At the age of fifteen, many Kalenjin boys are sent through a month-long initiation. This involves leaving their homes to stay in a nearby forest. Elder Kalenjin men lead teachings as part of the month, preparing boys to move into adulthood. Boys in small groups live in seclusion away from their families, undergoing training and lessons that remain largely secret to the outside world. Sleeping in camps on animal hides, the boys are taught what is described as "teachings in discipline and facing life with positivity." Only rarely are the boys allowed to venture outside their camps, and only when dressed in sheaths made of rice sacks with their bodies covered in white clay to disguise their identity from one another.

They're made to crawl through stinging nettles, beaten, and at the end of the month, circumcised with sharp sticks. Often the circumcision ceremony requires the boys to endure the operation in complete silence, compartmentalizing the pain in a way that some say is similar to the way in which long-distance runners need to mentally override distress signals during races.

"It's like what you in the States probably imagine Basic Training to be. We are broken down, taught to adapt to challenges and then lifted as a community. It makes us stronger and more resilient," a Kalenjin man describes. "The circumcision part itself is far less common in the past decade with operations in hospitals becoming more accepted, but even today many young men still opt to go through the month-long ritual because it builds mental toughness."

Irrespective of diet, genetics, the altitude, or cultural upbringing, perhaps the most striking ingredient impacting the success of the Kalenjin is the way they approach running. Rather than focus on the competitive aspect, running is viewed as a joyful celebration. It is, according to Kipchoge, "not so much about the legs. It's about the heart and mind."

Self-reliance, a familiar measure of success in other parts of the world, is far less valued than community building when it comes to running. The life of a Kalenjin runner is one of simplicity with few distractions and much support from others. With more of the country invested in this philosophy, a greater proportion of the population has sought to work together to take up the sport and thus, a higher percentage have ascended at the international level. Whereas the average schoolkid in the United States may look at Kipchoge and think, "No way, I could never do that," the average Kenyan schoolchild is more apt to think, "With help from my community, why not me?"

It was January 2010 and the day before he was scheduled to leave for the United States. John Tirop and Shadrack leaned up against a chain link fence at the Nairobi airport. John had started the morning by announcing there was no better place to spend the day than watching planes land and take off. Of all places, it seemed absurd, but John argued it would help with Shadrack's departure. After all, he argued, Shadrack had never been on an airplane. Good to just see what was in store.

"That one's probably heading to Mombassa," John said as a puddle jumper took off in front of them.

"I've got this, Baibai," Shadrack assured his father. "I'll be on a much bigger plane and Titus will be there on the other end."

According to NCAA rules, only the head coach of his team could pick him up, but Shadrack planned to live with his brother, so Titus would be the second person to connect with after landing.

"Even still, it's good that we're all here to show you off," his father said. "You've done well, son. I wish I'd had your courage when I was young. Or the opportunities you've had."

Displaying restrained Kenyan emotions, his father patted Shadrack's back. The gesture was plenty to let him know his father was proud.

"You'll visit, Baibai?"

John shrugged. "We'll see. International travel isn't exactly easy and it's expensive. Your mother's a better candidate than me. She's ready to get in your suitcase tomorrow."

The contingent from the Tirop family was impressive. Every sibling and their grandmother had made the six-hour haul from their homes in northern Kenya to Nairobi to see him off. As the sun rose the next morning, the clan gathered in the main terminal. Each one with a few words of advice. Most of them crying. For joy or sadness, Shadrack wasn't sure. Leading their family in prayers, John and Rose searched for the ideal blessing to send another child around the world for an undetermined period. Perhaps forever.

"A little something to get you started," John said slipping three crisp twenty-dollar bills in Shadrack's palm. He'd gone to the bank in Eldoret to special order the currency.

Shadrack folded the bills carefully, easing them into the pocket of the Nike backpack that Alfred had given him. His brother-in-law stood in the back of the group, arms crossed and sporting a grin. Practically every stitch of clothing Shadrack was bringing had belonged to Alfred. They were gifts from running sponsors and races he'd run all over the globe. A black technical t-shirt. A hoodie with the emblem of a French running company. And a stack of bright white socks that were so new that Shadrack was loathe to put them on.

Before him, a moving staircase. He knew it was called an "escalator," but he'd never been on one. He watched as each person stepped on and stood still as the stairs lifted all on their own like a gift from the ground. Reaching for the handrail, Shadrack stepped on cautiously, then froze. He turned, seeing his family wiping tears and waving. Then, with all the mystery of the universe, the magical stairs lifted him upward, his family disappearing below.

Masses of people in every shade walked purposefully through JFK International Airport. Shadrack had never seen such a rainbow of humanity. And they all seemed to know exactly where they were going. With help from strangers, he made it to his gate. Nashville, Tennessee, was the destination. He found a lady at the check-in counter.

"I need to call my brother," he said. He'd practiced the sentence several times, but his English still seemed clunky here in the United States.

The woman behind the counter looked surprised at first, then softened. She'd seen versions of this moment before and knew the proper protocol.

"Come here, young man."

She pulled a cell phone from under the counter.

"What's the number? I'll dial it for you."

Titus picked up on the second ring.

"American brother! You made it. Lots of crying at the Nairobi airport, right?"

"You know it," Shadrack said.

"Well, you're here now. Can you get yourself a little something to eat until your flight leaves?"

"Baibai gave me money, so I guess that's possible. I bought a Sprite, but I'll get something to eat soon."

"Yes, do that. Coach will be at the airport to get you and I'll see you soon. Do you have a sweatshirt with you?"

"I do. Why?"

"Good. You're gonna need it. It's snowing."

"Man, I'm glad I brought extra layers for this one," said Titus.

He wrapped his arms around himself, shivering as his feet sank into the soft ground. Ten months had passed since Shadrack had arrived, and in that time, Titus had tried his best to attend as many of Shadrack's races as he could. Now that Titus was working on his master's degree at Western Kentucky, he could be a full-time cheerleader for his brother on the weekends.

The job was a piece of cake. Shadrack's first track season had been outstanding from the start, and cross-country season was going even better. Now they were at pre-nationals for cross country, a lead up to the national cross-country championship at this same course in a few weeks. This course was close enough to Western Kentucky for Titus to drive.

Shadrack's first few months had gone according to plan. At first, Titus needed to walk him to every single class. His introduction to American college coursework had been a geology class. The professor had a heavy American accent, and it was mixed with complex academic terminology; the hour had been a test in Shadrack's listening skills.

The running had gone better, though it included a day of being desperately lost as he tried to walk home on the first day of practice.

On the fields of a cross-country course, Shadrack always felt at home. Western Kentucky had been a good place to start his collegiate career, but Shadrack was already looking ahead to a transfer. A bigger school with a better program. As usual, his brother had advice. The two walked the fields, the November air whipping through their jackets. Tents were set up on the perimeter of the racecourse, which was flat and open.

"Let's see how you do today, but I'm thinking it's time. Time for me to start making calls, though hell, at the rate you're running, I suspect teams will be coming to *you*," Titus said.

"Yeah, I agree. They've been good to me here, but I think it's time. I can go bigger."

"Definitely. I think Dave Smith will be interested. I haven't talked to him in years, and I bet he's been watching you progress but probably has no idea you're my brother. After all, I'm still a Tirop and you're a Kipchirchir," Titus added.

"I know and Baibai will never let me forget it!" Shadrack responded, laughing.

"Okay well let's table it for the time being and just get you to the starting line."

"Agree. I need to connect with the rest of the team, but check that out," Shadrack said, pointing to a group of runners.

On the crest of a hill, six to eight of them had gathered, and all of them were speaking Kalenjin. This was starting to happen more frequently, as more Kenyans were being offered scholarships to run and study in the States.

Titus and Shadrack joined the group, a mix of athletes wearing warmup suits of all colors, representing universities from around the country, but bound by language and culture.

Chapter Eight

Bring Me the Shoes

Kapchorwa, Eldoret, and Iten, Kenya
2009–2010

Gogo held Elvin's wrists.

"Too skinny! I may not be able to see anymore, but I know a skinny girl when I feel one. What did they feed you at Moi Girls' for the past four years?"

Elvin laughed and scooped rice and beans onto a plate for Gogo. She was back in the village after graduating high school. Following a long wait, she'd received her marks from final exams. Among the highest in the country, her scores were somehow still a disappointment to her.

"Dear one, it's time to stop fretting about those scores. Surely there are a million opportunities for university studies here in Kenya with scores like that?"

"I'm sure, Gogo, but I wanted to do just a little bit better. Maybe I study another year and take the tests again?"

"Absolutely not. I forbid it. You cannot have your sisters pay for your studies one more year, and you shouldn't stay here in the village."

"Then what?" Elvin asked.

"Then figure it out, dear one. Stay a couple days here and then go back to Iten. I know Hilda is running overseas now, but talk to Sylvia. Talk to Hugo. Come up with a plan. I dare say it might involve running."

"And leave you here?"

"Yes, leave me here. It's only Ian and Daisy home now. Compared to the ten of you there once were, two is easy. We'll be fine."

"Only because you say so, Gogo."

"I say so. And I say return someday with a handsome man. That, too."

He'd left behind the SAT book. Her favorite cook had made it to America and in his old bedroom in Iten at Sylvia's house, Elvin flipped through its worn pages. The questions were difficult, but manageable, she thought. Moi Girls' had given her a top-notch education, and her English was far superior after four years there.

Sylvia came in, plopping down on the bed. She was deep into her training. Long runs in the morning with at least a dozen other runners trailing behind every day. Shorter runs in the afternoons. Sometimes the group would travel to a track in Eldoret. The track was the place foreign coaches occasionally showed up for time trials. They'd arrive with stopwatches around their necks and clipboards in hand. Always looking for the next great talent, the perfect mix of brains which would survive at their universities and the kind of athletic talent that could help raise the profile of their cross-country and track teams.

"You could easily score high," Sylvia said, nodding to the SAT book.

"You're right. I think I'd do okay on it. I want a better education, and I know I'd get that in the United States, but I'm not sure I'd be as strong a runner as you and Hilda. Can't I just get good grades and go there with that alone?"

"Sissy, that's not how it works. You need to be good at both. They've got plenty of smart kids in the United States, but the running part . . . that's what they need. That's why they're here to look at runners. But of course, yes once you get there, you can study whatever you want. You can become a doctor if that's what you want. You just must run . . . if only a little bit."

Elvin leaned back on the desk chair, tugging at her hair, which had grown long enough for braids. She considered her options, hearing Gogo in her head. Her choice was clear.

"All right. I've got nothing to lose. Bring me the shoes," she said.

Hugo stood on the side of the track in Eldoret, surrounded by a group of fifteen young women.

"Okay 3,000 meters, team, and this one is timed, so do your best," he called out.

Elvin's first few months of running had been a wild learning curve. Not only did running involve the actual running part, but an entire process of treating one's body with kindness. Sylvia schooled her in the proper nutrition, how much sleep to get, and when to stretch. There were massages and videos to watch on the proper running form to use. She'd tried to go back up to the village to run, but the intensity and environment of training in Iten brought her back.

Running was surprisingly easy for her, she found. In the moments her body was working, she found time to daydream. After her runs were finished, she loved the way her heart felt stronger. She slept better, ate more, and found pleasure in pushing herself at the end of workouts. What had started as a means to an end, Elvin was slowly discovering she might love.

Hugo had watched her intently and though he hadn't said much, she could tell he was pleased with how she'd progressed. Today was her first timed race. She wore a pair of long tights and a t-shirt as the group settled in on the starting line.

"On your mark, set, GO!"

As she'd done the past few months, Elvin fell into the middle of the pack. With each lap, she could see Hugo making notes as he checked a stopwatch. With a lap to go, Elvin moved to the front and opened a gap, her short but strong legs carrying her around the track. She could hear her breath, her lungs straining for air. At the finish she leaned ever so gently forward, as she'd seen other runners do.

Hugo stared at the stopwatch, not looking up. The other girls had finished well behind her and lay on the track in a tired heap.

Elvin waited, but Hugo wasn't looking up. She walked over, expecting the worst.

"How bad was it, Hugo?" she asked.

"Well, I'll be damned if that isn't one of the fastest time trials I've ever seen. It was a 10:50, Elvin, on your first try. That's enough to get a scholarship today, to one of the smaller schools in America, I'm sure."

Elvin shrieked, pumping her arm in the air and hugging Hugo so hard his cap fell off.

"It's time for me to make some phone calls," he said.

Two months later, in December 2009, a huge portion of the Kibet family crowded the track in Eldoret. Elvin had focused on her running seriously, hoping to bring down her 3,000-meter time closer to ten minutes, the time she knew would grab the attention of a bigger American university. The University of Arizona cross-country and track program was coached by James Li, and Hugo had contacted him to gauge what a full ride scholarship required. As the younger sister of Hilda and Sylvia Kibet, she'd caught Coach Li's attention, and now he'd made the journey to Kenya, where he was planning to watch several time trials for different groups of runners. He was looking for an "up front" female distance athlete and told Hugo that he'd watch Elvin race as long as he was coming.

Elvin's 10:50 had already resulted in a scholarship offer from a United States university. Coming in the form of a National Letter of Intent notice, the offer sat on her dresser in Sylvia's house, unsigned. There was a better school out there for her, she thought. One with a strong public health program, perhaps. A big school like Arizona would be a dream.

It was hard to miss Coach Li as he entered the stadium. He wore a bright red collared shirt with an Arizona logo on it and carried a notebook. With a handful of potential athletes to look at, he was instantly swarmed with local Kenyan coaches and other runners, most of them boys. Elvin stood to the side with the ten other girls who'd race the 3,000 with her. She'd let Hugo navigate the introductions.

One by one the pack around Coach Li dissipated and he made his way over to her, led by Hugo.

"Elvin," Hugo said, "this is Coach James Li from the University of Arizona."

Coach Li held out his hand, which Elvin took. He squeezed firmly and flashed a warm smile which faded just a tiny bit of her nerves.

"Elvin, it's so fantastic to meet you. You're smaller than I'd imagined. Just being honest. Gosh you're small. How old are you?"

"I'm twenty, Coach."

"I see, I see. Well just go out there and run your best today when it's your turn. I know these races can be stressful, but just take it in stride. I've heard about your talent and obviously I know your sisters have done well, so there's nothing to be nervous about."

She could feel the other girls in her group hovering, trying to hear the conversation. Elvin knew they'd give anything to be sized up like this by an American running coach and it made her self-conscious, as much as nervous for the actual race. She thanked him and moved behind the bleachers where she could stretch and watch the boys' races.

An hour later, it was go time. The race felt strong from the start. She was more in control of her pace than during her first time trial. Standing next to Coach Li, Hugo called out her splits as she passed him each time. It seemed faster than her first race, but not enough to make the time she'd hoped for.

Never mind, she thought. *I'll go as hard as I can and if it's not Arizona, then at least another school. One more choice would be good.*

With two laps to go, Elvin's legs began to feel heavy. She stopped listening to Hugo and took herself back to the village. Gogo's voice willed her forward. *My child, never give up. Come home, but first, go out and see the world.*

One of the slower women pulled into the second lane as Elvin lapped her, cheering softly, "Yes, yes . . . you can do it, Elvin."

With 200 meters to go and lactic acid racing through her legs, Elvin focused on Hilda and Daisy who were jumping up and down at the finish line.

"10:30 Elvin! Nice work!" shouted Hugo as she crossed.

The time was slower than she'd hoped, but she'd won by a significant margin and done her best. Putting her arms on her head to catch her breath, she walked over to Coach Li and Hugo.

"Not bad, not bad, Elvin," Coach Li said.

She shook his hand and tried to concentrate as he talked about how competitive it was at the division one level. So much talent in Kenya, and very few scholarships to give, he said.

"This kid Lawi who I saw today . . . the kid's going to be a superstar. He'll get an offer from me right away, but sometimes I need time. That's the case here with you, Elvin. You're clearly the best here today, and you've got potential, but I'm looking for certain things. Your running mechanics are incredibly sound. You don't look like you'd have any risk for injury. I can see your passion and your drive. But I also know you haven't trained very long. And you'd need a full ride, unlike some of the American kids I offer scholarships to. I can offer them partials, but I know you'd need a full ride, so I'll need time to think about it."

Elvin nodded. No matter. She'd given it her best, and surely her 10:30 would attract attention from other coaches. It would have to be enough.

One week later, Hugo picked up the phone in Iten. Nearly 11:00 in the evening, it could only be someone from overseas.

"Hugo, it's James Li. I know that Elvin's sometimes up in the village, so thought I'd try you. I can't stop thinking about the look in her eyes. She's hungry. Absolutely spectacular focus, not to mention her extraordinary biomechanics. And the humility. I like that. Add it all up and throw in the fact that she's got something special being Hilda and Sylvia's sister. As long as she's done okay on her SATs, I'm signing Lawi Lalang and I'd like to sign her to a full ride, as well."

Hugo motioned to Hilda, who came over and listened to the conversation with one ear.

"Oh no worries there, Coach. I'm happy to say she's crushed her SATs."

"Perfect. I know her time wasn't quite there, and goodness she's just so damn small, but given that she's running at altitude on a dirt track, I'm confident she'll get to the place she needs to be. There are too many things in her favor. She was quiet, but even the short conversation we had seemed important. I connected with her. Tell her I'll see her in Tucson."

Hugo navigated his car into the parking lot. He and Elvin were in Nairobi to apply for her passport. It was a full two days of running around the city and it was making her head hurt.

"Let's park and run in to see if we can find you a decent suitcase," Hugo said.

"Can't I just take the bag I took to Moi Girls'?" she inquired.

"No way. Not overseas. You need something sturdy that will survive a trip that long."

"You know I don't have much to bring, right?"

"I do. That's fine. You don't need much. Some clothes to run in. Things that will remind you of home. Other than that, the school will take care of you."

The pair parked and then walked into the mall, with Hugo leading the way. He led them to a staircase that moved, then he paused, letting others go in front of them. He eyed her, knowing that this was a first for her at age twenty.

"Elvin, this is an escalator. It'll take us up."

"Up where?"

"Up to the next floor, where there are different stores we need to check out."

A steady stream of shoppers walked past them, each stepping on the moving staircase.

"I'm not sure Hugo. Can't we just take the regular stairs?"

"You're gonna have to get used to this sooner or later. Here, hold my hand."

Hugo reached over, grabbing her hand and pulling her gently onto the first step.

Chapter Eight

August 2010 had arrived, and Elvin was ready. She'd brushed up on English slang, maintained a strict training schedule, and listened to plenty of American pop songs. Now if she could just get herself through this airport.

Her goodbyes in Kenya felt a blur. She was sure with the amount of travel that Hilda did that she'd see her sister soon. As for the rest of her family, there was uncertainty. With promises to keep in touch through Facebook, she simply hoped for the best and prayed that Gogo would still be alive when she returned.

Ivy tried hard to keep it together. She and Baba were at the matatu stop as the driver loaded suitcases onto its roof. The minivan was covered with bright images of pop singers. Elvin's ride to Nairobi to catch her international flight started here in Eldoret with this leg, a six-hour journey that would be uncomfortable but affordable.

Elvin handed her suitcase to the driver and turned to her sister and father.

"Ivy, you're going to make me cry, too."

Elvin put an arm around her sister, who leaned her head on Elvin's shoulder.

"Girls, you're both going to be fine. Ivy, you're not far behind your sister," Baba said.

"He's right, Ivy. You're going to work hard, and you'll join me soon in America. Just keep up with your studies and I know you'll be discovered just like I was."

Ivy smiled weakly. Her resolve was strong, though in the moment all she could see was her sister leaving for some unknown place she'd only heard about through movies.

Elvin lifted a plastic bag into Ivy's arms.

"I need you to take care of these things for me. Can you do that?"

Ivy nodded, peering into the bag. Inside was a collection of clothing, a stack of photos, and at the bottom, a pair of running shoes.

"Your shoes? You can't leave these behind," Ivy said.

"I can and I will. The university will have running shoes for me when I get there. This is the pair that Sylvia gave me, and now they're yours."

Dusty and caked with dirt, the shoes had seen hundreds of miles, but on Ivy's feet they'd feel brand new.

A horn sounded and the matatu driver waved passengers onto the bus.

Baba embraced Elvin and shoved a warm round of chapati into her shirt pocket.

"Don't forget to eat, small one," he laughed.

The matatu pulled away, leaving a crowd waving. Through the cloudy van window, Elvin watched the streets of Eldoret fade into red dust.

Chapter Nine

Arizona

Tucson, Arizona
2010

The Istanbul airport must have been constructed by the devil, Elvin thought. Its signs pointed every which way. Did an arrow pointing up mean she had to go up a floor on the moving staircase thing or did it mean straight ahead? Her stomach groaned from not enough food. She'd been too scared to eat anything on the plane, including the chapati that Baba had sent with her. To her left was a group of loud, white people dressed in short skirts and tank tops. Behind her was a Middle Eastern family whose women all wore head coverings and spoke in some unrecognizable language.

Holding her backpack, Elvin looked up at the signs again. It's possible she'd be stuck here forever. She and Sylvia had gone over every conceivable challenge to her trip. This included how to go to the bathroom on the airplane and which piece of paper was her boarding pass and which was her visa. Sylvia said being on an airplane was like being in a house, and true to her word, the first flight had been easy. But this. These signs were going to do her in. Wandering over to a corner, Elvin leaned against the cold wall, slumping to the ground in a ball of tears.

After twenty minutes, she stood up, realizing she wasn't getting anywhere by sitting on the airport floor. This was only the first of so many unknowns ahead. Getting stuck now wouldn't do her any good. Following the signs as best she could, Elvin found her way to the proper gate.

The passengers on her flight to Chicago were a mix of all ethnicities and languages. They eventually packed together onto her second flight ever, a journey over the ocean that touched down in the middle of the country.

"Welcome to Chicago O'Hare International Airport" the sign called as Elvin walked the carpeted corridors. By the grace of some higher power, she'd made it to the United States and was now trying to find her last flight, a short hop to Tucson where she'd be met by Coach Li.

Again, with the signs. So many signs with so many arrows pointing in all directions.

"Excuse me, but how do I get to gate B-15? I have another airplane," Elvin asked a group of people standing in line at a coffee shop.

It was the first time she'd spoken English outside Kenya, and she felt self-conscious. Her British-Kenyan accent sounded awkward.

"You've gotta take the train. That'll get you to the B-Concourse," one of the men replied.

"Train? Oh no. I'm sorry my English isn't great. I'm getting on another airplane, not a train."

Two of the men gave each other a glance and one repeated, "It's the train first. Then the plane. That's how it works here."

Elvin thanked the men, wandering off in search of a different and much better answer. Surely, they were lying. Who'd ever heard of a train to get to a plane?

With a bit more luck and the help of a passerby, Elvin landed in Tucson and stumbled out to baggage claim. She'd been studying Coach Li's photo the entire journey, worried she wouldn't remember what he looked like. He was there, arms wide open and giving her a warm hug and welcoming smile. He was the only one allowed to pick up international athletes, but it was part of the job he loved. Seeing him, Elvin sensed the load she'd been carrying since Kenya lift.

"Here she is, the famous Elvin Kibet!"

"I'm famous?" Elvin asked, confused.

Coach Li laughed, "Not just yet, but with a little hard work, perhaps."

It was taking all she had to stay awake. She saw her suitcase and when Coach offered to grab it, she sensed relief. Pulling it off that moving conveyer belt thing seemed crazy, and all she really wanted to do was sit down and sleep. She leaned against a wall, her blurry eyes watching Coach pull it off the conveyer belt.

"Elvin? Elvin are you awake?" Coach asked.

Elvin blinked. Minutes had passed. She must have nodded off leaning against the wall.

"I've been standing here for 15 minutes, but the baggage has stopped coming out and there aren't any more with your name on it. I think we should go see if they can track them."

"Track them, Coach?"

"Your bags. The rest."

"But that's it, Coach. Just the one."

"Just this one little bag? Holy smokes, you travel light. You should've seen the piles that Momo and Hanna came with last week. I swear they brought their entire closets. Eight pairs of shoes, each, I'm guessing."

The two walked to the parking lot, finding Coach Li's car, a sparkling SUV with leather seats. Elvin paused.

"I can't get in," she said nervously.

"What do you mean? Why not?" he asked.

"I'm not clean. I've been traveling for days and I'm going to get your beautiful car dirty," she said.

"Don't be ridiculous! Get in . . . you're perfect!"

Elvin could already tell that her hope to remain unnoticed here in Arizona might be hard to achieve. There was so much new. So much to learn. It was overwhelming.

Outside, the road from the airport stretched toward campus.

"I love this part. I love picking all of you newbies up at the airport. It's only eight miles until we get to campus but it's just enough time to let you know how happy I am that you're here," Coach said.

Elvin began to relax for the first time since leaving home. With a free hand, Coach Li gestured outside to the light posts, each of them adorned with a banner. They featured different University of Arizona athletes in motion.

"You see those banners, Elvin? As head coach, I get to decide which of our runners gets to be on one of those banners every year. Every now and then, I get to tell a recruit that one day, I hope to see you there. It's not something I say to everyone, but I've got a feeling about you, Elvin. I see you up there one day."

With only a night of sleep in a hotel under her belt, Elvin managed to get to the very first workout. Coach Li had arranged housing for her, and it was with other runners from the team. She'd find out today at the workout where she'd live and who she'd live with. Baby steps, she thought.

Her teammates seemed welcoming, though an immediate problem presented itself.

Oh God, they all look the same.

The cross-country team sported women of every hair and eye color but to Elvin, they were one big mass of sameness. Fair-skinned, surprisingly thin, and identical to the next.

"Okay gang, you have the workout from me, so after stretching, give it a go. You freshmen, be sure to link with an upperclassman on this run so you don't get lost. Elvin, you're gonna go home with Hanna after the workout today."

It seemed a simple direction. Go home with Hanna. Yet it seemed a bigger task than sending a man to the moon. To make matters worse, there were two Hannas on the team.

Oh no, I swear I met Hanna an hour ago. I met both. Which one is the Hanna I need?

The team set out for a long run; Elvin's ears tuned to the conversation to pick up cues. Her anxiety grew as the run progressed.

What if I get left behind?

How am I going to figure out who Hanna is?

As the miles passed, her concentration on the running waned. It was taking every inch of mental energy to focus on who she was meant to connect with.

Rounding the corner into the lawn that stretched out in front of their fieldhouse, Elvin saw Coach Li. He looked concerned, no doubt because his star freshman was bringing up the rear.

While the team lay on the grass catching up on summer happenings, Elvin made one final push to determine her Hanna. Without any further clues, the women stood up and dispersed. In a leap of faith, Elvin followed a tall runner with a brunette ponytail. Noticing Elvin, she turned and said, "Oh, I think you're supposed to go with Hanna, Elvin."

Pausing, she saw Elvin's mortified look.

"It's okay. You can't tell who is who, can you? That's okay. And there are two Hannas. But they live together, so that makes it easier."

Does it? Elvin thought. *They have the same name, they look alike, and they live together. And now I live with them. Does this really make it easier?*

The moment of confusion was enough to draw the attention of Coach Li, who came over and guided Elvin to Hanna. She wore a slightly shorter, slightly less brown ponytail and Elvin was sure it would take months to understand how she looked any different from the teammate she'd assumed was a match.

"Of course, yes. Sorry, of course I should have known better. You're Hanna," Elvin said.

"No worries," Hanna replied, smiling broadly. "It's confusing. The other one we call 'Momo.' So that helps. You'll get the hang of this before too long."

Hanna put her hand on Elvin's arm.

"It's a little intimidating at first. I was there last year, too. But really, we're all harmless."

Hanna's eyes were bright, and she seemed to be a focal point for the other women on the team. Several of them approached her, providing extended hugs and sympathetic looks. Elvin took note and chalked it up to more dynamics she'd have to learn.

Coach Li called the women together.

"Okay gang before we leave, a couple of things," he said.

Walking over to Elvin, he put his arm around her shoulders, and she wondered where he was going with this.

"So, here's the deal. I know you're gonna do great at this, so this is just a nudge. Elvin's brand new. Not just to college like some of you, but to running. And hell, to the United States. So now she needs you. It's not easy. So can you step up, please? This is where our season starts and it's not with running or time trials. It's here. In this moment with her. Some things are just bigger than running, team."

Elvin pushed down her embarrassment at being singled out. The gesture from Coach was thoughtful, and the women on her team nodded in affirmation. Things were going to be okay with the team by her side.

On her third day in Tucson, Elvin resolved to go for a run on her own. It was a rest day, but she thought it wise to try to explore a little of her new home by foot. Coach Li had pointed out a place off campus where she could run. There was a traffic light and he'd stood on the corner with her, showing her how to press the button which made the light change and allow her to cross safely. The route was a straight line and back again from her new apartment. How hard could it be?

Several miles into her straight line on the way back, she noticed a home ahead of her with a little blond girl of two or three years old playing in the front yard. Looking up, the girl noticed Elvin running toward her, and screamed. The noise startled Elvin, who reached the girl, bending down to apologize.

"Oh, I'm so sorry I scared you," she said, speaking to the child at eye level.

The girl looked at her with uncertainty, until her father appeared, scooping up his daughter.

"I'm sorry I scared her. I'm just out for a run," Elvin repeated, backing away.

The man didn't respond. Taking a couple steps back into her run, Elvin could see the father consoling his daughter, then spoke in a voice loud enough to hear. The words entered Elvin's tired, jet lagged brain and scattered, not making sense.

"No honey, it's not a monkey. You can tell because she doesn't have a tail."

Father and daughter watched Elvin run away, her footsteps barely making sounds.

The words seemed wrong, but also unfamiliar. For a moment, she thought she'd heard incorrectly. Should she have asked what he meant or rather stood up for herself? This situation was as foreign as the baggage claim, the traffic light, and the fancy SUVs from the past several days.

Hours later, she was still thinking of the incident as she saw Coach Li. He'd decided to take her to all her classrooms in advance, so she'd have an easier time on her first day of lessons. Despite her protests that she'd surely forget and get lost all over again, he insisted. The two of them walked on campus reviewing her schedule. English, political science, and a few gaps to fill with classes she hadn't picked yet.

"Something weird happened on my run, Coach," she said. "Somebody said something as I was running but I didn't understand it."

Coach Li looked left and right, trying to recall which way the political science buildings were.

"You mean you didn't understand the context, or you didn't literally understand the words?" he asked.

"The context, I guess. I feel like in the three days I've been here, I'm really missing a lot. A lot of context."

"Okay that's normal. Plus, college kids have their own language sometimes, so it can be tricky. Let's see if I can help. What did you hear?"

Elvin repeated the story. The little girl screaming at her. The father assuring his daughter that Elvin wasn't a monkey. None of it made sense.

Coach Li had halted, his face reddened and contorted in a mixture of horror and anger.

"This cannot be happening," he said.

"What is it? I mean . . . I'm not a monkey and I don't know why she thought I was. I didn't know what to say but it's not right, is it?"

"Elvin, it's not right. It's awful. Terrible. Racist in every way. We need to go back to that house right now. Tell me where they live. I want you to show me the house."

His voice was raised now, bringing attention from passing students.

He put his arm around Elvin's shoulders and began swiftly leading them away from campus. She pulled back, looking at him. The last thing she wanted to do was make waves. All she wanted was to blend in.

"No, Coach I can't do that. I don't want to make a fuss. I just got here. Can you just help me understand?"

Coach Li paused, assessing his options.

"Can I help you understand? Oh Elvin, what a question. What a beautiful, big, and impossible question. I can start, but this is so much larger than a conversation here with just me."

"So that was racist? Those words?"

"Jesus, yes, I'm afraid they were. On day three, you got a bigger dose of it than almost anyone I've ever known, Elvin. And I'm so damn sorry."

Coach's words made everything clear, and with it, brought her an urge to understand more.

"Well, that's terrible. Just terrible. Should I have said something to them? What would that even be? Holy cow, I have a lot to learn here, don't I?" she asked.

Coach Li had resumed walking her to the political science building.

"I'm afraid so. We can get you into an African American history class if you want. That's a start at least. It'll teach you about slavery and how it's stuck around in all sorts of ways."

"I want to do that, then. I need to do that, rather. Need. I'm here now, so I need to figure this part out. I didn't know slavery was here at one time. I don't know anything about this. Oh my gosh I have so much to learn."

He stopped again, looking at her.

"We'll have things to learn from you, too, Elvin. I'm sure of it. In the meantime, I need you to tell me if anything like this happens again. Especially on campus or in classrooms. The university won't tolerate it."

"I will. I'll tell you," she responded. "I just can't believe people can be so cruel. Nobody told me about this. I wasn't prepared."

Coach Li surveyed the campus and walked in silence, preparing himself and all that was to come for this small girl from Kapchorwa.

Three months later, Elvin had become skilled at airports. The University of Arizona cross-country team had traveled several times by plane and had arrived in Terre Haute, Indiana, for Pre-Nationals, a tune up for the national championship meet. With the help of her teammates, her adjustment had gone as well as could be expected. A series of hilarious misunderstandings, wondrous discoveries, and aching for home.

Her roommates Hanna and Momo had been instrumental in helping her. They never judged and put up with her million questions.

They explained salad to her, which Elvin claimed was like eating leaves, as if they were rodents. It was confusing that salad wasn't cooked, she thought.

Momo and Hanna had trained others to avoid giving Elvin ice water, which gave her headaches.

There were instructions on the proper use of all the kitchen appliances, with special attention to the microwave which Elvin continued to think was safe for metal spoons.

They helped her find ingredients for chai and chapati after finding her nibbling on the one-week-old chapati she still had from Kenya. Soon Lawi Lalang would arrive, and they'd begin cooking together.

She'd been lost in her political science class until she resolved to read the book cover to cover and scored an A.

She'd wowed Coach Li and her team by handily winning her very first collegiate cross-country race.

She'd been unsure of her shoe size when she arrived and told the equipment manager she probably wore the same size as Hanna. A month later the assistant coach noticed her toes poking out the tips and put her in a proper shoe, a full size larger.

She'd found herself several times in the office of Coach Li, teary and homesick, telling him she was ready to go home. Each moment with him showcased his ability to connect with his athletes beyond sport. He seemed more invested in the athletes who were struggling than those who were thriving. She'd leaned on him so heavily that she'd begun to call him Papa Li.

Elvin bounced along the soft terrain. She and her teammates were taking one last jog of the course the day before the race. Each of them checking out the tangents and visualizing the race on their own. This one was a flat course without a single tree getting in the way of the view for spectators. Still adjusting to the soft grass of American cross-country courses, Elvin's eyes lingered on a herd of cows in a meadow beyond the grounds of the marked trails. Distant relatives of Cheptelit, she thought to herself. Much better fed, but not nearly the views that Cheptelit had from her pastures in the village. From her right, the sounds of chatter caught her attention. The loud, boisterous English that she'd adapted to had been replaced with Kalenjin.

Elvin had interacted with a few other Kenyan runners along the way during this cross-country season. It was becoming more common for teams to have an occasional East African on their roster, and she relished the chance to speak Kalenjin.

Today, though, the voices were numerous. She spotted a group of Kenyans from different teams talking in rapid Kalenjin. In the mix, she spotted a man with a shaved head and broad shoulders. From the side, he looked familiar. He spoke with his hands, in gestures that were measured and serious. She walked closer to get a better look.

Turning to wave goodbye to one of the runners, he came into profile, and she knew immediately.

"Titus! Is that you?"

Elvin took a few wide skips to reach the man, confirming he was the same boy she'd met at Sylvia's guesthouse years ago. At least five years, she thought. The boy with the SAT book had somehow made it to the United States.

"Elvin! Oh, I can't believe it," Titus shouted in Kalenjin.

He gave her a giant hug, American style.

"You made it to the States!" he said.

"I did indeed! You left behind your SAT book, and I picked it up and look where it got me! I can't believe you remember me. I was just a girl."

"Well as I recall, you told me not to forget you and how could I? You're all grown up now. Look at your jacket! University of Arizona. With James Li? Nice. Very nice indeed. Proud of you, Elvin."

Behind Titus, a slender runner stood silent. He had wide, dark eyes, a similar shaved head, and was wearing a uniform from Western Kentucky University.

"So, tell me, you are long since graduated and I don't see you in running clothes, so how is it that I'm finding you on a field in Indiana?" Elvin asked.

"My brother. I tried to bring several of my siblings over, but this one's the first to succeed."

Titus put his arm around the runner behind him, who looked more a boy than a man.

"Elvin, this is Shadrack. Fellow runner and my baby brother."

Part II

United States of America

Chapter Ten

Together

2010–2011

Runners cruised by, checking out the course conditions in Terre Haute, Indiana. Tucking into the slipstream of faster teammates, a few stragglers made their way past Elvin, Titus, and Shadrack who stood off to the side chatting. Twenty minutes had passed, and Elvin still couldn't believe she was on a field in the United States talking to a friend from home. The fact that they'd run into each other in the middle of a collegiate cross-country course seemed fateful. Titus had left Kenya so many years ago that he was anxious for in-depth updates. Mutual friends. The scene in Iten and Eldoret. Who else had made it out of Kenya and into foreign universities.

She shared a few of her favorite stories from her first few months in America: How she'd tried to fly well under the radar despite her steep learning curve. The day she went to the University of Arizona Athletic Department equipment room and was given new shoes, a uniform, and all the socks she needed. How she'd overslept for a workout, assuming teammates would wake her up like her family did in Kenya. Alarm clocks were foreign to her until Momo taught her how to use one. Washing machines, which were only slightly less confusing than stoves. How she'd made chai one day and it bubbled over, putting out the flame on the gas stove. Nobody had mentioned the importance of turning off the gas, so she left and hours later when she and her roommates returned, the entire apartment smelled like gas.

"I was like a fish out of water," Elvin said. "I feel like I'm just now getting the hang of it. I've been constantly dehydrated because the water here is always served cold. Ice water, refrigerated water, freezing water from the tap. It gives me a headache. I can't do it."

Titus smiled. "Well, I suppose if you haven't grown up with a refrigerator, that's kind of how it goes!"

"Exactly. The first week I overheard Coach telling one of his interns to give me a chance. 'She's just come from the village,' he said. The reminders are hard to miss; try as I do to fit in."

Shadrack listened, rapt. He'd only met other Kenyan men in the States. No women. Hearing Elvin's bubbly descriptions of her experiences felt sweet and intoxicating. The University of Arizona jacket she wore was bright red, and she was swimming in it. He wondered how she survived the stampede of runners on dusty cross-country courses. She'd mentioned winning her first meet only a few weeks after she'd arrived. Surely she was a fighter if she'd made it this far. He held eye contact with her when he was able, finding it hard to concentrate when he did.

"I'll be honest, the transition hasn't been easy. I'm in Coach Li's office once every few weeks crying and telling him that maybe it's time for me to go home. But I think I'm getting there."

Elvin turned to wave at Hanna and Momo who were across the field stretching. She was sure they'd ask who she was talking to.

"What's your deal, Shadrack? How's Western Kentucky?" Elvin asked.

Shadrack snapped himself into chat mode.

"It's been good, but I think I've got potential to go a little bigger."

"A bigger school, you mean?"

"Yeah, possibly. Depends how I do at nationals in a couple weeks."

"Well, if you've been here for almost a year and figured out how to hydrate and feed yourself, I feel like you've already conquered the world!" Elvin joked.

"I've got a car here, so maybe we grab lunch tomorrow after the race?" Titus suggested.

"A car! I'm even more impressed," said Elvin. "And that's another thing. This whole driving thing. Our assistant coach picked me up in an SUV on my first day here and I couldn't believe it. A woman. Driving a car. With a dog in the back. Can you believe it? Dogs inside cars and houses? It doesn't get crazier than that," she laughed.

Following the race the next day, Elvin settled into the front seat of Titus' car. A quick lunch out was in order before she would be required to depart for the airport with the rest of her team. She ordered her usual lunch of pepperoni pizza with a side of French fries. The women on her team were constantly amazed by her pizza consumption, complaining that they couldn't look at a slice without gaining five pounds. Elvin laughed the comments off. Her gratitude that she could enjoy food like this every day brought her back to pizza and fries frequently.

"It's nice to see you eating more than salad," Shadrack commented. "That's pretty much all the women on my team eat."

"I know! It's weird, right? What's the deal with the salads and uncooked food? Rabbit food, I call it. When you've come from a place with so little to eat, why eat all that salad when there's meat everywhere? So much meat!" Elvin said.

She folded her pizza in half the way she'd seen the men on her team do. Shadrack and Titus were eating burgers, the grease dripping down their fingers. Shadrack's race had gone much better than hers, and he seemed more talkative than the day before. There was something different about him. Different from American men for sure, but also the Kenyan men she'd met here in the States. So many of them had inflated egos, but Shadrack seemed down-to-earth and not remotely self-absorbed. Almost painfully humble. When he laughed his voice went up into his throat a little bit, catching in a higher octave. It was cute, she decided.

Back in Tucson, Elvin entered Coach Li's office after practice. Sitting in his cozy side chair, she reviewed her race at Pre-Nationals with him. As she often did, she lingered on the ways she could've been faster. The tactics she could've used to get to the finish line just a few seconds sooner. She began to feel teary but fought hard to keep them at bay. Coach Li stood up and closed the door.

"Oh Elvin, it's so hard to see you like this. Tell me what's bugging you? Is it really the race or something else? The teammates? Or just the whole 'this-isn't-Kenya' part? You know I get it. I was in your position years ago when I came here from China."

"It's not the teammates. They've been amazing. Hanna is taking me to her house for Thanksgiving in a couple weeks."

Elvin dabbed at her eyes.

"I think I'll go home with Momo for the summer. I'm just homesick. It's getting better, but I still haven't adjusted. Thank God I have the women on the team. Momo and Hanna, in particular."

"Super. I would've been surprised if they'd been anything less than welcoming. Hanna has had a hard year. Having you in her life has been important, I think."

Elvin learned through conversations with Hanna that she'd lost her brother Kyle in a car accident the previous spring. Kyle had been only twenty-two years old, and newly enlisted in the Air Force. While off duty, he was a passenger in a car which hydroplaned and was hit by an oncoming vehicle. He'd suffered massive internal injuries, losing his life and years of future adventures with his little sister Hanna. Hanna's loss left Elvin constantly thinking about her baby brother Collins, and how much she missed him. If only she could find a way to bring both him and Ivy to America. At times, the weight in Elvin's apartment was heavy with Hanna's grief, Elvin's own adjustments, and the pressures all of them were carrying from college athletics.

"As far as your running, you've had a few highs and lows, but I think you'll be on the upswing soon. An adjustment period is normal. You've had a lot coming at you," Coach Li added.

Coach Li walked over to a CD player on his side table and looked through a stack of discs.

"I met a bunch of Kenyans at Pre-Nationals, too. I think it'll help to keep connecting with them," Elvin said.

She thought about Shadrack and heard an upbeat song coming from the CD player.

"You know I care more about your emotional well-being than your athletic performance, don't you?" Coach Li asked.

"I do."

"Okay then. We're going back to Terre Haute for the national championship race, so let's just focus on that part. Your heart and mind being healthy. This song is a good start."

Through the door of Coach Li's office, staff walking by could hear the familiar sounds of Bobby McFerrin singing, "Don't Worry Be Happy."

Back in Terre Haute for the national cross-country championship race, Elvin felt more at ease. She saw Shadrack the night before the race at her hotel, and as he left, they shared a brief kiss. Simple but natural, it both took her off guard and scared her a little. Everything in her world was new, including these feelings. Gogo surely would approve of him, but for the moment she kept the kiss and her feelings to herself. The rules on how romance worked were different here in America. She still needed time to figure it all out.

Running, on the other hand, she was nailing. She placed first for the Wildcats, helping them to eleventh place. Shadrack had an unbelievable run as well, and what she saw impressed her. He ran effortlessly, with a long stride and a slight, crossbody hitch in his right forearm. At the finish line, he'd placed twenty-seventh overall. It was an impressive showing, and enough for him to consider a transfer to a bigger program.

"Can Titus and I call you over break?" Shadrack asked as he and Elvin did a cool down run after the races.

"Yes, of course. I'd love to chat. By video? I'm not going anywhere, so I'll be all alone and it would be nice to have the company."

She knew that the calls would be with both Titus and Shadrack, but secretly hoped Titus might be gone for a few of them.

From a hundred yards away, they saw Titus waving his arms. He was behind the rope that separated spectators from athletes and their coaches. Shadrack and Elvin exchanged a quick hug goodbye.

"Bro, that race was unbelievable. You are on FIRE!" Titus exclaimed as Shadrack approached.

He gave his brother an embrace.

"Felt good," Shadrack replied.

"You hear? Oklahoma State won the whole damn thing! My man Dave Smith is over there with his team, but I'm gonna try to grab his attention."

A large group of runners had gathered nearby, all of them dressed in orange. As they made their way to the waiting spectators, Titus cupped his hands to the sides of his mouth, screaming to get the attention of the coach in the middle of the sea of orange.

"Dave! Over here! Coach Smith!"

Dave Smith, the Oklahoma State University cross-country coach, glanced over and saw Titus behind the rope. It had been years, but he recognized the smile of the man who'd driven him around Kenya looking at promising athletes. He walked over, momentarily tearing himself away from the celebration of winning a national championship.

"Titus! Good to see you. It's been years," Dave stuck out his hand and Titus grabbed it.

"Last time I saw you was in Kenya. And here you are winning a national championship!" Titus said.

"What can I say . . . those men got it done today!" Dave responded.

"Dave, I want you to meet my brother Shadrack."

Shadrack smiled and shook Dave's hand. Dave noted his Western Kentucky jacket.

"He's not one to brag, but my baby brother only arrived in January and just placed twenty-seventh. Top freshman in the country."

"Twenty-seventh! That's a decent first outing," Dave exclaimed.

Shadrack nodded, as Titus continued. Shadrack knew that there was a fuzzy ethical line when talking with other coaches about transferring, so he let his brother take the lead.

"He's looking to transfer. Get somewhere bigger where he'll have a more significant impact."

"Well, I can't say I'm not interested. I'd have to look at our scholarship pool and get Western Kentucky to release him. Any other nibbles so far?"

"Not sure. Maybe Florida State."

"Okay, well, keep me posted," Dave said as he shifted his attention back to his OSU men's team.

They were in full-on celebration mode, cheering at him to rejoin them.

"I can't promise anything but keep in touch. Shadrack, nice to meet you. Great race today," Dave said.

Shadrack flashed a wide grin, the kind that lit up rooms. Dave returned the smile, taking note of his gut feeling. This was a kid to watch. He made a mental note to follow Shadrack's spring track season and was then swallowed back into a sea of orange.

There weren't enough blankets in the apartment to cut the chill. Winter break had only begun, and Tucson temperatures dipped into the forties at night. With all her roommates home for the holidays, Elvin's days were filled with running and talking on the phone or video chatting with family in Kenya. She'd discovered a data plan which gave her unlimited minutes, a mind-blowing concept when she was used to a world in which she paid shillings for every minute of time on the telephone. Talking to friends back in Kenya kept her connected, but the calls she lived for were those with Titus and Shadrack. Their video chats went for hours, and typically included a barrage of questions that Elvin had hesitated to ask Hanna or Momo out of embarrassment.

How to use the bank's ATM machine.

How to use a debit card to buy groceries.

How to book a plane ticket.

"Is the heat turned on?" Shadrack asked late one night.

Titus had gone to bed, leaving Shadrack and Elvin with their own conversation. Though she enjoyed her chats with Titus, it was getting harder to deny that she'd started to have feelings for Shadrack. He represented more than a connection to home and more than a new friend. The simple kiss they'd shared at the national championship races in Terre Haute had been a first for both. While this might not have been a big deal for some American women, it carried a ton of weight in her world.

"What do you mean the heat? We don't have a fireplace. This is Arizona, silly," she replied.

"No, I mean the heat. Have you turned up the thermostat?"

Silence from Elvin. Shadrack suspected he knew what the issue was.

"Walk around the apartment and look for something on the wall with numbers on it," he directed.

Elvin took his advice, finding a small box on the wall and pushing a button that made the numbers climb higher. Five minutes later her chills abated as Shadrack tried to keep a straight face.

"It's okay," she assured him, her bright smile making him ache to be closer.

He was already counting the days until he'd see her again in person.

"Go ahead and laugh. Heat in the house was something I didn't know about. I didn't exactly get a set of directions when I got on the plane in Nairobi," she added, bursting into laughter at her own ridiculousness.

"So, what's the story with us, Elvin Kibet?" Shadrack asked, transitioning their conversation.

"What do you mean?" she replied, stalling for time to figure out how to respond.

"Well, I mean, are you and I, you know, dating now?"

Elvin went flush. Aside from getting on an airplane and coming to the States, this was more foreign than anything. This conversation. This relationship.

And also, it seemed perfect.

"I guess we are, but I'm not really one to advertise it, if you know what I mean."

She saw him laugh a little in a sweet way. Once again, he seemed undeterred by anything she could throw at him.

"No advertising. Got it. I promise not to announce it on a billboard."

Elvin smiled, resting her chin in her hand. She tilted her head to see him from a different angle on the screen. He looked good from every vantage point. In the early morning hours after finishing their call, Elvin realized she might make a life for herself here in the United States. She was less homesick, and her sadness was lifting. Slowly, with the kindness of friends, a loving coach, the connection to home through Titus, and new feelings for Shadrack, she began to see in equal parts both the beauty and the madness in this place she now called home.

Chapter Eleven

Oklahoma

2011–2013

Of all the things that perplexed her about this new world, the relationship the women on Elvin's cross-country and track team had with food was at the top of the list. She didn't understand it and for sure couldn't explain it, but there was something odd with food. Something mysterious that she couldn't put her finger on.

Every time the team would go out to eat, the women would all order salads and Elvin would order her usual. Fettucine alfredo or pizza with fries. If the team went out for ice cream, inevitably the women would all order the smallest scoops with the lowest fat content. Then without fail, one or two of her friends would order cones and hand them directly to Elvin, who'd enjoy all of them herself.

In America, food was everywhere. Abundant. It had been in such short supply in the village that here in Tucson, Elvin intended to enjoy every bite. Women back home were praised for large tummies and big behinds. Considered a sign of wealth, it seemed the opposite of the way things were here. In America, she'd discovered that meals at home were rarely eaten together, nobody talked about the joy of eating, there was a scale at the gym that felt like God—like it was the most important thing or being in the universe—and then there was the bizarre matter of the food in the cupboards that just . . . disappeared.

At first, Elvin wondered if she'd been dreaming. She made an entire platter of chapati, but the next morning it was gone. She bought two boxes of cereal and found the empty boxes in the trash twenty-four hours later.

The answer to what happened, and the ways food impacted her teammates came one January evening in the middle of the night. Elvin's bed was adjacent to Momo's, and close enough to hear her crying. She woke to the sounds and in the darkness reached out for her friend.

"Momo, are you all right? Why are you crying?" Elvin said.

Her arm wasn't long enough to touch her, but Elvin's sleepy voice oozed compassion.

"I'm so sorry, Elvin. I did it again. I can't help it when I get this way."

"What do you mean? What did you do? Are you sick?"

"No, not exactly. I mean, yes, I think I am. The other day I ate both boxes of cereal you'd bought. And just now I ate all the leftover dinner you made and had put in the fridge." Momo sniffled. "I know we were saving it for the next few nights."

Through the shadows, Elvin could see Momo sit up in bed.

"All of it? But there was so much left over. Why are you so hungry? Should I make more? I can make more tomorrow."

"No, no, it's not that. I don't need more. I think I just need some help."

"Help with food, you mean?"

"Yes, help with food. Because what I do is eat and eat because I feel bad about myself, and then I make it go away."

Elvin's silence said everything. She had absolutely no clue what Momo was talking about and suddenly had fifty more questions. Patiently, Momo answered each one until nearly daybreak, both stopping several times to cry.

By the time the sun rose, Elvin had undergone a crash course in bulimia, binging, and purging. Momo talked about the way she saw herself and her body, which wasn't remotely how Elvin saw her. She talked about how running felt addictive at times and was perhaps part of the problem. There was the matter of her scholarship and the stress of needing to run well to maintain it. Clearly, this wasn't just a problem for Momo. Other women on the team were suffering, too. Mostly in the shadows.

All of it seemed foreign and desperately sad. Elvin thought back to the many magazine ads and television commercials she'd seen since she arrived in America, all featuring thin white women who looked nothing like most of the women she saw every day walking around campus and Tucson. For Elvin, this was just a funny observation, but for her friends, she suddenly realized they were aspiring to a social construct. It seemed to help both Elvin and Momo to talk through how they viewed food. Momo saw each day of eating as full of landmines, while Elvin looked forward to what new culinary delights she could find to fuel her body and her running.

"You only have one body, Momo. I think you're perfect just the way you are."

"I really want to believe that. I do. It's just that my mind is telling me something different. I know I should be seeing a therapist. Maybe it's time."

Therapy was something Elvin had heard about. It sounded like it involved people whose entire job it was to sit and listen to others when they were sad or frustrated.

"Coach Li helps me when I'm sad. You've talked to him too, right?"

"A little. It's not something I like to talk about, so mostly I try to hide it. He has too much on his plate. I don't want to stress him out. But you're right. I should talk to him. He's good with this stuff."

"You're right. He'd be upset to see you like this, Momo, but he'd help you get to the right people. He cares more about you than he cares about the steeplechase record," Elvin said.

"I want to live in Kenya. It sounds so much easier. Can you stick me in your suitcase the next time you go?" Momo said.

Elvin laughed. "Oh, believe me when I tell you there are plenty of problems, there, too. Different problems, but big ones just like here."

Elvin resolved to keep an eye on Momo. She couldn't do the work for her, but she could listen and learn. That had to count for something.

In early 2011, the spring semester of Elvin's first year in Tucson started. She and Shadrack were communicating regularly, though the concept of calling him a "boyfriend" felt scandalous and very American. Girls from tiny villages in Kenya didn't have boyfriends. They were either married, or they were not. Hanna had caught on, gently teasing her about the boy from Kentucky who she spent hours on videocalls with.

"Even Coach Li approves of Shadrack, Elvin. I think he did his homework on him," Hanna said.

"I don't know what on earth you're talking about," Elvin responded.

"We're just happy for you, that's all. Shadrack seems very cool. We'll see if he pulls anything together for your birthday," Hanna added.

Though Elvin had tried to keep the budding relationship under wraps, it was clear that she wouldn't be able to much longer. Nor did she want to. He made her happy, even if it had to be from hundreds of miles away over videocalls. There were several track races coming up in the spring that they'd both be at, and they'd already planned how to steal time together.

Elvin's birthday was just a few days away, but it was nothing she intended to celebrate. In fact, she'd never celebrated and wasn't even sure her parents would remember the date she and Ivy were born if pressed.

She found herself thinking of Ivy on their actual birthday several days later. Ivy was still in Kenya, and with technology they'd been able to start chatting more. They'd been brainstorming ways for her to get to America. She hadn't taken to running like her sisters, but there must be other paths. Lost in thought, Elvin was sitting in the passenger seat of the assistant coach's SUV. This time, no dog in the vehicle. They'd been running errands but instead of taking Elvin back to the house she shared with Momo and Hanna, the coach had announced a quick stop at her own house. She needed help carrying something inside, and with Elvin to assist it would take no time at all, she insisted.

Elvin walked the path up to the front door, stepping inside after her coach. A chorus of "Surprise!" startled her, and popping out from behind couches and chairs were her teammates, a dozen of them, all wearing silly, colorful, pointed hats. They looked at her, clapping, with grins stuck on every face.

"What?! What's this? What's the surprise?" Elvin shouted, totally oblivious.

"It's you, Elvin! It's a surprise for you!" shouted Momo.

"But what did I do?" Elvin asked, truly confused.

Her teammates began yelling, "Birthday! Birthday!"

"You were born," said Hanna. "Happy birthday! It's a surprise birthday party."

A mix of shock and gratitude washed over her as someone strapped a purple hat on her head. The living room was covered with streamers, pink balloons, and a banner that said, "Happy Birthday." A table on one end was filled with food and a cake with her name on it. In the corner there was a pile of gifts, more than she'd ever seen in one place. And plastered on one wall, what looked like a cutout of a small horse with its tail missing and stuck a few inches away with masking tape.

"But is this all for me?" Elvin asked, surveying the scene.

"Yes, unless someone else on the team has a birthday today!" Momo responded.

Elvin began to cry. The hats. The food. The cake. The decorations. The gifts. Especially the gifts. She'd never had a birthday party, and certainly not one with gifts. The kindness and the joy had done her in.

Hanna glanced at Momo who made a motion for her to take Elvin away from the chaos. Hanna put her arm around Elvin and led her away from their teammates who'd turned to the food and music. She'd known Elvin long enough to know what was wrong but needed confirmation.

"Is it that you miss your family or . . . is it just too much?" she asked.

"It's too much," Elvin said.

"I get it. I do. But sometimes here people like to go a little overboard. It makes them feel good to give. And you've brought so much already to *us*, Elvin. Your delicious chapati-cooking. Your funny stories from Kenya. The way you thought that big dog last week in the field we ran past was a horse," Hanna laughed.

"I'd never seen a horse!" Elvin said, slowly wiping away tears.

"I can't believe you thought it was a horse," Hanna added.

She joined her in laughter and hugged her friend.

"You've brought life to this team, and we really love you. We just wanted to show you and today seemed like a good time to do that."

"I love all of you, too. I'm grateful. You've taught me so much. I can't believe what I've learned in just six months," Elvin said.

"How to cook pasta, where to buy groceries, when to set your alarm clock," Hanna joked.

"And that's not even counting all the classes I've taken. Political science, African American history," Elvin added.

Hanna tipped her head and scrunched her nose.

"Yeah, I'm afraid you're learning all the good and all the bad about the United States, aren't you?"

"You're not kidding. This country is messy."

"You're finding your big, old American voice, Elvin. We're all becoming much better people by listening to you and seeing things through your eyes."

"I hope so. Mostly I just feel like I don't know what I'm doing here," Elvin laughed.

"Come out to the patio. I've got my gift for you out there, and I can't wait to show it to you."

Hanna took Elvin's hand and led her to the patio door. She covered Elvin's eyes and counted to three. In front of them, a green bicycle. The handlebars were covered with purple and silver streamers and tinsel. A brand-new lock and helmet were propped against the pedals.

"A bike! It's for me?" Elvin asked.

"It's for you. Everyone here has bikes to get to campus and I know you've been walking all these months. This will get you there faster. Momo and I will teach you how to ride it this weekend."

Elvin reached out and stroked the seat. The bike would make things so much easier. It looked like it had miles on it, and perhaps stories.

"Oh, Hanna it's amazing! I love it. Thank you, thank you. I can't wait to learn. Where did you get it?"

Turning back to Hanna, she noticed her smile had left, replaced by eyes that had welled with tears.

"Oh no . . . So much crying today. Why are you crying? Hanna, where did you get the bike?"

"It was Kyle's," she said.

They'd talked about Kyle a few times these past months. Hanna's brother had been gone less than a year. In frequent visits to Hanna's nearby home, Elvin had gotten to know her parents, sister, and grandmother. Hanna's mother had made sure to document every visit and Hanna always put the photos on Facebook, a visual scrapbook of Elvin's first months in America.

"He'd be so happy to see you riding it, Elvin. My mom wanted you to have it. It's really helped us to have you here the past few months. We wanted to do something special. Plus, it'll keep Kyle with us a little bit longer to see you scooting around campus on his bike."

The two hugged, both awash in tears and laughter. It was well into the next day in Kenya late that night when Elvin finally got on a video call with Ivy.

"Happy birthday, little sister. You're not gonna believe my day."

Standing with the men's cross-country team inside a conference room near the coaches' offices, Dave Smith minced no words. The Oklahoma State University coach had gotten wind that his team had done a second workout on the down low the previous day. Their first had been sub-par, and Dave suspected he knew who was behind the secret second workout. He glanced over at Shadrack.

Dave had succeeded in bringing Shadrack from Western Kentucky the previous year. Now it was the fall of 2012 and Shadrack was a junior, but he was still learning how to accept disappointment. Workouts that ended poorly often meant he'd see Shadrack in his office in tears and asking about the possibility of a transfer. It wasn't that he didn't feel happy at OSU, but rather that he couldn't bear to think about the money Dave had spent to bring him on scholarship, only to perform below his capabilities. It was an unusual display of vulnerability and emotion from one of his athletes. It took time, but Dave had learned that the emotions were only because Shadrack hated letting him down.

"Look guys, this just isn't how I want you to handle crappy workouts. First, it wasn't that bad. Second, we're only a few weeks away from

Nationals. It got away from us last year and we learned. Don't screw it up by killing yourselves with a second workout."

The team nodded in affirmation. Dave was a well-respected coach with the accolades to back up his training methods. The way he studied other teams to find tactical advantages was legendary, but none of it would help if his men were overtraining on the sly.

"Shaddy, you hear me? Tom, I'm serious here. Girma, you, too. This is a team effort. I need all of us on the same page here."

The men acknowledged their coach and scattered, leaving Shadrack alone with Dave. Shadrack stretched his legs out in front of him while Dave leaned against the desk, arms crossed. Shadrack was still wearing the clothes that his brother-in-law Alfred had given him so long ago in Eldoret when he was living with them and running for the very first time. It was eons ago. He'd found a brotherhood here in Oklahoma, and it seemed so special that he'd tried to bring in one of his Kenyan friends who was looking to transfer. Paul Chelimo would be a great addition to the team, he thought. The two of them would make a strong partnership. The team and Coach Smith had become family and he wanted to share it with Paul.

"You've been here a year now, Shaddy. You're a huge part of this team. I know it frustrates you to have poor workouts and even more so to have bad races, but you've gotta listen to me when I remind you that we want you here. You contribute so much more than scores for us."

Shadrack had heard this before from his coach, and each time felt like an elixir.

"You bring people together and you make them feel good about being a part of this team. That's a much more important goal here than running."

"I hear you, Coach."

"I know the guys kid you about the way you arrived here. I had to chop up everyone's scholarships to bring you on here and they joke about it. I get it. But let's stay the course. Trust the training. Good God, let's run like we're in college and not professionals. I'm not training you for the pros right now."

The words were simple, and finally sinking in. There would be plenty of time to think about his post-college plans. He assumed running wasn't in the cards. He'd worked hard on his degree in construction management technology. Perhaps he could finally put it to good use. Meanwhile, his younger brother Nicholas had been in the States for a few years and recently dropped out of college to join the Army. That seemed a respectable path, in Shadrack's mind, and he was considering it.

Elvin wouldn't like it, but maybe she would warm to it. After all, running was only temporary for both. Her own running career in Arizona was on the upswing, having earned All-American status earlier in the year. They'd been together over a year now. The long-distance thing had forced them to take things slowly, but it was clear they were meant for each other. The love they had for each other and for running grew constantly.

Yet once college and running were done, they'd surely have to look at real-life options together, either in the United States or Kenya. Elvin and Shadrack had trained all summer together in Boulder with her sister Hilda, who'd been there preparing for the 2012 London Olympics. Concentrated, in-person time together gave them space to be a regular couple, doing regular things. Shadrack taught Elvin how to drive and she told him story after story from her days in Kapchorwa. Days flew by, each of them feeling like they'd been around each other forever. Their path together seemed clear. The only question was what that path looked like.

Shadrack's brother Nicholas seemed transformed by the Army, and in a good way. Every time they'd chat, Shadrack could see how the experience of joining the military had helped his brother grow. If they were back in Kenya, the Army would be one of the first options they'd consider after high school. Doing so in America could only serve to solidify his gratitude at what the country had given him. A life in Kenya would be the easy choice. With an American degree, he'd easily find a job. Staying in the United States for Army service meant more time away from his family. Then again, his family was starting to look like . . . Elvin.

Oklahoma State University took the 2012 NCAA Cross Country championships with a wave of orange jerseys crushing the competition. The win propelled Shadrack into the end of his junior year, and with it, thoughts of where he'd go after college. By the time the calendar hit the summer of 2013, he was certain. It was time to break it to Elvin during one of their nightly video chats. She was gearing up for her own cross-country season and with Elvin in the lead, the University of Arizona women were ranked number one in the country.

"So, I've been thinking about next year. After graduation," he said via video chat one night.

Elvin was rolling out chapati circles on her kitchen counter in Tucson.

"Something here in the States, yes? Your grades have been fantastic. I'm sure you could find someone to hire you and sponsor a work visa."

She focused on Shadrack, dressed in sweats with an OSU logo on the chest. The long-distance thing had worn them both down, but the end was near. One more year until he graduated, and they'd find a way to be closer.

"I think I have a better plan. Something more secure. Better benefits."

"Sounds awesome. What is it? Tell me it's in Tucson, please!" Elvin laughed.

"Not exactly. I'm a little nervous to tell you. I don't think it would be your first choice."

Elvin stopped rolling the dough and stared at the screen.

"Tell me this instant, Shaddy."

"The Army. I'm going to enlist."

"Are you? Is this happening?"

"It's happening and it feels like the right thing to do," he replied.

"What does that mean for us?"

"It means you'll finish your senior year and I'll go to basic training, focus on a specialty, and then get placed in a unit. When you graduate, you can move to wherever I've been sent."

Elvin thought about her father and all the years he was gone. She'd be willing to consider this option for Shadrack, but with hesitation.

He could tell the entire thing made her nervous.

"One step at a time, as they say. For now, just keep rolling that chapati dough, babe."

Chapter Twelve

Enter WCAP

2013–2014

Dave Smith and Shadrack walked along the Oklahoma State University cross-country course. The team had just finished an early season workout. Shadrack's senior year had begun, and he'd broken the news to Dave. He was planning to enlist shortly in the United States Army and follow in the footsteps of his younger brother Nicholas. Coach Smith wasn't taking it well.

"Shaddy, I'm telling you, the world isn't in a great place right now. 2013 has been a mess so far. Truly tumultuous and it's bound to get worse. You realize you'll be deployed if you enlist, don't you? It's inevitable."

"I understand. I do. And I won't lie. That part makes me nervous. It's Elvin's biggest concern, too."

"Plus, you've worked so damn hard on your degree, Shaddy. Don't you want to use it when you graduate in May?"

"I do and I know I will. Someday. Here's the thing, Coach," Shadrack continued.

He pushed the sleeves up on his OSU running shirt, using his hands as he spoke. Dust kicked up around them on the trail. Each turn and incline had become so familiar to him that he was sure he could run the course blindfolded.

"This country has given me a ton of opportunities. My life is different because I'm here now. Clearly. That's not something I take lightly, and it's important for me to give back. I don't know where I'll end up. Maybe it'll be back in Kenya. Now, though, I feel I owe it to this country to serve."

Coach Smith found it hard to push back. He knew Shadrack's leadership on the team over the past few years would translate well in a military setting. It would surely spell the end of his running career, but running professionally was never the goal.

"Well, Shaddy. If you really feel it's the direction you want to go, I'll support you."

"I'm sure. This is going to be the end of my running career, but the Army is the ultimate team, Coach."

"That it is, Shaddy. You'll be an outstanding soldier. In the meantime, let's make the most of your senior year. Exciting stuff ahead for the next few seasons of running. I want you to go out on top."

Spring of 2014 arrived, bringing Shadrack's final semester of college and his last outdoor track season. He spent long hours on the phone with his friend Paul Chelimo, who was also heading to the Army. While Paul hadn't ended up running with him at OSU the way he'd hoped, Shadrack was excited that they'd both picked the Army for their next moves.

"I don't know, man, my legs are strong, but I've got the upper body strength of a toddler. I can't even do five pushups. I'm not sure how I'm going to make it through boot camp," Shadrack confessed on the phone one night.

"You've got some work to do, but I've got faith you'll survive," replied Paul.

Shadrack and Elvin were seeing each other as often as they could. He'd grown certain that she was the one and only for him. Her energy was infectious, her sense of humor witty. She was his favorite person in the universe. His best friend. How in the world it happened that they'd met all the way in America after growing up so near to each other in Kenya amazed him every day.

Elvin felt the same way about him. She loved everything about him. Every moment they were together made her feel safe. Their conversation was natural and flowed as if they'd known each other since childhood. His laugh made her melt, with the way it came so easily and always ended up in a high-pitched, airy giggle with his head tilted back a little to catch air.

It was his decision to enter the Army which concerned her most. Her childhood had been marked by an absent father who was gone because of his own military service. There was no chance she'd want that for her own children. So when Shadrack posed the hypotheticals that involved them married, she brushed them aside. His response to her dismissiveness was relentlessly patient.

"You lead the way. When you're ready, I'll be here waiting" was the refrain. Always.

Midway through the year, a twist arose in Shadrack's plan to leave running behind and focus on a military career. A program called the World Class Athlete Program popped onto the scene as an option for distance runners in the Army who were interested in pursuing their sport professionally. Poking into it, Shadrack learned that the program was its own unit in the Army. Soldiers who met qualifying time standards were entitled to receive orders directly to the WCAP unit. The program's history was primarily with boxers, wrestlers, and shooters but it looked like distance runners were getting more involved. It all seemed a possibility if Shadrack could achieve the qualifying standard in the 5,000 or 10,000 meters set by the program. If he could be assigned to a unit whose main function was to compete for the United States it would check two boxes. Running and service. And if he avoided deployment at the same time, at least in the short term, it might mean he'd convince Elvin to finally consider tying the knot.

The US Army's World Class Athlete Program (WCAP) allows top-ranked soldier-athletes to perform at the international level while also serving their nation in the military. Our members train and compete throughout the year—and aim for the Olympic and Paralympic Games.

WCAP Soldiers come from the Active, Reserve and National Guard components, and are selected for their ability to perform at the highest level of their sports. After joining the unit, they hone their skills with elite civilian and military coaches at America's best facilities. Meanwhile, they keep current with Army requirements, attend military schools and stay competitive with their uniformed counterparts.

WCAP Soldiers also conduct essential outreach activities. They hold clinics, speak to high school and college audiences, talk with athletic teams and make appearances in support of Army recruiting stations. They become a training asset to the larger Army, too, through Total Soldier Enhancement Training (TSET), which sends Mobile Training Teams of WCAP Soldier-athletes to lead units through customized resilience and performance enhancement skills training.

WCAP also grants the Army important national visibility, and reinforces public pride in our Armed Forces. Especially during high-profile competitions like the Olympics, WCAP Soldiers provide positive role models, motivate their fellow Soldiers and give Americans another reason to get excited about the Army. Since 1948, 446 Soldiers have represented the United States at the Olympics, earning 111 medals in a variety of sports. WCAP continues that proud tradition.

—Official US Army World Class Athlete Program website

It's a Sunday morning just outside Colorado Springs. Long before church or house chores, the distance runners who are part of the United States Army's World Class Athlete Program attack their weekly long run.

They wear standard running clothes. Athletic caps to keep bare heads warm in the early morning hours. Loose t-shirts of high-end fabric to keep cool once the sun hits hard.

Among the group, several are wearing gear with the U.S. Army logo. A few have on olive-green t-shirts with the name of their program. A torch with a yellow flame underlays the end of the acronym WCAP. On the sleeves, the American flag is embroidered in white and gray.

Fancy running watches are started.

The pack tightens, a group of ten today. Nine men and one woman.

Running shoes that were once clean are instantly coated with dirt as the group tears through the miles. Seven minute miles turn to six minute miles and then five. These aren't runs for conversation, but rather they are the high-speed bread and butter of any long-distance training group. A hundred miles north and west, professional training groups in Boulder, Colorado, are likely having similar mornings.

What's not similar are the responsibilities outside of running that members of WCAP hold. Professional runners in other groups focus their days around training and rest. While regular life often overshadows running, running itself is their only job.

For the distance runners who are part of WCAP, running is only part of the job.

They're athletes but also soldiers, and it's impossible to separate one from the other. Nor would they want to.

The lives of these soldier-athletes started with basic training the way it did for all Army recruits. This was followed by specialized training and then a first assignment. For those athletes who knew about WCAP when entering the Army, perhaps they'd already met the qualifying times for entrance into WCAP and were assigned directly to the WCAP unit. For others, it took time and years working in regular Army positions while training hard on their own before they qualified for a spot in the WCAP unit. All the while, the soldier-athletes continue to receive regular Army pay and maintain regular Army responsibilities, attend ongoing military classes, and face the possibility of deployment with their unit if needed.

Ninety minutes elapse and the group stops, assessing the workout. Coaches give feedback. One of the coaches who holds a military rank higher than his athletes gets a playful salute. Shoes are unloaded into cars. Families are waiting at home for the rest of their Sundays to begin. Music blares from car stereos as the athletes pull out of the trailhead parking lot.

Kenyan pop songs echo from each car, a cacophony of guitars and drums filling the dry, Colorado Springs air.

The Army's World Class Athlete Program began in 1978 and became fully supported by the Pentagon in the 1990s. Headquartered in Colorado Springs, personnel continue basic military work, balancing their duties as soldiers and as athletes. They train full-time for the Olympics and other national and international competitions. Programs covered include track and field, wrestling, boxing, tae kwon do, judo, modern pentathlon, biathlon, and bobsledding.

Joining the American military has long been a path to citizenship. Non-citizens are allowed to join the military if they have permanent residency status, also known as a green card. For a U.S. immigration system that's well-known for lengthy delays in paperwork, it's an attractive option. Soldiers typically have shorter residency requirements and their application fees are waived. In the late 2000s, an increasing number of legal immigrants joined the Army through a special recruiting program (Military Accessions Vital to National Interest, or MAVNI) designed to deepen the Army's skill set. If they possessed skills in essential languages, their applications were fast-tracked. Enter the launch of the Army's WCAP distance running program. Swahili, a language native to East Africa, was deemed essential. It was an easy way to make the puzzle pieces fit. The United States gained quality talent in its military force and the Army began to see hopes of becoming a distance running powerhouse. Likewise, new college grads who'd arrived from Kenya on distance running scholarships and now felt America was home had found a way to remain.

Regardless of their ability to qualify for the WCAP unit, the Army had ample new recruits who were motivated and eager to jump on the legal path to citizenship. The MAVNI program lasted from 2008 until it was suspended in 2016 by an administration less sympathetic to expanded immigration policies. Today, athletes who want to try for the WCAP unit continue to join the Army with their hopes high. There are rarely exceptions made in terms of entry standards, and many new soldiers will never achieve their goal of serving in WCAP. Instead, they will live out their military careers while serving in traditional Army roles.

While the benefits of citizenship are valuable, for successful young distance runners coming out of college, the ability to continue in their sport and get paid a respectable salary is often just as thrilling. The Army's World Class Athlete Program provides an unparalleled, potentially lifelong measure of security. Most first-term enlistments require a commitment of four years of active duty, a manageable time period that often corresponds with prime athletic capabilities. A military commitment isn't one that most Americans would consider, but for newer arrivals who can make the WCAP standard, the path to citizenship plus the financial payoff is a hard-to-ignore duo. The alternative would be to enter the regular citizenship path while also trying to find a traditional shoe company sponsorship.

For any college athlete, making the leap to the pros is a long shot, and for track and field athletes, it's truly an uphill battle. The post-collegiate athlete willing to take a shot at the pros enters a universe designed for failure. With no professional coalition or union in place such as those provided in other major sports, track athletes are essentially freelancers without health insurance or protections. Though some money can be earned through prize purses, it's almost always in the hundreds of dollars and not the thousands of dollars it would take to earn a living wage. Sponsorship opportunities are the only real way to make a living, but they're notoriously hard to obtain. A very few big-time college standouts may draw $100,000/year deals for multiple years from shoe companies, but more common are the contracts for second-tier runners, which pay far less. Less than $15,000 is what 50 percent of track and field athletes who rank in the top ten of their sport earn annually. Should an athlete have an agent, another 15 percent is sliced off. On top of this, sponsorships usually come with built-in performance goals. Make the Olympic team or a podium at a major championship and you're in good shape. Miss out and you can start thinking about your options outside of sports.

As if the difficulties aren't great enough, the challenges for athletes of color or those who were born outside the United States are even more significant. The undeniable reality is that white runners draw the biggest contracts, while those with dark skin or unfamiliar names have to work twice as hard to get noticed.

As one professional runner of color states, "There's no way around it, those of us with brown or black skin are at the end of the line when it comes to sponsorship dollars, especially if we weren't born in this country."

That's true universally, even for American runners as recognizable as Meb Keflezighi, who's become a beloved representative for distance running in the United States.

"When Meb came out of college, there were many companies who passed on him because he looked unlike other distance runners and it was just too hard to pronounce his name," says Hawi Keflezighi, his brother and agent.

"Honestly, what it took was a gatekeeper to see the potential that he could become a star. Skechers took a chance on him and the gamble paid off. That's what it takes. Companies or people who are willing to use their platforms to elevate athletes who otherwise wouldn't get a chance."

It's inescapable in the world of sponsorship dollars, as it is in so many other arenas in America. Deeply engrained and misplaced standards of beauty make the fight for shoe company dollars challenging for people of color, particularly new Americans. WCAP can provide what sponsorship dollars usually cannot.

Elvin (second from left) holding her sister Daisy in Kapchorwa. PHOTO BY HUGO VAN DEN BROEK.

Shadrack at the 2018 USA Indoor Track and Field Championships. COURTESY OF THE UNITED STATES ARMY.

Elvin and Shadrack training in Black Forest, Colorado. IMAGE COURTESY OF SEAN RYAN.

Elvin in 2019. PHOTO BY SHADRACK KIPCHIRCHIR.

Shadrack leading the 10,000 meters in the rain at the USA Outdoor Track and Field Championships in Des Moines, Iowa, in July 2019. IMAGE COURTESY OF SEAN RYAN.

Sammy prior to the Tokyo Olympics. PHOTO BY KARL SCHULTZ.

Elvin post-workout. COURTESY OF THE UNITED STATES ARMY.

Elvin and Shadrack in 2016. PHOTO BY SHADRACK KIPCHIRCHIR.

Shadrack at Garden of the Gods, Colorado Springs. IMAGE COURTESY OF SEAN RYAN.

Elvin in 2023. PHOTO BY MIKE HUNNISETT.

Chapter Thirteen

The Standard

2014–2015

Taking his collegiate athletes to run with professionals was a privilege that not all of Coach Smith's athletes received. The races were almost all in California. A plane ride and hotel costs added up. When athletes *did* get a shot to race with the pros, Coach Smith only offered it one time during their outdoor season. Shadrack was offered a chance to make the WCAP standard by running at a race in California in April 2014. He was prepared and hung with the pros as long as he could, but the pace still managed to outclass him. With his future on the line, he'd fallen short of the WCAP standard by only six seconds.

Coach Smith tried to console Shadrack with his usual upbeat talks about running and life lessons. Nothing seemed to work. This time was different.

"Coach, can we talk?" Shadrack asked.

The team had spent the night in California and was now on board their flight back to Oklahoma. Shadrack knelt in the aisle next to Coach Smith, speaking in a loud whisper.

"I want another chance. You gotta give me another chance, Coach."

"Oh Shaddy. You know that's not my style. You left it all on the track out there yesterday. You totally went to the well. And you know I only take you guys out to Cali once per season."

"I know, I know. But I think I'll do better at the 10,000. The WCAP standard is 28:15 and I think that's possible. It's possible if I come back to California."

"In two weeks, you mean?" Coach Smith asked. "At Payton Jordan?"

The Payton Jordan Invitational was the second of two California meets that the coach traveled to with different groups of athletes, and both were well-known for producing fast times. The meet was loaded with professional runners and select outstanding college athletes who had a chance to hang tough with the pros.

"Oh man, Shaddy, your best is 29:08 in the 10,000. And it's twice as far as you just attempted with the 5,000. And in less than two weeks."

A flight attendant squeaked by as Shadrack inched closer to Coach Smith, who could tell that Shadrack was becoming emotional.

"This is my life, Coach. This is my dream. I've always done what you've asked. Please. Give me this chance."

Coach Smith could see the welling in Shadrack's eyes. He'd seen it many times before, though always in private. At 30,000 feet above the ground, he decided to take the odds, knowing how desperate Shadrack was to not disappoint him.

"Okay, Shaddy. Let's go back to California in two weeks. You can give it one more shot at Payton Jordan."

Standing on the starting line two weeks later, Shadrack could see Coach Smith on the opposite side of the track at the Payton Jordan Invitational. The race was one of the last of the day, scheduled late at night to avoid the heat. Shadrack had been placed into the fast heat of the 10,000, with only two college athletes in his race. The starting gun went off, sending a pack of men around the track. At the halfway point, Shadrack was at 14:02, a pace destined to fall short of the 28:15. With the second half of most races inevitably slower, Dave suspected he'd lost his opportunity, but shouted to Shadrack to stay focused and stick with the pack. The men in front of him were professionals and racing for a world standard time to ensure their places at future competitions in the season. It was the same time Shadrack needed, and he didn't intend to be dropped.

Well if I blow up, then I blow up, Shadrack thought. *I've just got to hang onto the pack.*

The pace began to ramp up as the runners started the last two miles. Coach Smith looked at his watch, realizing there was still a chance to hit the standard.

"You can hit the standard, Shaddy! Stick with them!" he yelled as Shadrack passed.

Four laps and one mile to go.

Six men broke away, widening the gap on the rest of the field, with Shadrack hanging onto the back. He could see the leader, Cam Levins, trying to push the pace faster.

Shadrack's stride lengthened, his breath quickening. He imagined the miles he'd run in Eldoret that had launched him on this journey. He envisioned his father standing over him as he worked on his studies. His first days in Kentucky with Titus taking him out for pizza. Meeting Elvin on a field in Indiana. Taking the oath of enlistment months ago in Oklahoma. He trailed the lead pack and could hear one of the men grunting as they approached Coach Smith, who was now jumping up and down.

"Shaddy! That's it! You're gonna negative split this thing!" Dave shouted, leaning on the fence that separated him from the track.

One lap to go. The bell rang, indicating the lead pack was running their last 400 meters. The giant digital clock on the infield read 26:38. It would be enough, Shadrack knew. Holding on, he pumped his arms, passing Coach Smith one more time, who was now screaming encouragement louder than the din around him.

Down the homestretch he ran, all the way across the line, with a finishing time of 27:36. He'd crushed the WCAP standard, running his fastest 5,000 meters in the middle of a 10,000 and set a school record. A breakthrough.

"Shaddy! How the hell did you do *that*?" one of his teammates yelled, hugging him as he was swarmed by his coach and teammates.

"I almost denied you . . . God damn that was amazing!" Coach Smith added, giving him a hug.

Other coaches were coming over now, congratulating both.

Shadrack looked up at the stands. He knew Elvin wasn't there and yet he wondered if someday she would be. It looked as if his running career just might continue. All of it, he wanted to share with her. The disappointments and especially these celebrations.

"Bro, that was off the hook!" one of his competitors said, fist bumping as they passed.

"Thanks . . . you, too. Tough out there, but we got it done," he answered.

"That's all that matters!"

Shadrack pulled his phone out of his warmup jacket and saw that it was blowing up with messages from people who'd been following the race. He scanned the texts looking for a message from Elvin but saw none.

At 1:30 in the morning, Shadrack was just arriving back to the hotel after a night of celebrating when his phone buzzed. He picked up and heard Elvin. She sounded flustered as she described how she'd gone out to visit a friend and managed to drive into a pole by confusing the brake for the gas pedal.

"Oh my God, are you okay?" Shadrack asked.

"Yes, I'm fine. The airbags came out and everything. You know I'm still kind of new at this driving thing. Obviously."

"Babe, you'll get the hang of it. Keep avoiding poles and traffic lights," he responded.

"I guess so. Anyway, how was your day?"

Shadrack smiled to himself as he answered.

"Well, remember I'm in California and I had that little race?"

"Yes! Oh Shaddy where's my head? I can't believe I forgot. How did it go? Did you make the standard?"

"I did."

Elvin screamed, and he pulled the phone away from his ear.

"That's fantastic! What was the time?"

"27:36. A school record."

"No way. A school record . . . Oh Shaddy, I can't believe it. So proud of you."

"I'm pumped. We both know I needed this. I guess I'll just wait now and see how this plays out with WCAP. It's not clear when I'll be assigned to the unit, but I hope all of this happens soon."

"I want more certainty, but this is a start, Shaddy."

One month later, Elvin and Shadrack were together again. They'd just run the NCAA National Championship Outdoor Track Meet, where Shadrack had placed second in the 10,000 and Elvin had placed fourth in the same distance. Meanwhile, Elvin had worked hard to get her younger brother Collins to the States, and he was now at Arizona on scholarship running with her. He'd even met Shadrack a few times and approved. With only days until he shipped out to boot camp, Shadrack decided to bring up marriage again.

"Things will be better soon. I'll do boot camp and training and then we can get married. I'll probably get sent to Oregon to train with WCAP, and a few months after that, you'll graduate. There's light at the end of the tunnel. Can you see us married yet?"

"Hell no, Shaddy. I'm not ready yet. What if you get sent to Germany? You know how I feel about military men."

"But I made the standard. My orders will send me to WCAP, not Germany."

"I want to know with 100 percent certainty that you'll really get a spot in WCAP. I'm tired of being apart and crying when you leave. I couldn't handle it if something went wrong, and you got sent overseas."

"Elvin Kibet, you drive me bananas. But I love you, so you lead the way. When you're ready, I'll be here waiting."

Days later, Shadrack shipped off to boot camp, followed by specialized training in finance. It was many weeks of breaking him down and building him back up again, not unlike his years in Kenya or his time as a collegiate athlete. At the end of boot camp, the orders to Germany arrived, along with conflicting orders to the WCAP unit.

After a short wait, the WCAP orders were elevated. He'd be sent to Oregon to train with several other distance runners, including his friend Paul Chelimo who'd also gone through basic training and met the standard.

In November of 2014, Shadrack hatched the ultimate engagement surprise. With Elvin's brother Collins as an accomplice, he booked a flight to Arizona and lay in wait for Elvin in the parking lot of the library where she was studying. When she emerged at 9:00 p.m., Shadrack was there, on bended knee holding a bouquet of flowers. The months without him while he was in boot camp had driven her mad, and he now had clear orders to be in Oregon and not Germany.

Her answer was finally yes.

Two days later they arrived at the courthouse in Tucson. Shadrack was dressed in his new Army dress blues, while Elvin wore a bright red dress with a thick gold necklace. With all of Elvin's close friends graduated and Titus too far away to participate, only Elvin's brother Collins and one friend were present to bear witness to the ceremony, which lasted no more than ten minutes.

Elvin's running at the University of Arizona was still a source of joy, and so were her studies. Leaning into everything she thought she knew nothing about, Elvin had taken classes in psychology and public health. Armed with new knowledge about disordered eating, depression, and mental health, she'd started volunteering at the student health clinic to help students who were struggling the way Momo had. She'd begun to craft her senior thesis which would focus on bulimia. Before Momo had graduated, the two of them had spent a summer in Flagstaff training until Momo's body and mind finally gave in. Suffering from stress fractures and a broken spirit, Momo stopped running competitively. Elvin helped convince her to get help at a treatment center. Now that Momo was gone, she regretted not having learned faster to help her friend and others who'd been wrestling with disordered eating. With her husband off to Oregon, Elvin buckled down to crush her last semester at Arizona.

On January 12, 2015, the Oregon Ducks lost the first-ever College Football Playoff National Championship to Ohio State. Though much of the state was wallowing, at least one Oregon resident was in celebration, as on that day Shadrack Kipchirchir went through his citizenship ceremony in Portland to become one of the newest citizens of the United States.

Chapter Fourteen

Oregon

2015–2016

Transitioning to life as a soldier-athlete based in Oregon had its challenges. Though Shadrack's days were spent focused on running, there were also military duties to attend to. He'd learned early on in his service that it was important for WCAP soldiers to remain competitive with their uniformed counterparts, and thus, receive all the same information other soldiers did. With many of the other WCAP athletes based at Fort Carson in Colorado Springs, he made periodic trips to Colorado where he was required to take military classes and attend formations, where he'd go through review from higher-ranking soldiers. WCAP members were also frequently assigned to essential outreach activities, holding clinics with high school and college audiences, and appearing at Army recruiting stations. Lastly, Shadrack and other WCAP soldiers were sent around the country to train members of other Army units in customized resilience and performance enhancement skills.

For Elvin, a long-distance marriage wasn't what she'd hoped for, but by April 2015 the separation was nearly over. Elvin and her teammate Lawi Lalang navigated the smooth road leading out of campus. He drove while she talked about the upcoming race in California which would be one of the last of her college career. She'd earned NCAA All-American status several times and had led her team to the podium as runner-up to the national championship in cross country in 2013. Coach Li's gamble on her talent had paid off. The fact that Elvin had her brother Collins with her at the University of Arizona made the last year racing that much more special. He was focused on the shorter distances and would be with her in California as she took one more shot at improving her 5,000-meter time.

"Holy crap, Elvin, there you are!" Lawi said, swerving slightly right as he left the campus gates. He pulled over and checked over his shoulder before doing a U-turn.

"What are you doing, you crazy man?!" she laughed.

"There! You're on one of the banners!"

"Look at that! That's me!" Elvin shrieked.

Hanging on a light post on the side of the road was a huge, vertical banner with an image of Elvin in mid-stride. On it, she wore her white and red University of Arizona singlet and a pair of red shorts. She was smiling, and one of her arms crossed her body as she ran. A huge letter "A" topped the banner and on the bottom the hashtag with the university's battle cry, "Bear Down."

"Get out of the car . . . we need a photo of you underneath it," directed Lawi.

Elvin jumped out and stood underneath the banner grinning, thinking back to the evening she arrived on campus with Papa Li in his fancy car. He'd hoped at the time that she'd grace one of these someday, and years later Elvin found it hard to believe.

The track at Mount Sac in Walnut, California, filled with the twenty women running the women's 5,000. Elvin took her place on the starting line. The evening race would last less than twenty minutes, but Elvin knew each moment would test everything she'd learned in her years at Arizona. How to pace herself. Where to sit in the pack. How and when to pass competitors and how to finish a race. Hanna had graduated the previous year, and Elvin thought about her, wishing her friend was still here to warm up with and cheer her on. A decent time in this race would improve Elvin's odds of getting a contract to run professionally. She was about to graduate with a degree in public health, but if she could continue running a little longer, she would. A life running in Oregon with Shadrack sounded heavenly.

Coach Li stood behind the fence and opposite the starting line at the 100-meter mark. He was prepared as always to watch Elvin's splits and have a little time to process before she passed him on each lap. As the race started, Elvin settled into the middle of the pack, one of the only collegiate runners in the group. Approaching the halfway mark, she moved into the second lane to inch up closer to the front. Feeling good, she threw in a surge and positioned herself in second place.

"Pace is great, Elvin! Stick with it!" Coach Li shouted from behind the fence.

The noise in the stadium had heightened, and he wasn't convinced she could hear him. Her splits were looking hot, maybe even on pace for a personal record. He began to make calculations about what the next few laps would need to be.

Elvin's legs began to feel heavy, with lactic acid building at every step. Each lap she heard Papa Li screaming. The tone in his voice felt urgent, matching the time on the race clock which showed she was running the race of her life. She started an internal dialogue, telling herself to take one lap at a time. With two laps to go, she was in a good position. Though she was no longer in second place, the lead pack hadn't gotten away from her. Stride for stride, she was keeping up with the professionals in the race.

"Elvin, this is it! You're on pace for a PR. Stay with the pack! You're doing fantastic!"

The sound of the bell in her ear caused a surge of adrenaline to rush through Elvin's body. She was in fourth place and knew all she had to do was hold on. One more lap. Pumping her arms, Elvin willed her body around the track. 300 meters. 200 meters. Holding off a late challenge from another member of the pack, she charged all the way through the finish line. Her time appeared on an electronic stadium scoreboard. 15:36:08.

"Elvin! Yes!"

Coach Li jogged from his spot across the track, cheering all the way.

"15:36, Elvin! That's a PR by a long shot!"

Elvin nodded, still catching her breath. A race official came over and handed her a bottle of water. Coach Li hugged her, lifting her body off the ground a couple inches in the process.

"That was a fast one!" Elvin said, wiping her brow. "You told me to run relaxed and with confidence. I think I did it!"

"You did. It was awesome. Elvin, it's a school record."

"What?! Oh my gosh. Yes, it is. By just a couple seconds, right?"

"That's right. But a record is a record. So proud of you."

Collins ran over, dressed in his warmups.

"Big sister, you crushed it!"

He put his arm around her.

"Now you and Shaddy both have college records," he added.

Brother and sister walked off the track together. She'd call Shaddy as soon as she could.

Back in Tucson several days later, Elvin picked up a copy of the school newspaper and turned to the sports section. She looked at the article highlighting the California track meet with a mix of confusion and frustration. Elvin was at the end of her senior year and though she loved him dearly, she was a vastly more decorated athlete than her brother Collins.

Yet somehow the focus of the meet was on Collins, who placed fourth in a race with multiple heats. In the last paragraph of the article, Elvin was referred to as "Collins Kibet's sister." Meanwhile, she had set a personal record, a university record, and her time was the fourth fastest in the United States that year. None of it made sense to her. After four years in America, she knew that athletes of color were treated differently than those who were white. But somehow, she'd wanted to believe that there was at least equality between the sexes. Perhaps that, too, was an illusion. In life, and apparently in the media coverage of female athletes.

With her graduation from the University of Arizona looming, Elvin had a choice. Jump right into a career or try to make a career out of running professionally. Her body was in top shape, and her dreams of going into a career in medicine could always happen later. With all that she'd learned at the University of Arizona, she knew the journey ahead to get a sponsor would be a challenge. Even so, it was time to try to make the leap to the pros.

After a few months of pitching herself to shoe sponsors, Skechers had expressed interest. None of the big shoe companies had nibbled, but Skechers signed her to a one-year contract. The compensation was barely enough to cover food for the year, but it was something. The contract called for her to endorse and wear Skechers apparel and footwear exclusively. Her name and likeness would be used in advertising, and she'd be required to promote the brand in social media and be available for photos and video shoots. She'd be able to train anywhere she wanted, and she picked Portland. Finally, she and Shadrack were together. They'd started to plan a long-overdue trip back to Kenya together. Eventually they'd need to have an official wedding ceremony, but now, all that mattered was getting back to see family after so many years away.

The pair settled into a quiet life of running, working on their apartment, and traveling to races. Shadrack had qualified for his first World Championship Team, an honor only comparable to a spot on the Olympic Team. Elvin ran with him at times, and with some of the women training at the nearby Nike facility, including Shalane Flanagan and Emily Infeld. The resources the Nike women had were superior to those Elvin had, but she was grateful for the training partners and access to the Nike trails.

Driving to the Nike campus one morning for a run, Elvin thought ahead to her workout. She was still getting used to driving and swung wide on a left turn as she approached her destination. A siren interrupted her thoughts. Her eyes scanned the rearview mirror. Flashing lights lit up behind her, as she realized she was being stopped by a police officer.

Oh my God, oh my God, what did I do? she thought.

Elvin pulled over, heart racing. She'd never been stopped by a police officer before and sensed panic over what traffic error she must've made. A laundry list of options filled her head.

Bad turn? Taillight out? Forgot my blinker?

She put the car in park. And then, because she'd never been schooled in traffic stop protocol, she did the first thing she thought of. She got out of the car.

Her car door had barely slammed when she saw the police officer jumping out of his vehicle.

His drew his gun from the holster, and pointed it at her, walking toward her and screaming.

"Ma'am! Get back into your car! Put your hands where I can see!"

Elvin froze at the sight of the gun, just a few feet away and pointed directly at her.

"Oh my God! Oh my God!" she yelled, throwing her hands in the air.

"Get back in the car NOW! And stay there! Stay right there!"

Elvin backed into the car, sliding in, and closing the door, then putting both hands in the air. Her fingertips were nearly on the ceiling and her whole body shook.

The officer walked over to the car. She turned her head slowly, hardly breathing. Through the window, Elvin noticed how young he was. Not much older than she was, Elvin thought. His face had flushed, and his voice sounded unsteady.

"Ma'am, roll down your window," he said, briskly.

His gun was now out of sight, but to Elvin the threat was still real. Her hands stayed up as she listened to him again ask her to roll down the window.

Finally, her left hand dropped, and she opened the window. The officer was out of breath from nerves. He looked as scared as she felt, and his face was bright red.

"What's going on this morning?" he asked.

"I'm a pro athlete and I'm going for a run at Nike," Elvin replied, voice quivering.

The officer was shaking, absorbing Elvin's answer. It hit Elvin that he'd miscalculated the threat she posed, realized his error, and was now uncertain what to do. Neither of them spoke to each other as the moments passed. Elvin tried to process what she'd done wrong, while the police officer likely tried to find an exit plan.

"Just go! Just get out of here. Go!" he finally shouted.

She rolled up her window, then eased back onto the road and finished the short drive to Nike. Running in a daze, she added to the list in her head all the things she had yet to learn about the United States.

By early 2016, it was clear that the WCAP unit training in Portland might have a shot at some of the Olympic distance running spots available for the 2016 Games in Rio. The group was still relatively unknown outside the Army, and they liked it that way. An energetic new leader of the team had arrived, and she was based in Colorado Springs. First Sergeant Jennifer Williams visited the team in Portland. Impressed by the bond the athletes shared, she made a mental note to keep tabs on them to make sure they had the gear and training supplies they needed.

Though they seemed to lack clothing and shoes, both Paul and Shadrack had made a point of finding the money they needed to invest in altitude tents. The devices were sealed tents which fit over their beds and simulated the higher altitude environments that produced more oxygenated red blood cells. When they weren't running, they could be found at home sitting inside the tents for hours a day, often just hanging out and watching television.

Elvin found the entire thing ridiculous.

She woke up one morning with a screaming headache.

"Shaddy, I've got a massive headache. What do you have this thing set on?"

Shadrack stirred as she leaned over to look at the adjustable dial that controlled the settings. It read "12,000 feet."

"Babe! It's at 12,000 feet! What the heck? Shadrack, this is insane. I was born at 9,000 feet, but even I can't adjust to sleeping at 12,000 feet like this. I'm outta here."

She unzipped the tent and slipped outside into the air of the master bedroom, which was at its natural, and much lower, fifty feet of altitude.

"My goodness, I can breathe," she gasped, half laughing. "You guys are crazy. I can't believe the lengths you're going to here."

"What do you mean? I love this tent! Worked for Alan Webb and he gave it to us for a steal. Who's gonna be laughing when we make the Olympic team?" he joked, propping himself up on pillows in the tent.

"That may be right, and it will for sure help us when we go to Kenya in a few weeks, but for now, I'm just going to enjoy the lovely, headache-free air of the rest of our house."

Chapter Fourteen

For the first time since college, Shadrack and Elvin carved time away from the United States to return to Kenya. Elvin arrived first, and unlike her departure which had featured a long matatu shuttle ride to Nairobi, she flew directly into Eldoret. Her siblings swallowed her up at the airport, all of them crying first and then each inevitably commenting on how tiny she looked.

"Why are you not eating? We need to feed you here. Eat! Eat!"

Elvin's days in Kenya were spent mostly in Iten. Ivy had skipped college and was being coached by Hugo, who was working hard to get her into a college in the States. With Ivy pacing her, Elvin struggled to keep up at first until her body adapted once again to the altitude and rituals of training in Kenya among the top distance runners in the world. The rhythm and joys of running were different here. Her days were focused on runs, eating, and sleep. There were no traffic jams, no million television channels, no endless strip malls. Everything here seemed uncomplicated.

When it was Shadrack's turn to come back, he decided to make a splash. Enlisting Paul, who was also going to be there, Shadrack launched a plan to keep his visit secret. On the day of his arrival, he hid in the trunk of Paul's car as they arrived in Shadrack's village. Popping out, he caught his parents and siblings by surprise. From a mile away, neighbors could hear the joyful hoots, tears, and laughter of a family reunited.

It was the first time Elvin and Shadrack had been together in Kenya. For Elvin, there was just one person she needed him to meet. The two spent a day in her village, where she showed him the fields she'd worked and the spot where she'd been bitten by the snake. Gogo was over one hundred years old, and almost unable to hear or see. Taking Shadrack's wrists, she scolded him for being too skinny. Even at her age, she was still full of life and Elvin was still one of her favorite grandchildren.

Though they were legally married in the United States, the couple still was inclined to keep the marriage on the down low when they were in Kenya. The elders were still negotiating Elvin's bride price and how many cows and goats would need to be exchanged for an official marriage ceremony sometime in the future. While Elvin was happy staying with Ivy and Sylvia in Iten, when Shadrack arrived he preferred the traditional mud hut in his village. They negotiated, eventually renting an apartment for a few weeks.

As their flight back to the States gained altitude, Elvin turned to her husband.

"I don't know why you pressed so hard to stay in the mud hut, babe. At home you require sports drinks and altitude tents. How can you be so happy here in a mud hut?" she said.

"That's where I'm most comfortable," he replied.

"But you're American now," she said. "And those homes remind me of the poverty we endured. It's traumatic for me to think about all those years. I don't want to go back to that life."

He took her hand.

"We're not going back. Not to that life. But we can keep the best parts of it and take those with us into this next life, can't we?"

"We can. We can take the food and the naps and the simplicity. I'd like to take the simplicity," Elvin said.

"That's what I mean. We might eventually end up with a big house and fancy jobs in the States, but do we really *need* all that?" he answered.

Chapter Fifteen

Chasing the Torch

2016

"Shaddy, you gotta keep drinking," Paul said, handing Shadrack a plastic jug of water.

Paul leaned over, catching his breath from the long run they'd just completed.

"It's brutal. Altitude is crushing me, Chelimo," Shadrack responded, gasping.

"We need to take an ice bath today for sure. The creek will feel amazing," he added.

"And sleep. A three-hour nap for me is on the agenda before this afternoon's workout," Paul said.

Mammoth Lakes, California, stretched out from all sides. In preparation for the 2016 Olympic Trials, their Army coach had brought them here to train for a month. Other WCAP distance runners had begun to train in Colorado Springs, but Mammoth was the place their coach believed gave them the best chance for success. At nearly 8,000 feet, the dry, thin air gave them frequent nosebleeds. Track workouts were run at 11:00 a.m. to mimic the heat they might feel when they got to the Trials. Their hard workouts on the track usually ended with the two of them laying flat out with the scent of the track's synthetic rubber piercing their senses. It was a grind as they pushed each other into uncharted territory and extreme physical condition. Nights were spent recharging with massage therapy sessions, and meals of ugali, beans, beef, milk, and rice.

Though they'd both been with WCAP for eighteen months, the program wasn't yet on the radar of the elite running community, nor the Army brass. Even with significant running accomplishments under their belts, Shadrack and his WCAP teammates struggled to get proper gear. They'd sifted through bins at the local donation clothing store to find shorts and tops to run in. Only recently had they been given proper warm clothing, thanks to their First Sergeant Jennifer Williams who'd flown to Oregon and seen their struggles firsthand.

All of it was enough to light a fire in each of them. Their careers as soldier-athletes involved races all over the world and of all sizes. Competing was a year-round job, peppered with regular Army training to keep their skills relevant and ensure they'd be prepared for future deployments. But somehow the magnitude of what they did boiled down to one competition held every four years. The Olympics mattered exponentially more to the public and to those in power in the Army and was the benchmark for success. In the world of sports, the totality and longevity of an athlete's career was usually celebrated. But for track and field athletes, it came down to signature accomplishments, the Olympics being the crown jewel.

Qualifying for the Olympics would put the WCAP team on the map. Now, keeping a low profile was to their benefit, but the weight of their need to perform at the Olympic Trials was heavy. Paul had begun finishing races with a salute across the finish line, which became his signature.

While the WCAP team was in Mammoth Lakes, Elvin spent her summer in Colorado. She'd tagged along with Shadrack in April when he was there for an Army training session. In her extra time, she sought out a coach she'd heard about through the running grapevine. Scott Simmons was based in Colorado Springs, not far from Fort Carson and the Olympic Training Center. Elvin had been coaching herself, using old workouts from Coach Li, but found she needed more volume and intensity. Scott seemed attentive, laid back, and even scientific in his approach. The two of them hit it off, meeting for coffee one afternoon. Scott had already studied her training and race history and came prepared with a plan.

"Elvin, I really think you can be running seventy-one minutes in the half marathon by the end of this year," he told her.

"What? No way. Scott, I'm not that good."

"Oh Elvin, you've got so much potential. You *are* that good. Training at altitude here in Colorado Springs and progressively increasing your volume now that you're more mature will be a game changer. You'll see."

His confidence in her was enough for Elvin to announce that she didn't want to return to Oregon after Shadrack's Army training was over. Instead, she'd stay in Colorado and train with Scott. After all, she argued, he was going to Mammoth Lakes and she wasn't allowed to join him there. Shadrack had met Scott as well, and warmed to him. The Army coach they'd been assigned to in Oregon knew his stuff, and was an accomplished athlete himself, but there was something missing. A new coach might not be a bad idea. Scott and Shadrack had begun texting frequently when he was in Mammoth, and he was acting as an unofficial coach. Race strategy, thoughts on his training plans and fueling concepts. He assured Shadrack he'd be at the race, and he hoped that perhaps the team in Oregon might move to Colorado at the end of the season. For now, the 10,000 meters at the Olympic Trials was only weeks away and listening to Scott, it became clear to Shadrack that there was only one person to focus on when he got to the starting line.

Galen Rupp.

Galen had been dominating the men's American distance running scene for years. A silver medalist in the 10,000 at the 2012 Olympics, he was known for pushing a hard pace from the early stages. Both Shadrack and Scott had studied his strategy and crunched the numbers. The workouts the team had been doing in Mammoth were enough for Shadrack to be able to keep pace with Galen. While other runners in the pack might let him go, Scott had instructed Shadrack to hang in Galen's slipstream as long as he could. If Scott believed in him, Shadrack knew he could hang on for dear life, letting Galen do the work, and make the Olympic Team.

Elvin had already been to the restrooms at Hayward Field in Eugene, Oregon, three times. Her seat remained empty as she paced the stadium waiting for Shadrack's race to start. Though his 10,000 was taking place in the early evening, she couldn't believe how hot it still was. Shadrack had told her the plan was to stay controlled and let Galen go if he surged, but Elvin suspected that her husband had lied to protect her from the truth and the stress it would cause her as she watched him race. He was never planning to stay controlled. It wasn't his style in races like this to be safe. He was going all in and there was nothing she could do to stop him.

Scott Simmons was there, too, sweating underneath his baseball cap. He'd given Shadrack and Lenny ice vests to pre-cool their core temperatures prior to their race. At eighty-two degrees, keeping cool before taking one foot onto the track was going to be critical.

First Sergeant Jennifer Williams looked up at the jumbotron as the athletes began to enter the stadium. Her leadership of the WCAP unit had been an unexpected pleasure toward the end of a long career. She recognized the humility and selflessness of the men representing the Army here at the Trials and considered it a beautiful testament to everything good about military service. These men had trained for years to succeed in this one race of less than thirty minutes. She glowed like a proud mother as she waited for Shadrack's name to be announced, along with Lenny Korir.

On the track, the athletes lined up and the announcer called out introductions.

"Don't let him go, Shaddy. Just don't let him go," was the last thing Lenny had said before they'd left the call room and entered the stadium.

"Representing the United States Army, please welcome Leonard Korir and Shadrack Kipchirchir."

Polite claps gave way to a roar as the next athlete was introduced.

"He was a silver medalist in the 1,500 meters at the 2004 Athens Olympics, and here to try to make his fifth Olympic team, it's Bernard Lagat!"

Shadrack looked over and smiled at Bernard. They knew each other well. Bernard was coached by Elvin's beloved Papa Li and still trained in Tucson. At age forty-one, many track fans weren't convinced Bernard had enough in the tank to make the top three spots needed for an Olympic berth, but Shadrack considered it an honor to be racing with him.

"Also, please welcome former Oregon Duck and silver medalist in this event at the 2012 London Olympics, Galen Rupp!"

This was Galen's home track, and it was obvious. The crowd was on their feet cheering. Shadrack had studied race videos night after night, preparing his strategy and becoming comfortable with Galen's race tactics. He turned and waved at the 20,000 fans packed into the stadium. The last to be introduced, he toed the line and waited for instructions.

"All right, men, let's have a clean race," the starter yelled.

He stood on the infield, two steps up on a riser. Lifting his right arm, a starting pistol pointed to the sky. A slight pause stilled the crowd, then the command "Set," and with the starting shot, a puff of white smoke dissipated over the infield. The two groups of athletes converged after a hundred meters, settling into an easy pace. Rhythmic clapping greeted the pack as they came around the first lap, followed by more from the stadium announcer.

"Twenty-five laps around the track for this race," he said.

Shadrack tried to calm his mind as the first few laps passed. Jostling for position, the pack of men watched the digital stadium clock. Sweat covered each of them, and as arms grazed one another, it mixed in slippery patches. *One lap at a time*, Shadrack thought. *You're here to fight.* He imagined himself an hour from now, holding Elvin's hand as they walked through Eugene or perhaps eating pizza with the rest of his teammates. Breathing from the other men quickened as they finished the first mile.

Six laps in, Galen picked up the pace. Shadrack hung back, aware of his strategy to create distance on the field but not yet ready to take the bait. He saw Galen's coach behind the blue fencing, shooting Galen a look of caution as he passed. Within seconds, the pack was back together as Galen slowed his pace. The men could feel each other grinding, and as they reached the halfway mark, the field began to stretch out. Unrelenting, the sun refused to hide, and several of the runners began to falter. Shadrack tried to channel himself back to the days in Mammoth Lakes—Lenny and Paul grunting on either side, the three of them collapsing on the dirt path at the end of their fifteen-mile runs at noon. Stealing a glance on the turn, he saw Lenny still in the hunt ten yards behind him. *Hallelujah, brother. Don't go anywhere. I need you.*

With twelve laps to go, Galen pulled away again. It was the move Shadrack had prepared for. He was in the big leagues now, and Galen was trying to break him. Shadrack could feel the crowd watching as they tried to see who'd respond. He knew they would be scrambling if he followed Galen, looking in their race booklets to try to figure out who he was. Right now, he suspected he was just another runner with the phrase "Kenyan-born" distinguishing him from the rest. Bernard Lagat gave chase, passing Shadrack and catching up with Galen. Bernard and Galen were Nike teammates and had likely worked on this plan a hundred times.

Shadrack considered his options, which weren't plentiful. In a matter of seconds, the distance between the Nike duo and the rest of the pack would grow. With it, any chance of hanging on would disappear. His spirit would be crushed. He looked up, and seeing an American flag flying over Hayward Field, he accelerated, reaching for the unknown.

Shadrack surged to the second spot, a stride behind Galen and close to the rail separating the lanes from the infield. There was no need to do anything but remain steady and use as little energy as possible. Drifting into lane two would waste fuel he'd need in the last laps.

The race continued until it was ten laps and two and a half miles to go. Shadrack rounded the bend at the 300-meter mark and sitting on the grass inside the track was Bernard. He cheered as Shadrack and Galen passed. The heat had gotten the best of him, and along with several other athletes, he'd dropped out. Looking up at the jumbotron, Shadrack could see the enormous image of himself and Galen projected on the screen. They were beginning to lap other runners.

You're not going anywhere, Galen. I think I've got this. Oh my God, I think I've got this.

In the stands, the crowd was on its feet as the pair approached two laps to go. Elvin had managed to make it to her seat for the whole race and now looked over at Scott. He was bright red, his fists clenched. Out of the corner of his eye, he saw her.

"Elvin! I think he's got this! My God, he's so wildly gutsy."

Scott's voice was barely audible above the cheering, and Elvin raised hers in response.

"Well to be fair, you instructed him to go with Galen, didn't you?" she yelled back.

Elvin shot Scott a look. He smiled and shrugged, clapping the whole time.

Three rows below them, Paul screamed, "That's it, Shaddy! Put the hammer down! That's it, Lenny! You got this!"

Paul could've been back at the hotel resting for his own race, a preliminary round of the 5,000 meters in a few days. But there was no way he was going to miss this.

With just over one lap to go, Shadrack pulled ahead of Galen. Whatever Shadrack had left in the tank he was pouring onto the track. Galen matched him step for step, waiting until the last 200 before pulling ahead. Shadrack took one more glance up at the screen and saw Lenny far behind him but in a secure third place. They were both about to make the Olympic team, representing the United States. He couldn't believe it. There was no need to close in a sprint now. Merely surviving the last hundred meters and crossing the line would be enough.

Elvin's lungs felt on fire as she roared for Shadrack and Lenny. Their entire cheering section was alive, arms waving and people hugging. The crowd was celebrating Galen, but in their little section of the universe at Hayward Field, the U.S. Army had just broken through and put the distance running team of WCAP on the map. Jennifer Williams let the tears flow, pulling up the hem of her black Army shirt to dab her eyes.

On the track, Shadrack had collapsed across the finish line and momentarily lost consciousness. He woke up seconds later, with Galen looking down at him,

"Kipchirchir, wake up! You made the team! Kipchirchir, you're going to Rio, dude!"

He reached down and gave Shadrack his hand, pulling him upright and onto his feet.

"Holy crap, that was one of the hardest Trials races I've ever had," Galen said, giving him a hug. "Maybe the hardest. You tried to break me."

"I tried, but you're unbreakable. Nice job, man," Shadrack replied.

Lenny approached, carrying a small American flag. He handed it to Shadrack and the two of them embraced. Sweat and salt oozed from every inch of them and onto the track.

"We got it done, Shaddy. We got it done."

"Battle buddies got it done. One race down. Two of us in," Shadrack said.

A race official came over with cool towels and bottles of water.

"Congrats to both of you and congrats on being selected for drug testing," she laughed, handing them the water.

Shadrack and Lenny smiled, aware that it was standard for both to go through routine drug testing after placing so well.

"You've got a presser first, then testing. Nice work out there. Impressive of you to stick with Galen, if I do say so," she nodded at Shadrack.

A coach from another team walked past, overhearing the comment, and adding,

"Good lord, yes. What were you thinking going with Galen?"

Looking up in the stands, Shadrack strained to see his crew and thought about what was ahead. In the immediate hours, a drug test if he could even produce the needed sample given his dehydration. A reunion with Elvin. Pizza for dinner. Responding to a million text messages, he was sure. There would be no sleep tonight, as he'd be too pumped on adrenaline. He'd stay and help pace Paul in the 5,000 meters later this week. Then it would be back to training, a trip to Rio, and probably a visit to the White House and President Obama in the fall. Not a bad start to 2016.

As he walked off the track, Shadrack remembered all the people who'd lifted him up and brought him to this place. He'd need to make sure to thank them when he came back down to earth. It took a few days, but eventually he put fingers to keyboard.

July 6, 2016

Dave,

Hey Coach . . . This is Shadrack. I want to thank you for believing in me. You told me at Payton Jordan that you'd see me in Rio and

it stuck in my brain the entire time until I crossed the finish line on Friday. I knew what you told me was true, because it's always been true, but it's taken time to believe in myself. My view about running changed when I moved to Oklahoma State. I made the right decision by transferring there and selecting you as my coach. You inspired me a lot and I won't forget those days. Thank you so much for everything.

V/r
Shadrack

Shadrack,

I am so proud of you! Amazing! Just amazing. Who could've imagined in 2011 when you were out there on the dirt roads that five years later you'd be going to the Olympic Games?! You're a fantastic ambassador for our team, for Oklahoma State and our country. And your best qualities in that role have nothing to do with running. Keep up the great work and enjoy this time in your life. You will tell your grandkids about this. My advice is to keep a journal over the next couple months and write a little in it every day about what you're experiencing and feeling, the things you see and do. Someday you'll really value being able to go back and read it.

Dave

An afterglow settled over Shadrack and Lenny in the days following the race. Bombarded with media requests, the secret was out on the abilities of the WCAP athletes. A third soldier-athlete coached by Scott, Hillary Bor, made the team in the steeplechase. With the 5,000-meter final not until the last day of the two-week competition, Paul tried to remain level-headed, but at least once Shadrack caught him mumbling,

"I'll die if I don't make the team and you guys do. Absolutely die."

"You're in, Chelimo. I can feel it. We've had the same training."

"I hope you're right, Shaddy. I trust you more than anyone else in this world. In life and on the track. Get to the front and up onto the rail if you can and block for me until I can take over."

"Plan. That's the plan."

Shadrack had qualified in the 5,000 meters as well, and though he had no illusions of finishing in the top three to grab an Olympic spot, he felt enough juice in his legs to race and help pace Paul. Both sailed through their qualifying heats and were on to the finals on the last day of competition at Hayward Field.

Shadrack had been offered a pair of high-end Nike track spikes by one of his racing buddies who was sponsored by Nike. The spikes were lighter and nimbler than the version he'd been wearing. He'd heard that Nike was developing technology for a vastly improved shoe for distance running. It had been a reminder of the many variables in success on the track, including products that he wouldn't have access to as a member of WCAP. He suspected these spikes weren't related to the new shoes in development by Nike and opted out in favor of his regular pair.

On the last night of competition, Shadrack attended to his pacing duties, with Paul squeaking out a third-place finish to make the team. Bernard Lagat, who'd dropped out of the 10,000, made his fifth Olympic team at age forty-one, winning the race in a blistering sprint to the finish and then falling onto the track after crossing the line.

Dropping out of the 10,000 a few days earlier had been crushing for Lagat. He and Coach Li had left Eugene, spending several days regrouping in Portland before traveling back for the 5,000. This victory was sweet. Making five Olympic teams was practically unheard of, particularly in the sport of distance running.

Paul leaned over and gave Bernard a hand to lift him off the track, with Bernard asking him, "Did you make it?!"

"I did! I'm in!" Paul shouted.

He was in, securing the fourth spot for WCAP track athletes at the 2016 Olympics.

In post-race interviews, Bernard Lagat praised his coach. James Li stood off to the side talking to a reporter from *Runner's World*, tears of happiness and relief running down his cheeks as Bernard spoke with NBC.

"My coach, man, he's genius. He told me to stay relaxed and be patient. I did that. He's genius."

Back in Colorado Springs, Elvin's blood was boiling as she read through the message boards on a popular running website in the days following the Trials. The comments showcased the best and worst of the greater running community and perhaps in all of America, she thought. A plethora of praise for the WCAP athletes who'd qualified for the Olympics, but a smattering of detractors.

"My taxpayer dollars underwrite the U.S. Army WCAP when they should be focused on the nation's defense."

"I'm not a fan of people who were born outside the U.S. being American Olympians."

"They're fake soldiers."

"OUR Army scammed the MAVNI program and subsidized chain immigration that took Olympic/World Championship spots from real Americans. Those whose parents paid taxes!"

"A medal for Paul Chelimo would feel different than a medal for Galen Rupp."

Shadrack was still in Oregon, but anxious to get back to Elvin, who was now on a furious tear.

"What the hell, Shaddy? People don't know that you came into the Army with special language skills or that you can be deployed if you stop making the WCAP standard. What will they say when some of you stay in the Army for your entire careers, long after you stop running? Also why do people think that there's some unique quality that makes people American other than citizenship? The spots on our Olympic team are there for the taking, by any American citizen. I don't understand the concept of 'stealing spots.' And I can't believe the stuff people feel free to say on the internet."

"It's awful. No doubt. It's racist and we both know it's there. It's always there. But don't pay attention to it, babe. They're trolls."

"I know we should be used to it, but I still can't get there. I stayed up practically all night reading these shitty messages."

"Oh Elvin, I wish you wouldn't. It's not worth your energy. Focus on the positive comments. Or our military family we know has our backs. I don't feel racism in the military. At least not in the way I feel it in the outside world. The Army feels like the great equalizer to me and that's what we should focus on."

"Paul says it best, you know? Whenever he's asked about this 'fully American' thing he says, 'When I put on that Army uniform, I'm ready to die for this country.' It's the only way to respond," Elvin said.

"That's right. Joining the Army is a sacrifice most aren't willing to take, but we did it because we love America and what could be more American than *that*?" Shadrack responded.

As usual, Shadrack soothed her nerves. If only she could get him to Colorado, where she was convinced he and the rest of the team would be most successful in both running and in life. Elvin began planning her pitch as Shadrack and the rest of his Olympic teammates made their way to the Rio Olympics a few weeks later. Elvin couldn't join them, instead watching alone in Colorado. Shadrack's real joy had been making the team. As for the rest, it was icing. He had a respectable run in his 10,000, realizing that he'd probably hit his peak conditioning for the Trials rather than the Olympics. Meanwhile, Paul Chelimo peaked at just the right time, shattering expectations and won a silver medal in the 5,000 meters.

It was the first American medal in the 5,000 meters in fifty-two years.

Chapter Sixteen

Becoming Sergeant Schultz

2016–2018

Elvin slipped into the back of the pack as the men training with Scott Simmons ran another 800 meters on the track at Cheyenne Mountain High School. Only a week had passed since Shadrack had returned to Oregon from the Rio Olympics and she was still in Colorado Springs. A series of long conversations were leading to an inevitable move to Colorado. Elvin had made her case and was backed by First Sergeant Jennifer Williams. Shadrack and Paul would receive better support in Colorado than in Oregon. It would bring them closer to Fort Carson where they'd be able to complete their military duties more easily. The altitude in Colorado would benefit their racing. And Scott would be a better fit than their current coach.

Elvin pulled off the track to the infield after the 800 was done. Two minutes, twenty-five seconds. She'd have a two-minute break before the next one, and it was enough time for Scott to catch her for a chat. He walked up to her as she caught her breath.

"That one looked good, Elvin. Just stay right there. If you can just maintain contact with the back of their pack like that, you've got a great workout going."

"Right, I'll try. This would be a hundred times easier with a few more women, you know?"

"You're right, and I'm working on it. We should have a few women coming to train with us next month. In the meantime, you're only getting better and adapting to the altitude."

"I still think you're nuts to believe I can hit seventy-one minutes in the half marathon this year."

"Absolutely. You're progressing well with volume and intensity. You'll be ready. Trust me."

Elvin shook out her legs and swung her arms across her chest to loosen up. The men Scott trained were already queued up ready for the next repetition. They were joking with each other in a way she couldn't relate to. When she was in Tucson, she'd always had her friends to run with, but training as the only woman in the group made things a challenge. She wished she could transport herself back to Tucson and the many miles she'd covered with Momo and Hanna.

"Okay gang, ten seconds, five seconds. Let's do this!" Scott shouted.

The group leaned over into ready positions, Elvin at the back.

First Sergeant Jennifer Williams sat in her office in Colorado Springs with Paul and Shadrack on speakerphone in Oregon. The two had just returned from an easy run, still on hiatus after competing at the Olympics. They'd chatted with Jennifer many times about their desire to leave Oregon and be coached elsewhere. Jennifer had been a vocal ally. She rarely saw soldiers with the low rank that Shadrack and Paul had champion themselves in the way they had. It was noble and she intended to honor their desire to change coaches.

"I realize you moving out here to Colorado will be a big deal. It's unconventional to advocate for yourselves in the Army the way you have. Believe me, I'm a woman in a system that's not always easy for women. I'm unconventional, myself!" Jennifer laughed.

"Loyalty is important to us. Community is everything, too. We're American now, but we'll forever have a lot of Kenya in us, and we're all about teamwork, so leaving our current coach out here to move to Colorado feels a bit challenging for those reasons," Shadrack said.

"But we know we're not getting the coaching we need right now, so if this advances the team, we're in," added Paul.

"Listen, you're both natural-born leaders, and as you know there are other distance runners out here in Colorado Springs assigned to the WCAP unit now. All men, but hopefully some women coming in soon. So, think about this move as standing up for your men. The program is taking off and we need you out here. I think this'll work out for the best and I've got buy-in from senior leaders. I did all the hard work behind the scenes on this already, so I'm excited to see you out here training with Scott. Let me handle the Army logistics going forward."

Days later, Shadrack and Paul loaded their belongings into U-Hauls and drove from Oregon to new homes in Colorado.

A few months later on January 15, 2017, Scott's prediction came true as Elvin ran the Houston Half Marathon in seventy-one minutes and thirty-seven seconds.

Training with a larger group under Scott sent both Elvin and Shadrack into an upward trajectory. Shadrack made two World Championship teams in 2017, and Elvin continued to improve. The men of WCAP took her under their wings, and Scott took on a few non-WCAP athletes who were women, which helped her feel less alone.

Meanwhile, Shadrack had told Elvin about a WCAP athlete in the sport of modern pentathlon, Sammy Schultz. She'd just entered the unit and was hoping to qualify for the 2020 Tokyo Olympics. Modern pentathlon was a sport that totally baffled both Shadrack and Elvin. As if it wasn't enough to focus on one sport, pentathletes had five to master.

Occasionally Sammy would come run with the distance team and though Elvin hadn't crossed paths with her yet, Shadrack described Sammy as outgoing and strong.

"She's got a lot on her plate, so I'm amazed she makes time to come and do the warmups with us," Shadrack said.

"It's wild. Sounds like she does three workouts a day to get good at each discipline?" Elvin inquired.

"Four, sometimes, I think," Shadrack added.

"That's nuts. On top of formations and military training?"

"Yup. I can't wait for you to meet her. I told her we're married and that you sometimes come to our workouts, too."

Sammy slipped on street clothes and gave her swimsuit a twist to release water. Ivy Pool at Fort Carson had been a solid place to get her laps in the past few weeks. At twenty-six years old, Sammy was fresh out of basic training at Fort Jackson in South Carolina. She'd returned to her home in Colorado Springs feeling exhausted but resolved. In front of her, duties with the Army paired with training hard in the WCAP unit to make the 2020 Tokyo Olympic team in the sport of modern pentathlon. Beyond that, whatever time remained in order to finish her college degree and spend time with her husband Karl.

Picking up her duffel, she glanced at herself in the mirror on the way out of the locker room. The Army-issued track suit fit her 5'7" frame with room to spare. Her blond hair had matted from being shoved inside her swim cap. She noticed that the glow that she wore when she was with Karl was missing, replaced with a serious expression. Wide, green eyes with a slight crease along her forehead that looked more prominent after months of being berated by drill sergeants in basic training.

The months she'd spent at basic had disrupted her usual workout routine. Flipping sideways, she tilted her head to get a different angle in the mirror. There was more work to do, she thought, to bring her body to a place her coaches would be pleased with.

Her goals for the next couple of years were lofty by any standard, but Sammy's path was one that had been laid from a young age. She'd grown up in Littleton, Colorado. One of two girls, she and her older sister had been skiing since they were two years old. This was followed by a childhood filled with sports. Soccer, volleyball, gymnastics, tennis, and swimming. The family lived across from a pool, where her mother was a swim coach. In fifth grade, the family bought a flea-bitten, gray horse named Charmer. They moved closer to the barn so Sammy could indulge in her desire to ride. By sixth grade, she and Charmer were doing shows together. Her father, a hunter, taught her basic shooting skills and gun safety at age thirteen. In the garage, the two of them would gut antelope he'd bagged and identify organs, sometimes sending them to school to dissect in her science classes.

Sammy's family held emotions close, attended church faithfully, and valued both working and playing hard. The balance between pushing their daughters to try new activities and letting them call the shots was one they worked hard to achieve. Coaches played a role at every step, mostly for good, though occasionally their behavior shattered the confidence Sammy's parents had tried to foster.

Sammy walked to the sidelines of the soccer field after a difficult practice in middle school. The body language of her coach told her all she needed to know. Arms crossed. Scowl firmly in place. He pulled her aside, his eyes full of irritation.

"Look, Sam, you're never really going to amount to anything athletically because you don't really work hard at this," he announced. "You're slow, and honestly, the way you played out there was just stupid. Get it together."

She took it in. The words ran together like ice in her blood. Of all the thirteen-year-old girls on the team, she was the biggest people pleaser, and most assuredly not the slowest player. Of that, she was certain.

Her parents were dumbstruck. The dinner table was silent that night as they took a long pause to let the report of the coach's outburst soak in. Her father looked up from his plate. He rarely swore, but she could tell it was a struggle this time.

"Screw that. You can be done with soccer after this season," he said. "I always hated soccer anyway," he added, taking a bite of his steak.

When soccer fell to the wayside, running cross country took its place. The sport suited her and the balance with horseback riding and swimming clicked. During senior year of high school, college recruiters came calling, and Sammy considered taking a scholarship to run until her riding coach mentioned the sport of modern pentathlon.

"It's five sports in one, essentially. Swimming, horseback riding, shooting, running, and fencing," her coach said.

"Fencing? Is that the sport with the sword?" Sammy asked.

"I don't think they call it a sword but yeah, you get the idea. It might be worth considering taking a lesson or two. You've already mastered the other four events."

She decided to try it, and attended a pentathlon fencing camp to test out the event. Fencing wasn't a rhythmic sport, and the combative nature was disconcerting. There was an opponent steps away, jabbing at her constantly. Somehow Sammy managed enough skill to qualify for the Junior World Championships just after high school graduation. That was enough to be noticed by the national modern pentathlon team and at age eighteen, she was asked to train in Colorado Springs at the United States Olympic Training Center.

Entering Colorado Springs from the north, visitors are greeted with views of Pikes Peak, the Air Force Academy Chapel, and a sign at the edge of the interstate that reads "Colorado Springs, Olympic City USA." The branding is part of a long-term effort to cement the city as the nation's hub for all things related to the modern Olympic Games. Among the most notable pieces of this brand is the United States Olympic and Paralympic Training Center (Note: Name changed in 2019 to include "Paralympic" in its title). The center provides training facilities and living accommodations for some athletes in training for high level competition, including the Olympics. How much athletes can access the services at the USOPTC depends largely on the support and advocacy they receive from their coaches.

With only a short period of time until the London 2012 Olympics, Sammy began taking college classes at night and moved to Colorado Springs to train at the USOTC. She was training with modern pentathlon athletes who'd been in the four-year Olympic cycle for a long time, their bodies accustomed to multiple intense workouts every day of the week. The transition was brutal, as her body tried to adapt. The days were a constant rotation of weightlifting, running, target practice, fencing lessons, and swimming. Not merely one sport to focus on, but four, with horseback riding reserved for the weekends when she'd drag herself home to Littleton.

"Bug, this is feeling unsustainable," Sammy's mom said one weekend, using her daughter's nickname.

Sammy lay on the couch, eyes half open as she struggled to stay awake past 8:00 p.m. She'd spent thirty minutes crying from weariness when she'd arrived home. The relationships with the other women on the team weren't going well, as the women knew they were all battling for the same competition points that fed into the sport's ranking system. The coaches were all male, many decades older, and subscribing to training methods that seemed almost beyond her pain threshold. The workouts never ended, and Sammy's body fought to keep up as every muscle was taxed each day.

"Your sister is worried about you, and so are we, frankly."

"Mom, I think this is just how it is at this level," Sammy responded.

"The coaches don't seem like they're acting in your best interests. They see you every day. How are they not noticing how small you're getting?"

"I'm not small, Mom. I'm fit. There's a difference. They say I'm fit, and I think I just need to keep at it. I'll adjust."

"I don't know. Your father and I trust you, of course. But we also want you to be healthy. We're too far away to help you manage any of this on a daily basis."

"Don't worry, Mom. I've got this."

The buildup to the London 2012 Olympics continued, and with it, the rigorous training. Sammy's modern pentathlon coaches at the Olympic Training Center subscribed to the concept of more.

More running.

More swimming.

More shooting.

More fencing.

Though it was a long shot for her to make the London Olympic team, Sammy pushed herself harder and to the point of injury. It was a stress fracture in her hip, and it sent her into a meeting with coaches at the conclusion of a competition in Russia.

One of her male pentathlon teammates was there, and he hovered next to her on the sidelines as the coach raised his voice with disappointment over the injury.

"I'm just going to tell it like it is, Sammy. For a 19-year-old woman, your body looks fine. But as a female athlete, you're fat. Plain and simple."

Sammy leaned back in her chair, looking at the coach. She had a flash of one of her female teammates, who repeatedly called herself fat and had started to restrict her food intake in the Training Center dining hall. Is this where it came from?

"So that's the deal. The injury and your poor performance here came from your weight, so that's something you're gonna need to deal with," he continued.

Sammy looked at her teammate for a reaction and saw he had none. He glanced at her with sympathy, but not partnership.

"Focus on the fruits and vegetables. Ease up on the carbs. That's it. That's all I've got to say. Okay, consider yourself dismissed. You'll still be able to swim and shoot while you're fully healing, so let's focus on that. See about getting a little time on the horse, too."

"Got it, Coach," Sammy said, holding back tears.

At one year out of high school and in the physical push of a lifetime, it was all she could muster.

Those under the age of fifty won't recall a time before Title IX. The landmark legislation provided protection against discrimination on the basis of sex in any educational program or activity that received federal funding. The concept of sameness was an important and successful rallying cry when the legislation was passed in 1972. Though the language of

Title IX was broad, most attention was focused on the law's application regarding sports. While the majority of schools have sought to achieve greater equality in sports for both sexes, unforeseen pitfalls have arisen.

As the number of girls participating in sports increased, so did the dollars going to those sports. With money on the line, the coaching landscape shifted. While close to 90 percent of women's sports teams had been led by women before Title IX, the influx of dollars shifted that percentage. Men began to coach women's sports teams because money was available, slowly dwindling the number of female coaches. With fewer women leading teams of girls and women, there was then a natural shift in the dynamic between male coaches and their female athletes. This remains today, and it's most apt to be detrimental in puberty.

The physical changes girls go through in puberty, including the start of the menstrual cycle, are topics largely undiscussed by male coaches with their female athletes, and the lack of normalization of these changes in female bodies has led to a disproportionately high dropout rate for girls in sports. An astonishing 51 percent of girls will have quit sports by the end of puberty. It's no wonder this is a challenge. With a dismal 6 percent of sports science going to study girls and women specifically, male coaches over the past several decades have been unprepared for the influx of girls and the myriad of gender-specific issues they're dealing with. One reason for the lack of data is the perceived difficulty in researching girls and women. The female body and its ebb and flow of hormones has created a disincentive for researchers to dive into sports science focused on girls. In short, female bodies are perceived as too confusing. They're challenging from a scientific point of view, and therefore, rarely studied. This has become true even when there's research to be done for which a hormonal influx wouldn't be applicable to the study subject.

The result is that, instead of being armed with science and language to discuss with their female athletes what they'll experience in puberty, coaches often feel stuck. Both athletes and coaches are thus left without the tools they need to maximize their experiences in sports, especially through the teenage years.

Girls are too often trained in an identical way to boys, with workouts simply made shorter or easier. It's not dissimilar from the sports marketing model which has until recently been focused on the "shrink it and pink it" model to appeal to female athletes. While boys traveling through puberty see a hormone shift that maximizes their performances with age, the path for girls is non-linear. Because girls can see plateaus or dips in their performances, often peak performance doesn't appear until well beyond puberty. However, with a lack of attention being given to science-based research that would help coaches understand these differences and how girls and women should be trained differently, an alarming trend has developed.

The unacknowledged differences in how boys and girls develop naturally leads to a focus on purely statistics, times, and finishing places. Without access to data on the real reasons why their performances are suffering, athletes and coaches look for ways to improve performance. When girls who've been fast prior to puberty have natural dips in performance, a push towards maintaining a lower body weight can occur. It's a belief in lighter, leaner, and faster. The push is frequently couched as "healthy eating," but when layered on too aggressively can result in disordered eating.

Many are now calling for the shortcomings launched by the altruistic intentions of Title IX to be corrected. Only then, they say, will all genders have access to the correct information on injury prevention, training protocols, and nutrition that they need in order to maximize the health and performances of female athletes.

Life as an Olympian-in-training continued for Sammy. By the time 2016 rolled around she'd been put on bed rest for a stress fracture, had surgery for a torn labrum, and taken more control over her weight by restricting her food intake. She wrestled with finances, finding a few sponsors to cover basic living costs, and secured a job at the Olympic Training Center to support herself. Night and online classes continued in between competitions. The success she saw at international competitions was becoming more frequent and praised by her coaches as a direct result of being "fit."

Among the modern pentathletes she trained with, several had opted to join the Army and after qualifying, had entered the WCAP unit. It was a way to secure financial stability, and several of her male teammates encouraged her to think about it. The concept of a steady paycheck was enticing. So too was the knowledge that she'd be part of something bigger than sports. There was a sense of collaboration in the Army, her teammates said. They got to travel into the community to give talks to schoolchildren. The possibilities gnawed deeply at her belief in service work, which her parents had worked hard to ingrain.

In August of 2016, Sammy sat in the stands at Maracana Stadium in Rio de Janeiro watching the closing ceremony of the Rio Olympics. She'd missed making the team by only a few competition points and was there as an alternate. Devastated that she'd missed another opportunity, the experience crystallized her decision. If she was going to make it to the Tokyo Olympics in 2020, it was time to join the Army and try to make it into WCAP.

The United States Army Training Center at Fort Jackson, South Carolina, is where the military journey starts for half of all soldiers. Basic Combat Training, also known as basic, or boot camp, is a ten-week program laid out in phases. The goal is to train enlistees in the areas of discipline, teamwork, Army traditions, weaponry, first aid, navigation, and combat skills. Days are long and the physical demands grueling. Most new recruits are in the eighteen- to twenty-four-year-old range, and only 15 percent of the recruits are women.

Sammy arrived at boot camp in August 2017. She was twenty-five years old. Unlike the other recruits, she wasn't worried about surviving the next ten weeks, but rather concerned about how out of shape she'd become. Her body had been molded by rigorous training which would be completely altered by both the physical but also classroom requirements of a new routine in boot camp. If the goal was to enter the WCAP unit in good shape, she believed she'd have to keep her pre-boot camp athletic training while at boot camp, on top of the already packed days she knew she'd have with the other recruits. The balance proved hard to achieve, with her days and nights full of strife at all turns, as her journal entries showed:

> *Some of the girls are intimidated by me. I'm so much older than them, and I blew my physical training section out of the water. I think someone Googled me, so they know I'm an athlete trying for the WCAP unit. I have a target on my back now.*
>
> *Today we practiced throwing grenades. I need to work on this. I'm not great at it. But my shooting is good enough here that I've qualified to be a sharpshooter.*
>
> *It's crazy hot. We had boxing matches today and I got hit in the head bad a few times. The staff sergeant figured out who I am and pulled me aside to tell me that he wants me to stay healthy. I thought he'd be mean about it, but he'll take care of me.*
>
> *I'm always trying to find the beauty or the positive. Today I got to go to church and was able to see my sister. I broke into tears and didn't let her go. She took a photo of me and sent it to Mom and Dad. Mom said she started crying when she saw it because I look so tired and thin.*
>
> *We finished the gas chamber exercise and the wilderness camping test. I was sleepwalking one night in the middle of a march and one of the other soldiers grabbed my backpack and threw me back on the trail.*
>
> *We're getting to the end of boot camp, and I've really taken on a leadership role. Some of the girls look up to me now. A lot of them are just kids trying to help provide security for their families. It makes me realize how privileged I am.*
>
> *I feel like I'm putting on weight. I'm being so careful of what I eat, but I'm always so hungry. I dream of eating at night. I'm not sure what's going on. Maybe my metabolism is really screwed up.*

Sammy graduated from her training with honors. Reporting for duty with the WCAP unit after her basic and advanced training, she'd lost fifteen to twenty pounds from the time she'd entered. Her menstrual cycle had disappeared, and it would remain absent for many years.

Chapter Seventeen

Colorado

2018–2019

As the calendar turned to 2018, Shadrack was representing Team USA in another World Championship and was approaching the end of his four-year Army contract. It marked a turning point with two paths: the option to re-enlist versus the option to leave the Army to seek professional sponsorship with a big shoe company. He and Elvin weighed the options.

Staying in the Army would provide lifelong job security and benefits. He'd be able to retire early and honor the United States through his military service.

Leaving the Army would allow him to earn a potentially higher paycheck in the short term and give him more freedom in whatever career he transitioned to after running.

"The Army's been so good to us, Elvin," Shadrack said as they sat on their front porch.

They'd bought a house in the suburbs which had become a gathering place for their friends.

"I hate the idea of leaving something that's given us a real life here."

"That's understandable," Elvin answered. "You know I'll support you either way. My gut is telling me that from a professional standpoint, your career after running will be better served outside the military, don't you think?"

He nodded, pulling legs out in front of himself and sinking deeper into the porch chair.

As for the running part, it was a clear choice. If he could keep Scott as his coach and sign on with a shoe company and all their resources, his career would continue to soar. Paul had decided to leave the Army at the end of his contract and had signed with Nike. After looking at all the factors, Shadrack decided that leaving the Army was the right move for him, too. Finding a shoe sponsor seemed daunting, but given his stellar race results over the past several years, he received an offer from Nike. He accepted the deal. The moment had come to finish his Army service and began to focus on life as a full-time, professional distance runner.

The track at Cheyenne Mountain High School hummed with life. Scott's training group had exploded with the addition of Shadrack and Paul. Free from their military duties, they were able to focus on running. Training together under Scott allowed them to be together all day. As a bonus, Elvin's friend and teammate from Arizona, Lawi Lalang, had joined the Army and the WCAP unit. Ivy had secured a visa and arrived to run with Elvin. Life in Colorado suited them, as Elvin had predicted.

She sat on the concrete bleachers changing into her racing spikes in preparation for the workout. Lawi edged in beside her, removing his own shoes from a duffel.

"How goes it, soldier boy?" Elvin asked.

"It goes okay with me. Just happy to be out of boot camp and back to the track. Feeling totally out of shape, you know?"

"I've heard that, which always seems crazy to me. What kind of person goes into boot camp and leaves out of shape?" Elvin chuckled.

Lawi laughed, "Yes indeed. Only us insane, professional long-distance runners, I guess."

He slipped his racing spikes over each foot, tying them tightly.

"So, it wasn't too bad, then? Something I could handle, you think?"

"Compared to the workouts Coach Li used to run us through, and the ones we've got now here with Scott . . . definitely. Why? Are you considering it?"

Elvin thought back to her conversations with Shadrack the past few weeks. Though most pieces of life were on cruise control, her contract with Skechers was expiring soon. The thought of renewing it at a price that would barely cover their monthly grocery bill was depressing. She'd never seen herself in the military. Not after experiencing her father's life. But maybe there was a path for her in the Army. She had the WCAP standard already. Why would she bypass an opportunity to earn a decent wage and be able to continue training most of the day? Shadrack was at the top of his game and could draw a contract from Nike. She couldn't. At least not yet. Perhaps the security of the Army could get her there.

"Considering it. That describes where I'm at. I could keep training with Scott. The benefits are hard to beat. It would be nice to earn a little something better than what I'm making from Skechers."

"All those things are true. You'd sail through basic training. You're book smart and you'd do fine with the physical stuff."

"I don't need the Army to get citizenship. I can get it through Shaddy. But this would make it happen faster, right? Independent of him."

"That's true. And you could compete for the United States, which is something you can't do now."

The ability to put on a United States jersey someday in world competitions was no small factor. Elvin had imagined it, though it seemed far away. She'd been living in the States for eight years, first on a student visa and then on a visa through being married to a citizen. If she ever wanted to compete professionally for the United States, she'd need citizenship all on her own.

"First Sergeant Williams thinks I should consider it, too."

"I bet she would've loved to see you and Shaddy serving together," Lawi said.

Elvin smiled. "She did say that, actually. More women need to be in WCAP, and we all know it. And wouldn't it have been great if we'd served together, and I got promoted ahead of Shaddy?"

Lawi lifted a leg onto the bleachers and leaned over, stretching his hamstring. The rest of the group was gathering at the start line, fiddling with running watches. Shadrack came over, pulling off his shirt for what would be a grueling next hour on the track.

"This looks dangerous," he joked, looking at Lawi and Elvin deep in conversation. "What are you two Arizona Wildcats chatting about over here?"

"Running. Life. Elvin entering the Army," Lawi responded.

"All good topics. First Sergeant Williams was bummed when I left. She's pushing hard to get the other half of our family to enlist," Shadrack said, nudging his wife.

"So I hear," said Lawi.

Scott called for the group to gather for the workout.

"Well, hang in there, boys," Elvin added. "It's sounding like a legit possibility. I suspect you'll see me in uniform before too long."

In October 2018 Elvin Kibet shipped off to basic training at Fort Jackson in South Carolina, followed by several weeks of specialized training in finance. By March 2019 she was back in Colorado Springs, assigned to the WCAP unit as planned. She'd met Sammy Schultz at a training run, and the two of them had bonded over their shared experiences. Being women in the military had its challenges. Being women in the WCAP unit added yet another layer.

"How do you do it all?" Elvin asked Sammy one morning after a military training meeting.

They were dressed in their duty uniforms, both with hair pulled back in buns and tucked under olive green caps.

"It's five different sports including one with a horse! I mean . . . wow, Sammy," Elvin gushed.

Sammy grinned, adjusting her cap. Elvin hardly reached her shoulder, making Sammy feel like a giant beside her.

"It's not easy. Then again, I have no idea how you spend two hours running twenty miles!" Sammy replied. "Let's connect and do something shorter together. Maybe the Monument Valley Park 10k next year? I think I could handle that."

"Yes, definitely. It's on my radar screen!"

By 2018 there had been a change of coaches, allowing Sammy to settle into training without the worry of being constantly berated. She was promoted to sergeant, received her college degree, and made the finals at the World Championships for the first time. She'd won seven national championships and medals at the Pan American Games and the Junior World Championships. Karl was her biggest supporter and there to watch her win a silver medal at the Pan American Games. The medal secured her spot for the 2020 Tokyo Olympics. She became a darling on the speaking circuit, representing WCAP in the run-up to the Tokyo Olympics. By all outside appearances, the decision to join the Army had been a good one, and her ability to wear the Army jersey to competitions made her proud. In theory, she now had access to untold resources in the military. So, it was a surprise when her request for a therapist leading up to the Olympics was turned down. Mental health support didn't appear to be the priority Sammy thought it should be. She realized she had people around her to care for her body, but too few resources to look after her spirit, which was faltering after years of competition.

Physically, she felt strong.

Emotionally, she felt drained.

While Sammy sought the resources she needed to prepare for Tokyo, Elvin's first sights were set on the Army Ten Miler, an annual race that drew over 30,000 competitors. Though open to civilians, the race drew primarily from the military and was the crown jewel of road races for military members. She'd be able to wear the Army jersey and run with a team of other WCAP members. Of even greater importance was the fact that she'd have built-in pacers. Her career had been spent in pursuit of wins in races with only women. Road races were an entirely new ball game. A huge race with men pacing her and pulling her through the finish sounded heavenly.

In October 2019 she arrived at the start line of the Army Ten Miler full of nerves. The race began fast, with Elvin pushing the first few miles at a 5:20/mile pace.

Oh, I'm gonna pay for this at eight miles, she thought.

To her surprise, she held the pace, overcoming scores of her fellow soldiers, most of whom were surprised to be passed by a woman. Crossing the finish line as the first woman in 54:05, she stood on the podium with Lawi, who'd won on the men's side. Part of her prize package was an American flag, dressed in a wooden frame. The gift seemed odd, as it had been a year since she'd gone through boot camp, but her immigration paperwork was still lagging due to an administration which had cracked down heavily on immigration in all its forms. Yet here she was, the winner of the Army's most prestigious road race, holding an American flag. It was the culmination of a series of similar bizarre moments. Months before, she'd raced fast enough to qualify to compete for a spot on the World championship team, and yet, without her citizenship processed, she couldn't participate.

Imagine that, she thought to herself later. *I'm a United States soldier, but I can't represent my country.*

Chapter Eighteen

1:59

2019

While Elvin celebrated her victory in the Army Ten Miler, her mind was across the world in Vienna, Austria, with Shadrack. He was running the same weekend and it was the honor of a lifetime. She'd been there, months ago, as he'd received a phone call from his agent.

"Shadrack, I think you're gonna want to sit down for this one," his agent had said.

"This is top secret and huge. I just got a call from Eliud Kipchoge's management company. They want you for the INEOS 1:59 Challenge."

No matter how many individual accolades Shadrack had beside his name, nothing was as gratifying as team victories—the cross-country wins with his Oklahoma State teammates and the World Cross Country races he'd done with other Americans, to name a few. The wins were so much sweeter when shared with others. Though it was hard to imagine how the INEOS 1:59 Challenge would affect the rest of the world, by Shadrack's standards, running as part of Eliud Kipchoge's team was about as good as it got.

Considered by most to be the greatest marathoner of all time, Kipchoge had attempted to break the two-hour mark for the marathon in 2017, falling short by twenty-five seconds. Once thought to be an unachievable feat, the slim margin of defeat gave way to an even more massive, coordinated effort to try again in October 2019. The race would pit Kipchoge against only the clock. Because the conditions would be manufactured for one man rather than an open competition, the time wouldn't count as an official world record. This fact hadn't seemed to faze the public on Kipchoge's first attempt, and it certainly didn't faze those organizing the second. Backed by big sponsors and the science to help determine the perfect conditions, the INEOS Challenge designed a course in Vienna, Austria, for the occasion. To run 26.2 miles in under two hours would require every advantage Kipchoge could find. Securing pacemakers to help him span the marathon distance was at the top of the list.

And then there was the matter of shoes.

It had taken several years for the running community to wrap its head around the fact that shoe technology would be a major player in the bid to break the two-hour marathon. After the 2016 Olympics, there were rumors in the running world that Nike had secretly developed new technology for racing shoes which had an energy savings with the potential to improve times in distance races up to 3 percent. The new shoes were unveiled with much fanfare just before Kipchoge's first crack at the two hour marathon in May 2017. Researchers at the University of Colorado measured that the bouncy lightweight midsole foam combined with a carbon-fiber plate to improve running economy by an average of 4 percent, but those results had not yet been published in a peer-reviewed scientific journal. Thus, even after Kipchoge fell just twenty-five seconds short wearing the shoe in what was essentially a two-hour Nike commercial, it seemed impossible for many to believe that a shoe could have such an impact.

Just a few weeks after Kipchoge's attempt, the science behind the shoe was presented at the American College of Sports Medicine annual conference.

"The abstract laid out very clearly the testing we'd done to conclude the shoe reduced the cost of running by 4 percent as compared to other established marathon racing shoes. The data couldn't have been more clear. But I'll be damned if there were only fifteen people in the room who wanted to hear about it," says Rodger Kram, the lead scientist of the seminal study and professor emeritus in the Department of Integrative Physiology at the University of Colorado, Boulder.

"We were accused of being shills for Nike. People said it was all a giant Nike marketing scheme and the media hadn't caught on yet. Eventually, people realized our lab was the real deal. Other studies from other labs that weren't Nike-sponsored almost exactly replicated our findings, but it took awhile."

Shadrack and the rest of Scott's training group had gotten wind of the INEOS challenge months before the call came. The stars looked like they were aligning, as race organizers were pulling together Nike-sponsored athletes who were able to cover distances of a few miles at a pace that would keep Kipchoge on target. With two more World Championship teams on his resume in 2019, Shadrack hoped and assumed he was being considered. Still, the call from his agent caused a bolt of excitement to run from head to toe.

"They want you for the INEOS 1:59 Challenge, Shadrack. It's on. It'll be in October in Vienna, so you'll have to fly directly there from the World Championships in Doha if you want to be one of the pacemakers. Are you in?"

"Are you kidding? Of course! I'll do it for free! Correction. I'll pay *them* to do it," Shadrack replied.

"Super. They'll put you in the Nike Vaporfly for the run and you'll need to go to Vienna for a practice session on the course at the end of August."

"They could put me in flip flops and run the thing in Greenland and I'd still be in, so yes, definitely thumbs up on this one."

His agent laughed, reporting that he'd get back to Shadrack with more details. In the meantime, the news about who was being selected was beginning to spread, so his agent urged him to check with the rest of his training group.

"I got the call," he said as Paul Chelimo answered his phone. "I'm in. You in?"

"Me too. I'm so in and this thing is gonna be sick," Paul answered.

"How many of us do you think will be selected?"

"Guessing a few dozen. They won't have us run more than a few miles at a time."

"And a practice weekend at the end of August in Vienna," Shadrack said.

"Yup. There's no way they'll have Kipchoge there for that, though. He'll stay in Kenya training, I bet."

"You're probably right, but either way, it'll be a helluva practice weekend."

A month later at the end of August 2019, Shadrack was in Vienna. He stood with a group of pacemakers including Bernard Lagat, who he'd seen sporadically since their sweltering Olympic Trials race at Hayward Field in 2016. Bernard was a team captain, meaning he'd be placed directly in front of Kipchoge to block any wind on race day. In front of him on either side would be four additional pacemakers in a V-formation. Behind Kipchoge, two additional pacemakers. The team of pacers would rotate to ensure a steady pace the entire 26.2 miles. The act of transitioning teams was a dance, and the groups were spending several hours over two days mastering the art form. Making it easier was the fact that the course was a series of wide loops, rather than point to point.

Shadrack listened to directions from the organizers of the race, one who spoke with an iPad in his hand.

"Everyone looked good out there today," he said. "All of you can hit 4:35 minute per mile pace for the duration of the distances we have you running, so today was all about mechanics. We took lots of video and we think we have a better idea where you should be placed. Come take a look over here in groups to see what we're thinking."

Shadrack and Bernard inched closer, looking at the iPad which showed video from their practice run.

"Shaddy, I think we're going to have you up front on Bernard's team. At the top of the V on the right like this," he explained, pointing to the formation on the screen. "That'll mean you're a lead runner. And I think we'll have your team run the first leg."

Bernard gave Shadrack a fist bump.

"Sounds good. If the car is in front of me, I'll be good to go," Shadrack said.

"Well, yes it'll be there, but it might take a few minutes for it to settle into the exact pace we need it to be at, so you'll have your hands full for about 800 meters."

An electric car had been commissioned as a pace car to drive directly in front of the runners. Projected finish times would be illuminated on a digital clock and the car would carry a laser system which would glow on the pavement where the pacemakers should run.

"I just don't wanna be the guy who trips Kipchoge," Shadrack said.

He twisted the red, green, and black bracelet on his wrist, imagining the disaster it would be if he stumbled on a stone and accidentally toppled the greatest marathoner ever to live.

"You and the other forty pacemakers," the organizer chuckled. "Don't worry. You've got this. Get yourself to the World Champs in Doha and we'll see you after that."

120,000 spectators crammed the Vienna racecourse on the misty morning of October 12, 2019. In the days leading up to the event, Shadrack and his fellow pacemakers had traveled from around the world, many from the Track and Field Outdoor World Championships in Doha. Kipchoge himself had been flown on a private jet from Eldoret to Austria.

A true global event, an estimated 500 million viewers were tuned in around the world, including millions in Kenya. Big screen televisions had been set up in Eldoret, where people had packed shoulder to shoulder outside in open air stadiums and street markets to watch the run. In Vienna, the pacemakers spent a couple days on last minute preparations. Paul, who'd been assigned the role of captain, was demoted. His long, beautiful stride with the high kick in back worked perfectly on the track, but in the off chance he could clip Kipchoge in their formation, he was moved to a position as a pacer on the side.

Though many of the pacers already knew Kipchoge personally, others had never met him and now in Vienna their first moments together were oddly sterile. Out of caution, everyone was masked, abiding by strict hand sanitation rules, and asked to stick to fist bumps only. While bizarre at the time, only a few months later when COVID hit it would feel like a bit of a prophecy.

Shadrack barely slept the night before the race, but he wasn't alone.

"Bro, I hardly slept. What if I trip Kipchoge?" his training partner Hillary Bor said to him as they gathered in the lobby on race morning.

Hillary had also been selected as a pacemaker and he and Shadrack were on a team together in the middle of the race.

Shadrack smiled reassuringly.

"Dude, everyone's worried about that. That's all anyone is talking about. It's not going to happen," Shadrack promised him.

"I'm counting on it," Hillary replied. "I'll see you in the middle leg. Hope your first one goes well. Get off the bridge and get into the right pace."

Shadrack had secured peach assignments for the INEOS run. He'd start the race with Bernard's team for a few miles. Then transition to another team mid-race for a few miles led by American Matt Centrowitz with Hillary running to his right. Then finish with Bernard's team. Having a spot on the first and last legs seemed too good to be true.

The group of seven pacemakers on the first team was taken to the starting line, a spot on the Reichsbrucke Bridge they'd practiced at in August. Each of the pacers wore orange long-sleeved shirts, black tanks, black shorts, and a brand-new pair of hot-pink Nike Vaporfly running shoes. Kipchoge's long-sleeved shirt was white, distinguishing him from the others. He seemed in good spirits, smiling and talking with the pacers and race organizers. Shadrack imagined Elvin waking up and watching. In Colorado it was the middle of the night, but she was surely among the millions anxiously awaiting the start.

Unlike other road races, there was no chatter and certainly no joking around. They'd all come here for a purpose greater than themselves. If Kipchoge broke two hours, it would be a barrier that most never thought they'd live to see. The sides of the bridge were covered in posters with Kipchoge's tagline, "No Human is Limited."

With fifteen minutes to go until the start, the group gathered in a huddle, arms around shoulders. One of the pacers led the team in prayer, ending with, "God give us the strength to come through this."

Shadrack's heart was racing from nerves, and he tried to calm them. All that stood between the start and finish lines were Kipchoge himself, a couple of hours, and several dozen professional distance runners whose only job was to keep a 2:50 minutes per kilometer pace and not fall. How hard could it be?

Long-sleeved shirts were removed as the pacemakers were called to the start line. A few shook out limbs, while others took a moment for the sign of the cross. They stood, side by side under a banner reading "INEOS 1:59." With the fog lifting, the starting gun sounded, and the group was off. Shadrack looked up at the electric car in front of them. They'd made a last-minute judgement call which would affect the rest of the race, one way or another. In practices, the car's speed was too uneven in the opening minutes. Therefore, the team had decided to let it go, achieve the proper pace on their own, and then begin following the laser pace lights illuminating the road behind the car when it had stabilized. This left no room for human error in the first 800 meters.

800 meters passed and Kipchoge's agent gave them a shout of encouragement. He was on a bicycle next to the pacers. His presence was calming, and his words reassuring as the team passed the one-kilometer mark on pace.

"That's it, guys! Looking amazing. Perfectly paced!"

Shadrack took a bigger exhale on his next breath, happy to have the first minutes behind him.

The streets were packed with spectators, all cheering loudly and some of them banging hands on the INEOS banners that covered the metal barricades. Beautiful, expansive trees lined the racecourse, providing shade. Shadrack sensed his nerves settle. The green laser in front of him was all he needed to focus on. He had a moment of overwhelm as he realized his position in the front of the formation, leading the team through what could be the most monumental, and unifying race of his career.

With five kilometers under his belt, it was time for the first transition. Shadrack eased out of the formation with the rest of his team, letting another pacemaker fill his spot. The first leg had gone well. With little time to waste, the group of athletes was shepherded to a staging area to stretch, take fluids, and go to the bathroom. Anything but sit down, which might cause cramping.

At eighteen kilometers, with one of the race organizers gently pushing on his shoulder as a cue, Shadrack eased back into the group for the next leg. Kipchoge looked strong and the pacemakers had done their job, keeping nine seconds under their goal finish pace. The television commentator painted a picture for viewers, saying, "They have just run in front of our commentary position, and I kid you not, if you blinked, you missed them. It was an absolute blur."

Hillary was on Shadrack's right at the top of the V. They were far from Colorado Springs and the track at Cheyenne Mountain High School, but both knew that Scott was watching. Meanwhile, Kipchoge's agent continued to trail the group on the bike as their own personal cheerleader.

"You're crushing it, guys! Right on target."

Shadrack and Hillary were now leading the group, a step ahead of the pacers behind them and responsible for steering the pace. The looped course took them around a gradual turn, easing out and then running the straightaway for several more kilometers. During the turn, the green laser on the car was not visible and it was their job to run on instinct, keeping the correct speed until the laser appeared again.

"We gotta nail this turn, Shaddy," Hillary said, loud enough to be heard, but not so loud to distract the other pacers.

"Take it easy. Don't get carried away," Shadrack responded.

"Won't. I don't wanna be ahead of the light when it comes back to us," Hillary added.

Conversation while running at this speed was brief, but it was reassuring to have Hillary with him. They'd been training together since 2016, and his brother Emmanuel was now part of the training group in Colorado Springs, sidelined from joining the pacers at INEOS because of an injury.

By twenty-three kilometers, Shadrack and Hillary had completed their leg and were out and on the sidelines again. In the entire race, there had been only one small bobble on a turn as the light disappeared for a moment, and it was a nearly imperceptible error. Kipchoge had taken all his fluids, running at a metronomic speed. Shadrack prepared for his final leg. He and the last team were taking over for the last five kilometers.

"Guys, it looks like this is going to happen!" shouted one of the race organizers. His voice lifted over the crowd, which was now screaming at a deafening level.

"Remember what we talked about! If you continue to stay on target, let's race the last kilometer and peel away with two hundred meters to go so Eliud can take it home by himself!"

The pacers nodded, rolling their shoulders and shaking their legs as they prepared to enter the formation. Kipchoge and the next-to-last team approached, and Shadrack eased in, followed by Bernard Lagat who took his position in front of Kipchoge. The crowd was so loud that it was impossible to hear breathing or the sounds of feet on pavement. These were clues that would normally give Shadrack an idea about the strength of his competitors. Today, he didn't need it. Today was about unity. He'd seen Kipchoge's calm expression when he'd entered the last formation and Shadrack knew he was about to be a part of history. He felt himself swallow hard, pushing back a lump in his throat as the crowd roared. His emotions were battling to get the best of him. *Oh my God, I cannot cry until I cross the finish line*, he thought.

"We should enjoy this moment," the television commentator gushed. "My heart is pounding. The next fifteen minutes of this man's life and in the lives of these pacemakers could be life-defining, and that is not overstating it. It transcends running and sport and pushed the boundaries in a way we've never seen before."

Shadrack looked at the clock on the pace car as it peeled off the racecourse, leaving the pacemakers and Eliud Kipchoge alone on the streets of Vienna. The clock had confirmed that their pace had been on target the last kilometer. With one kilometer left, it was time to race. The noise from the crowds was like nothing Shadrack had ever heard. None of the pacemakers fell off as the pace dropped by ten seconds in the final kilometer. With 500 meters to go, Eliud used his arms to emerge from the middle of his cocoon of pacers and spread them to the side of the road so he could surge to the finish line alone.

Spectators hung from trees along the final hundred meters. Shadrack could see ahead to the finish line and hear Kenyan songs being blasted from speakers. The rest of the pacemakers were there, waiting and jumping up and down behind Kipchoge's coach Patrick Sang, the vice president of Kenya, and Kipchoge's wife Grace, who'd never watched her husband race in person.

Shadrack and the six other pacemakers on the final team looked at each other, incredulous at what they were witnessing. Talking would be fruitless, as the cheering was ear-piercing. They kept pace a hundred yards behind Kipchoge, all of their arms now pumping the air and screaming with the crowd as Kipchoge crossed the finish line in 1:59:40. His momentum carried him into the arms of his wife, who acted as a speed bump and brought him into hugs with his children and coach. Then he was swallowed up by the pacemakers and hoisted into the air, the crowd awash with screaming, tears, and music. Paul was there, a grin stretching from ear to ear as he screamed and wrapped Kipchoge in a bear hug. Shadrack stood meters away, catching his breath and his emotions. He could feel the adrenaline coursing through his body, as if he could run another ten miles.

In Iten and Eldoret, time stopped as people celebrated and danced in the streets. Both Elvin and Shadrack's families were watching the television coverage, glowing at the accomplishment. Elvin curled up on their couch in Colorado Springs with tears streaking her cheeks as she marveled at what she'd seen. She saw the images in Kenya and the jubilation of the people singing and dancing in the streets. The sun had not yet risen in Colorado, and her husband had just been a part of something monumental. Neither of them had been prepared for what an extraordinary spectacle this would be, and she was sure nothing could match it, not even the Olympics. As for Shadrack's role, it all made sense—the fact that his greatest athletic achievement was in support of another extraordinary athlete from Kenya.

It fit.

Chapter Nineteen

Sergeant Kibet

2020–2021

"So just a reminder that if you'd like to compete at the Olympic Trials in a few months, it's time to declare now so that we can get your paperwork in order," the WCAP captain said. "I've got a list here of those of you who've already declared, and I know most of you are on it, but let's get the rest of you on it, ASAP."

Elvin sat in a team meeting at Fort Carson with other WCAP athletes from different sports. Wrestlers, swimmers, and track athletes. It was early 2020 and the Olympics were only six months away. Elvin's paperwork with the United States Citizenship and Immigration Service had been filed long ago, but she hadn't heard a word. Compared to the speed at which Shadrack had received his citizenship in 2015, it seemed bizarre. Each time she called, she was told about a backlog. Be patient, they said.

The soldier-athletes were dismissed and began streaming out of the room.

"Specialist Kibet, can I see you up here please?" the captain asked.

"Yes, Sir," Elvin said, gathering her things and walking to the front of the room.

The captain was reviewing the list of declared athletes with a puzzled look on his face.

"I see you haven't given notice yet that you'll be competing at the Trials. Everything okay? You healthy and training going well?" he asked.

"Yes, sir," she answered, adding, "Just waiting on my citizenship, sir."

The captain stopped looking over the list and up at her.

"You're still waiting on citizenship?" he asked. "You can't very well compete at the Olympics if you're not a citizen, now, can you? Hasn't it been forever since you submitted your paperwork with USCIS?"

"Yes, sir, quite some time. Well over a year, I think," Elvin answered.

"Well, hell, that's not okay. And you've inquired?"

"I have, sir. They tell me there's a backlog. Paperwork pending, I think is the exact line I hear each time I call."

"My ass. This is important. You've been serving since what . . . 2018? Active duty that entire time. Let me make a few calls and see if we can get some movement. You want to be there at the Olympic Trials in July, I imagine? Hayward Field in Eugene, right?"

"Yes, sir. I'm training to run the 10,000 at the Trials. I hope to run it with Shadrack running in the 10,000 for the men."

"Damn shame we lost him to Nike, but I understand. I'd probably have taken the offer if Nike had come calling, too!" he chuckled.

A few days later Elvin received a call from the captain, who'd had a conversation with someone at USCIS. As soon as he'd said the word "Olympics" and "soldier" he'd gotten their attention. They'd be happy to see Elvin at their Denver office, he reported. Tomorrow. To make sure there were no further delays, the captain would drive her himself.

"And Specialist Kibet," he said, "wear your uniform."

The Rockies spanned the distance to the west as Elvin and the captain drove to Denver the next day. She'd never spent this much time with him and found him curious about the intersection of her past and present.

"So, what's different from a running point of view? Which is better, Kenya or the United States?"

"That's a tough question. I didn't run very much in Kenya. Only a few months after high school before I came here. But running in general is a big deal in Kenya. Lots of support. The big-name distance runners are celebrities. Everyone knows Shadrack, now, too. They recognize him from the Olympics and the INEOS run. That's not really the case in Colorado. He's just a regular guy on the street here," she said.

"Then again, the coaching is probably better here," she continued. "I've been fortunate since I got to the U.S. to have amazing coaches. I can still hear my college coach talking to me now when I'm in big races."

"Well that probably makes all the difference in the world, right?" he asked.

"For sure. Having a coach who sees you as a human and not a machine. Someone who knows you're more than an athlete. I was so serious in college. Obsessed with getting A's. Always scared of what I didn't know. Coach Li . . . yeah, he really helped me grow as a human. Shaddy had a great coach, too."

"You can't ask for more than that, I suppose," the captain replied.

They pulled into the parking lot of the immigration offices. As usual when she was out in uniform, she got stares and was never sure what they meant. Today, the official behind the plexiglass perked up as soon as they walked in, shuttling them to the front of the line. They were ready for her, and excited to have an Olympian, they said. Elvin smiled politely, knowing she was still quite far from that title. She was shepherded into a conference room where an immigration officer led her through a series of civic questions. Elvin nailed each one. The officer congratulated her, telling her she'd been approved for citizenship.

"That's it?" Elvin asked, amazed.

"That's it!" the officer said. "You can come back tomorrow for your swearing in, or you can hang out for a couple hours and do it this afternoon. We've got a group coming in."

"Oh, I'm not going anywhere!" Elvin said. "Pretty sure my captain will want us to stay and take this thing across the finish line, as we say!"

"Good plan," the officer said.

She stood to walk Elvin out, asking on the way, "You know, I was in the military once, as well. So, I understand a little bit of about how military assignments work, but what happens with your running after the Olympics?"

"Well, the goal is to just make it to the Olympic Trials. That's a big deal in and of itself. If I don't do that, then I think I'll be sent into a regular unit. My assignment with the WCAP unit is always dependent on meeting their time standards," Elvin explained.

"A regular unit in the Army wouldn't be bad, would it?"

"Definitely not. There's so much I can do in the Army," Elvin said. "I'm thinking of becoming a physician's assistant, and I know the Army would support that career," she added.

Elvin and the captain killed two hours with a long lunch, then came back to a room filled with elated, soon-to-be-new-Americans. After all that waiting, the last twenty-four hours had been a breeze, and on February 27, 2020, Elvin Kibet went through her citizenship ceremony in Denver.

She called Shadrack, who was equally stunned that it had happened with just one additional phone call up the chain of command.

"Come on back to the Springs," he said. "You and I have some training to do. Our first time racing together!"

The couple was planning to run their first professional race together, the New York City Half Marathon.

Two weeks later, on Tuesday, March 10, 2020, along with St. Patrick's Day parades, political rallies, and all NCAA postseason spring tournaments, the New York City Half Marathon was cancelled.

Months followed that seemed like an eternity. The WCAP athletes continued to train through the pandemic in small groups. In a stroke of fate, Elvin had been back to Kenya at the beginning of 2020 and had returned to the States with both Ivy and a pacemaker she'd hired for herself. Though the men of WCAP had each other, Elvin was once again the only woman in the group and needed someone to help her gear up for the Olympic Trials at just her speed. Her pacemaker had come straight from a running camp in Iten and now found himself stuck in the United States for months living with Shadrack, Elvin, and Ivy. The foursome trained together until the Olympics were postponed, when both Ivy and Elvin's pacer returned to Kenya.

In the summer of 2020, Sammy Schultz and Elvin ran with several of the other WCAP athletes in the Monument Valley 10k in Colorado Springs. Sammy watched as Elvin took off at a pace that she couldn't keep up with. The out-and-back loop allowed them to pass each other and exchange a quick smile. In the middle of the pandemic, it was the closest they could get to being together.

The country grappled with its new reality. Communities were both created and fractured. Almost without exception, everyone was weary. Some chose to rise. Others chose silence. Still others dug deeper into fear and hatred.

Shadrack came home from a run one morning in late 2020. Elvin heard the door close, and the familiar sound of his running shoes plopping down in the front hall. He appeared in the kitchen as she stood at the sink. His expression was flat, without the usual animation she saw after he returned from doing a job he loved.

"What's up, babe?" she asked. "Looks like it wasn't such a great workout."

"No, no . . . it's not that. That part was good. Something else. About a mile from home. A guy was outside his house just off the running trail," he said, then stopped.

"And? What happened? Shaddy, you're scaring me."

"The guy called me the n-word. I had just run by, maybe fifty meters, and he screamed, 'Run, n-word' and then he went back inside. I couldn't believe it. He just said it."

Elvin slammed her palms on the counter. "What the hell?!"

Shadrack knew she meant business when she swore in English. The two of them only spoke Kalenjin to each other. Gogo had never allowed her to swear and therefore it was only now in her second language that Elvin would let it rip when she was infuriated.

"I was debating whether to tell you. I knew you'd be pissed."

"We're going back there. Right now. To talk to them."

Elvin walked around the counter and headed for the front door.

"Elvin. Elvin! We're not going back. Leave it alone. It's not worth it."

She stopped and stared at him, a combination of anger and overwhelm on her face.

"I mean it. Don't give this guy the time of day. People like that won't change. We've been through stuff like this before here. We both know there are neighborhoods we avoid running in. We both see the racist stuff that's written in some of those tunnels we run through on the trails. It's just part of what we must put up with here."

"That's bullshit, Shadrack. It's bullshit to be scared when we run. Which I am. I just never know who's out there or what they think when they see me. You remember what happened when I was stopped in Oregon by that cop all those years ago? If I'd been a black man in a hoodie at that traffic stop and gotten out of the car the way I did, we both know I'd be dead."

Shadrack remembered the incident well, and how much it had terrified both of them.

"You're probably right. Some of this makes us stronger, I'm sure. More resilient."

"Resilient sure. All this adversity keeps us going and has made us bulletproof on some level, yes. But also . . . Blah, blah, blah. I just want people to be decent human beings, babe," Elvin said.

They'd wandered into the living room and sat on the sectional, their feet meeting in the middle.

"The question for me is whether this is a country where we even want to raise a family?" Elvin said. "That's where I land on all of this. We grew up in Kenya. We were poor. We struggled to get here. Uprooted ourselves to be in this country. We understand survival. But look at where we are now."

She gestured to the expansive living room, the large-screen television, and the adjoining kitchen of their 3,000 square foot suburban house.

"When our children grow up here in this place, not understanding exactly what it means to really survive the way *we* did, where does that leave them when shit like this happens to them?" she asked, realizing the answers were missing.

2020 slid into 2021. It looked as if the Olympics in Tokyo might finally happen. Though the military wouldn't let the WCAP team members travel out of the country for races, Shadrack was slowly beginning to race and train again overseas. With the return of the travel came the return of drug testing.

Shadrack could not love this part of his job more. He wanted the sport to be clean and relished being tested as often and as spontaneously as he could be. In Kenya, athletes were being popped for drugs frequently, for reasons that were different than in the United States.

One good race and a decent prize purse could turn the fortunes of a family in Kenya around in ways that were incomprehensible in the States. Sometimes crooked coaches and agents put pressure on athletes to dope. And sometimes it was just a plain old desire to perform well and escape the cycle of poverty that made Kenyans athletes turn to performance-enhancing drugs.

Testing by the United States Anti-Doping Agency (USADA) meant a required daily window of one hour in which Shadrack was to be at home, or within range of arriving home. His window was 8:00–9:00 p.m. To manage the window when he had social activities at night, he'd hooked up a video doorbell with remote access through his phone. Over many years, he knew that the drug testing crew always arrived at the stroke of 8:00 p.m. When he was away from home, he'd peek at his phone app at 8:00 to see if they were there. If so, no matter where he was or what he was doing, it was time to leave and get home to meet the testers.

The same USADA drug testers had been visiting him for years. He respected what they did and how professional they were. Perhaps the only thing that could've made their visits easier was if he was able to provide a urine sample more efficiently. Elvin coined him "Mr. Always the Last Guy" for his inability to pee on command. He felt sure he held the record for the longest period ever recorded for a urine sample to be produced. It was in Doha after the World Championships in 2019 when he was called for testing at 4:00 p.m. and couldn't produce a sample until midnight. Unsure if it was performance anxiety or constant dehydration, he only knew that he sensed relief every time the drug testers announced they were taking a blood sample rather than urine.

Though the selection process for drug testing was said to be random, Shadrack was fast becoming one of the most tested distance runners in the USADA testing pool. The reasons why were unclear. Was it because he trained in Kenya from time to time? Was he still seen as Kenyan rather than American? The answers were unknown, but as he rose to the top of the testing pool, all that mattered were his test results. Each negative drug test added to his "Athlete Biological Passport" which was described by USADA as a function designed to "monitor selected biological variables over time that indirectly reveal the effects of doping, rather than attempting to detect the doping substance or method itself."

Not only was his biological passport adding to his stellar reputation as a clean athlete, but he found the stories he could tell of his drug testing visits were getting better every time. Perhaps his favorite took place on a recent trip to Iten. Without Elvin, he was staying in a traditional home with his brother. A little step up from the home he grew up in, the tiny structure had a roof and walls made of iron sheets rather than mud. On a morning he intended to be filled with errands, he instead found himself having a conversation with a friend that went like this,

"Hey, I know we're supposed to get together at 10:00, but I just got a visitor," he said over the phone.

"A visitor? Can you tell them you have plans and ask them to come back?" the friend inquired.

"Afraid not. It's the drug testers. I've gotta be tested," Shadrack replied with a chuckle.

He nodded at one of the two testers, who was removing a urine cup from his duffel.

"You *must* be joking. They found you here? In Iten, in the boonies in that tiny little place you're staying? Which, by the way, Elvin will never stay at," the friend added.

"You're totally right. And yes, they found me, thank God. They went to my neighbor's house first because there's a 'Shadrack' there, as well. But clearly that 'Shadrack' wasn't ready for drug testing."

The two laughed and made plans to meet later, with the friend saying, "Give them my best. I'm impressed they found you. Neither rain, nor snow, nor sleet, nor oceans, nor crappy Kenyan roads or multiple Shadracks can keep drug testers away!"

With the world finally turning a corner on April 15, 2021, Elvin stood on the grassy infield of the Mesa Ridge High School track in Colorado Springs. This time, she wore her duty uniform rather than shorts and a t-shirt. Her teammates were there, including Ednah Kurgat who'd joined the WCAP unit. Having Ednah to train with was a delight. The men of WCAP had been Elvin's biggest advocates. Her battle buddies. The ones who'd get her all the way to the Olympic Trials in a few months. Yet having another woman to run with brought her a little extra joy that she'd been missing since college.

Elvin had spent much of COVID thinking about her life after running. She'd volunteered with a physician's assistant and taken classes to prepare her to start her own training in that field. She and Shadrack had talked about starting a family. And then there were the extra military classes she'd taken to gain a promotion. She could've picked wherever she wanted for her promotion ceremony. It just seemed natural that she'd do it here at the track before their workout of 400-meter repetitions.

The team and her immediate superiors were gathered on the infield with her. Just a few chairs. Everyone still in masks. Shadrack was in black sweats and under strict orders to go easy on the legs. He'd suffered his first major injury and wouldn't be competing in the Olympic Trials. Instead, he was spending his days supporting Elvin, making sure she stayed fueled and rested. Though he wouldn't be racing at the Trials and thus not the Tokyo Olympics, he knew she would be at the Trials, and he hoped it was as special for her as it had been for him in 2016. His injury had made him consider his own future in running, and he was thinking about a transition to the marathon. The progression to the marathon was a natural one for 10,000-meter runners. He'd been thinking about it for a long time, and ready to make the move away from the track and onto the roads for the marathon.

A few perfunctory words from various military officials, and then it was time for her promotion. She'd chosen Shadrack to pin her as the official ceremony script was read.

"The Secretary of the Army has reposed special trust and confidence in the patriotism, valor, fidelity, and professional excellence of Elvin Kibet. In view of these qualities and her demonstrated leadership abilities and dedicated service to the United States Army, she is therefore promoted from Specialist to Sergeant effective April 15, 2021."

Shadrack leaned in, pinning his wife with new stripes on her hat and chest.

"Congrats, babe," he whispered.

Sergeant Elvin Kibet gave him a smile and a wink. In the distance, she noticed the freshly painted white lane lines on the track. Underneath her uniform, running clothes clung to her body, aching to see the light.

Back at Hayward Field in Eugene, Oregon, the track that Elvin found herself on in 2021 was different than the one Shadrack had competed on in 2016. The stadium had undergone a remodel, making it one of the fanciest facilities she'd ever competed at. Just like Shadrack's race in 2016, her 10,000-meter run was a scorcher. The start time had been moved earlier in the day to increase the likelihood that the competitors wouldn't suffer heat stroke. She knew she was a long shot to make the team, but it was going to be a joy to compete, nonetheless. Shadrack had stayed home to nurse his injury and was watching the coverage on television.

Forty-one women started the race. The huge field required the women start in two packs and only merge after two turns around the track. Elvin's teammate Ednah moved to the front, with Elvin remaining in the back. On television, former pro runner Kara Goucher provided commentary as Shadrack edged closer to the big screen hanging above their fireplace.

"In the heat you need to protect your body early on. The more relaxed you can be, the less you press, the better you will be overall in the race," she added.

Elvin worked hard through the first half of the race. She moved up to the middle of the pack as the temperature on the track rose above ninety degrees. Her racing spikes gripped the red rubber as she tried to keep Ednah in her sights. It had been a fierce few months of training. Elvin had arrived at the track already feeling worn. Her natural inclination would normally be to press harder. But as she passed the four-mile mark with only two miles remaining, Elvin knew the race wasn't about her finishing time, nor the chance to make the Olympic Team. She'd come so far to even be here at all. It was a life she hadn't even considered a dozen years ago.

Thirteen hundred miles away, Shadrack saw his wife begin to fade, eventually stopping a lap short. She'd miscounted and when she realized her error she began to run again. It happened from time to time in races this long, and certainly in this heat. He stood up and cheered for his wife proudly as she continued.

One more lap.

Elvin wasn't alone in suffering from the heat. A handful of women had dropped out and thus she'd been able to remain in the middle of the pack, even with her miscalculation. She pictured Shadrack at home in Colorado Springs, watching her race as she'd watched so many of his. He was probably on his feet screaming at the television and telling her to take it one step at a time. He might even be crying. With tears of joy or stress, she wasn't sure.

Hot as hell, it didn't matter. She wouldn't make the Olympic team, but it didn't matter.

She and Shaddy both held records at their American universities that had stood the test of time. Her 5,000-meter run for Arizona and his 10,000-meter run for Oklahoma State were nearly ten years old and still intact.

And now she was running the Olympic Trials for the United States and wearing a United States Army jersey.

A dream come true.

Surely somewhere in the heavens, Gogo was smiling.

Chapter Twenty

Tokyo

2021

With the Training Center shut down in 2020, Sammy had moved her four-times-daily workouts to the garage of the house she and Karl had just moved into. Weightlifting, target practice, and long runs were all part of her routine. She and Karl were married now. She'd changed her name to Sammy Schultz and he had begun keeping watch over her physical well-being. With nowhere to go besides home and the grocery store, he knew she was spending too much time in her head and on her feet.

"How many times did you work out today, Sammy?" Karl asked as they finished dinner one night.

"Just twice," she lied.

It had been three if she counted the fencing session in the garage. The cement floor wasn't doing her feet any favors. She could feel the plantar fasciitis she'd battled for a long time beginning to flare again.

"I really think you can back off a bit. You do realize we're in a pandemic and you're not going to Tokyo just yet, right? This doesn't have to be all or nothing right now. You can find a balance, can't you?"

"I think so, but what if they reschedule the World Championships? I must be ready for that."

"You've been at this for years. Your body has muscle memory. Your weight is too low, and your coaches know it. They said so."

"Not true, Karl. All they said is that they want me to get stronger."

"Sam, wake up. That's code for 'you need to gain weight' but they just don't want to say it. Just like when you hear 'you're so fit' it means you're thin and they want you to keep it that way. That's just adding fuel to the fire and keeping you more active than you need to be. The whole thing is so fucking messed up."

Sammy was getting frustrated, picking up their plates and walking into the kitchen.

"I'm doing the best that I can. I saw that nutritionist they referred me to and all she did was hand me meal plans for foods I can't and don't like to eat. This is stressful, Karl. You get to go out and do your regular work, but I'm trapped here trying to stay in shape. People complain when I'm too thin and people complain when I'm fat. I can't freaking win, can I?"

"I get it. I know you're at the end of your rope, here. You've worked so hard for this and it's super isolating right now. I just think you're overcompensating."

He was fighting an uphill battle. His wife limped out of the kitchen and upstairs to bed, her foot aching. The MRI she'd scheduled with the staff at the Training Center couldn't come soon enough, and he secretly hoped it would show something to slow her down.

His wish was granted. The MRI showed a stress fracture in her foot, and Sammy went into a boot to heal it seven months before the rescheduled Olympic Games.

The studies of women in sports have been vastly limited relative to those conducted on men, though the studies that *have* been done have yielded important data. Within the past decade, medical clinicians have noticed an uptick in something that was eventually labeled as REDs. The condition stands for Relative Energy Deficiency in Sport. Three main symptoms are the key to its diagnosis. Disordered eating, increased risk for stress fractures/bone loss, and the absence of menstruation. When put together, REDs present a serious risk to the long-term health of female athletes. The monthly delivery of estrogen through menstruation in the female body helps build bone density in adolescence which is critical for the rest of life. If menstruation is missing, it means hormones are not acting properly to fuel the body and develop strong bones. By the time girls finish adolescence, about 90 percent of the bone mass they will have as adults has been collected. Once girls leave those precious years of growth, the opportunity to regain that bone density is lost.

REDs can be hard to identify even for those who might normally recognize symptoms. Likely this is because some of the early, short-term symptoms include faster times and better performances among the endurance athletes suffering. Losing menstruation during this process can be seen as a normal product of high-intensity training, almost a welcome exchange for enhanced performance. But in reality, it's the body's way of announcing a lack of energy stores to keep up with the level of activity it's undergoing. Eventually, REDs depletes performance, perversely inspiring the athlete to train harder without giving their bodies the rest they need to become stronger.

Conditions faced by girls and young women in sports throughout their teen years can make or break how they participate in sports for the rest of their lives. If they're lucky enough to have coaches who understand the complexities of female body development and hormones, girls can thrive. If they have coaches who lean into the belief that lighter means faster and better, the long-term damage can be a combination of body dysmorphia, disordered eating, and bone damage. To be surrounded by coaches and parents who understand that girls and young women cannot be trained the same way as boys and young men is key. The trajectories of success for female athletes will not be the consistent, upward path that it will be for their male counterparts. However, with time and attention given to developmental needs, girls and young women can thrive and become healthy athletes for life.

Inside the main dining hall in the Tokyo Olympic Village, the choices of cuisine overwhelmed. Sammy stood just inside the main doors and off to the side, trying to decide which way to turn. Her foot had healed properly. Competition would start in a few days, albeit an Olympic Games unlike any other. The athletes had gone through rigorous COVID testing prior to arrival, on top of all their other health screenings. Dispensers with hand sanitizer were placed every twenty feet and everyone wore the highest quality masks.

She could feel her heart racing. Thirty minutes had passed since she'd started walking around trying to decide what to eat and still her plate held nothing. Standing at the front door, she considered her options. The salad bar. Or the pasta bar, but she'd need to do another workout if she took in too many carbs. Frozen, she watched streams of athletes with full plates enjoying themselves and their moments of Olympic glory.

Sammy sensed a tap on her shoulder and turned to see one of the Team USA sports psychologists. After exchanging a few words, she gestured for Sammy to join her, then stopped, noticing that Sammy had no intention of going any further than the front door.

"There's so much food here. I'm worried. I'm not training as much, and all this food concerns me. I'm feeling anxious," Sammy said.

"Is it the number of people here? Is it nerves about the competition? What's causing you the most anxiety?" the sports psychologist asked.

"I'm telling you . . . it's all this food. I'm training less and tapering. I'm afraid I'm going to get fat here."

The psychologist gave her a puzzled look, then dismissed her concerns, saying, "You're not going to get fat in a few days. Let's just have you get through these next few days, and I'll see about getting you on an anti-anxiety medication when we get back."

An Olympic ring display reflected off the stainless steel food carts. Each tier of food encircled made Sammy dizzy.

Sammy sat in sweatpants and a t-shirt in her home office. Out the office window, a light dusting of snow coated the grass. It was March 2022 and eight months after the Tokyo Olympics. She and Karl were still trying to negotiate a path forward. Karl had believed that Tokyo was the end of the road for Sammy's career in modern pentathlon, but the reality had proved otherwise. WCAP leadership had offered her another three-year rotation in the unit to try and compete at the Paris 2024 Games. The offer and Sammy's pause to consider it had sent Karl over the edge.

He'd pleaded with his wife to turn the offer down. He couldn't watch what the training was doing to her, he said. If it were still enjoyable, he'd be on board, but she was physically spent, and the injuries kept piling up. Plus, though they'd talked about starting a family, she hadn't had her period in years. Karl gambled and offered to support her 2024 Olympic bid on the condition that she got a doctor's approval that she wasn't doing long-term damage to her body and its ability to carry a baby. Behind the scenes he'd buried himself in research about disordered eating. He knew there wasn't a doctor on the planet who'd greenlight his wife trying to get pregnant. And he was correct. A single visit to a fertility specialist resulted in Sammy being referred to her Army primary care doctor to start with a basic assessment of her health.

Sammy folded her legs underneath herself at the desk chair, trying to take up as little space as possible while waiting for her primary care doctor to join the Zoom.

"Hey there, Olympian!" the doctor said as he popped on the screen. "I haven't talked to you since Tokyo, but it sounds like you had a good showing!"

"I did well, all things considered. My fencing sucked and my horse almost bucked me off in the equestrian portion, but I crushed the swim and run, so that made up for it."

"Indeed, indeed. And I understand you're considering another run for Paris 2024? I mean, that's part of what I understand from the notes I've read from your fertility doc."

"That was on the table, but I'm not getting a good feeling about it, and Karl certainly isn't on board," Sammy said.

Her hands cupped a mug of tea, and she could feel her leg falling asleep underneath her.

"Okay, so let's talk. You know that as your Army primary care doctor, I've been able to get an overview of the care you've been receiving, so let's just review some of that."

The doctor put on reading glasses and looked down at a notepad.

"So, it's my understanding that your team includes a nutritionist, a massage therapist, a sports psychologist, your coaches, and the folks in sports medicine, is that right?"

"That sounds about right," Sammy replied.

"And have any of them expressed concerns about your health, your weight, anything like that?"

"Not directly, no. Sometimes the massage therapist says I'm too lean to work hard on. The sports psychologist suggested anxiety medicine. My coaches tell me sometimes they want me to get stronger. Stuff like that."

"I see," the doctor said. He looked at his notes and then up at Sammy.

"I will say that it can be hard sometimes to pull together any semblance of coordinated care for our soldiers. That seems to be the case here. I'm concerned about your relationship with exercise, but more than that, I think it's clear you have some work to do if you want to reach a place of better health. From what I've gathered from your file and talking to a few other people you've seen, I don't think I'm the only one to have noticed."

"I don't get it. What do you mean, exactly?" asked Sammy.

"Well, it sounds like there's been a degree of concern for some time, but that your case has fallen through the cracks. You've had a series of stress fractures and no menstrual cycle in seven years. I spoke with the fertility doc about a bunch of things, and he confirmed you're not ovulating. I know you told him that you didn't believe you have a negative relationship with food, but I've also spoken to your strength coach who indicated he believes there's reason to be concerned."

"But what are you saying? I get that maybe Paris isn't a good idea, but what about getting pregnant? Isn't that what we're talking about?"

The doctor took off his reading glasses, staring deeper into the screen.

"No. Sergeant Schultz. Listen. That's not what this is about. You're still training heavily and not ovulating. Even if you were to get pregnant, your chance of miscarriage is close to 100% right now. The issue we're talking about right now is more basic."

He paused, knowing full well that Sammy had left her body and wouldn't be able to process the next few words.

In her office, Sammy had the sensation of things around her unraveling. If the Zoom dropped now, she wouldn't have to listen to what was coming next. She could go back to her workouts and figure things out on her own.

"Sam, you're suffering from an eating disorder. Period. You need help. I have no clue how you made it through the mental health screening you needed to get to Tokyo. That's a failure on the part of Team USA. But even more than that, I'm sorry the Army has missed it until now. We've failed you. Apparently, we've failed you for years, but we've got you now."

The doctor opened his desk drawer and pulled out several official-looking yellow forms.

"It's time to get you in to see someone in mental health. You need a team of people to tackle this before we see more lifelong damage to your body. Let's get you scheduled and taken care of, Soldier."

Sammy noticed herself go cold. She bit the inside of her lip to avoid crying. Underneath her, the other leg had fallen asleep.

From miles away, the doctor looked at her, eyes locked on her expression and posture.

"Sam, I know this is a lot to process. Take your time. I'm going to stay here until you're ready to say something."

She felt exposed and could feel her whole body clenching.

And then, after a moment, releasing.

She was seen.

Eight months prior Shadrack and Elvin had watched the Tokyo Olympics from home. Paul won a second Olympic medal, a bronze. Sammy Schultz finally completed her dream of participating in the Olympic Games, and though Elvin didn't know much about her sport, she followed Sammy's competition and knew that she'd busted her ass to be there.

So it was a surprise when Elvin got the news from a mutual friend after the Games.

"Sammy wanted me to reach out to you, Elvin. This is going to be hard to hear, but she's been so appreciative of having you to lean on all these years. As a friend, a soldier, an athlete, a woman," the friend said over a call.

"This sounds bad. Just give it to me straight, please," Elvin responded.

Sammy's career as a pentathlete was over. Her body had crumbled little by little, and the stress of the Tokyo Olympics had been the breaking point. A series of stress fractures, a long-absent menstrual cycle, and years of disordered eating needed to be dealt with. She was in the process of being medically discharged from the Army and would be entering a treatment center shortly.

Silence spanned the distance between Elvin and the news.

"Elvin? Say something. She's strong. You know her. She'll get the help she needs; she'll make it through, and she's got a ton of life and adventure ahead of her. Maybe not in sport and probably not in the military, but in life."

Elvin pictured herself on the floor of the bedroom she shared with Momo in Tucson. Their late-night chat and the years Momo had struggled with food, exercise, and body image. There was probably no single reason that led Sammy to this point. It wasn't black and white. Life rarely was. It wasn't just the military or just the intense training or only the pressure to look a certain way but rather a combination of many things, most likely.

"I'd like to reach out to her. I have things to share. Do you think she'd be okay with that?" Elvin asked.

"Of course. She'd love to hear from you. If anyone understands some of the things she must be feeling, it's you."

The text was a start. They'd talk in person soon, but for now, a text was enough to let Sammy know that Elvin would be on her team forever.

Hello Sammy,

I hope you're well. It's been a minute and I just wanted to check on you and see how things are going. I've heard you've been going through a tough time and I'm so very sorry. I applaud you for staying strong and fighting. Speaking about it and seeking professional help is the first step to healing. I imagine it wasn't easy. So I guess I'm reaching out to show my support and even though I don't understand a whole lot about eating disorders, I'm here for you. I can listen or just sit with you and be there for you. I've struggled too, with body image recently and so did my college teammates. I'm not trying to compare, but I do understand how much of a struggle it can be and find it all so hard because there's so much we don't know about this topic.

Big hugs, Elvin

Chapter Twenty-One

Rising

2021–2023

"I'm sure he's going to be cool with it, Elvin," Shadrack said. "He's Scott. He's mellow about these things."

"Mellow? How would you know? Because Shaddy, this has literally never happened. I was the only woman on the team for the longest time and now I'm pregnant. I'm breaking the mold here. What the hell is going to happen when everyone finds out?" Elvin added, smiling.

It was November 2021, and the couple was at home brainstorming how to break the news to Scott. Elvin's pregnancy was both completely normal in some ways and yet a total outlier for the WCAP distance running team. She'd managed years of running identical but slightly shorter or slower workouts than the men. A pregnancy wasn't something that could be compared with any experience the men on her team had gone through. There was no training plan for this. Further, the Army's pregnancy and postpartum policies were designed for soldiers whose job had nothing to do with running competitively and logging eighty miles on the roads each week. WCAP had sometimes laid its own path by necessity to meet its athletes where they were.

This time was destined to be the same, wasn't it?

"My job is to run. We both know I'll keep running as long as I can. Even when it gets difficult. But I'm already feeling like a cow and I'm only in my second trimester."

"Elvin, listen to yourself. You're pregnant. Not sick. Not injured. And not overweight. You're perfect and healthy and that sort of crap would never in a million years have crossed your mind if we were in Kenya right now. You'd be elated at the weight you've gained."

Elvin took in his words. He'd crushed it, as usual. And he was right. If she were pregnant in Kenya, she'd be eating whatever she wanted with all sorts of people telling her to slow down and rest. Her weight would be lauded the higher it went. They'd thought about waiting until Elvin was done with competitive running to start a family, but she hoped to be racing for years more. Pregnancy and childbirth were a normal part of development for women that shouldn't have to wait until her career in running was over. The crowd of professional distance runners choosing to have babies in the middle of their careers was growing, and she intended to be among them. In fact, she thought, she owed it to future generations of women to model how it could be done just as she'd watched female athletes ahead of her do.

Olympian Alysia Montano had been one of the first to bring to light the disparity in professional sports between men and women. While the industry provided for men to have full careers, Montano illuminated the fact that women were often pushed out at their prime by deciding to have a baby. When she ran eight months pregnant in 2014, it was a watershed moment. Her sponsor, Nike, had responded to the announcement of her pregnancy by offering to pause her contract and stop paying her. She left Nike and went to Asics, who initially seemed more supportive, but then threatened to stop paying her as she was on her postpartum journey. Montano fought back, both by advocating for better standards for female professional athletes, and on the track, where she won a national championship six-months postpartum while still nursing.

The story was much the same for sprinter Allyson Felix and distance runner Kara Goucher, also both Nike athletes at the time of their struggles. Nike suspended Goucher's pay both during her pregnancy and as she came back from childbirth, all while praising her and claiming to be a brand that celebrated motherhood. Both women also faced performance-based reductions when they returned to competitive running, as well as confidentiality clauses in their contracts which prohibited them from discussing those contracts even after the life of the document had expired. It was a zone of silence.

Over the next ten years, sponsors and shoe companies began to shift. Policies were changed to guarantee pay for athletes before and after childbirth. Health insurance, often provided through athletic federations, could no longer be stopped due to pregnancy or the inability to compete at a high level because of a recent birth. Finally, the message was becoming clear that pregnancy shouldn't be treated as an injury but rather as a stage in an athlete's career to be embraced so it could lengthen the athlete's time in sport.

Elvin knew there was much work ahead. Despite some progress, most endorsement contracts still had clauses which allowed for reduction in pay for any reason if athletes didn't meet specific performance thresholds. No exceptions were made for pregnancy. In 2021, marathoner Aliphine Tuliamuk had to fight strict COVID travel restrictions which nearly prevented her from bringing her breastfeeding daughter with her when she was competing at the Tokyo Olympics. The limitations placed on women at every stage of pregnancy and postpartum journeys were fewer, but there were still improvements to be made.

Meanwhile, back in Colorado Springs, Scott had been supportive as she'd hoped, and they developed a framework for Elvin's postpartum return to running. The issues that other athletes had with sponsors started to feel less of an issue for her. The Army was in many ways one of the most progressive institutions she'd seen. It may not have the glitter that Nike did, but perhaps that was in her favor. She crossed fingers for less glitter and more actual support in the months and years ahead. As the days grew closer to her delivery, Elvin let go of her concerns to focus on the upcoming birth. Long walks slowly replaced runs.

She'd be ready when the time came.

"Shaddy, help! I'm not ready!"

Elvin called to her husband in the middle of the night in mid-April of 2021. Her water had broken, sending a rush of liquid down her legs that seemed unstoppable. Shadrack hadn't woken at first, but when he did, the sounds of his wife panicking were like giant buckets of ice water being poured on his head. The couple scrambled, scattering around the house looking for phone chargers and their overnight bags. In theory, they knew they had time to spare until the actual birth. In practice, it felt like the bell lap in one of their 10,000-meter races.

The drive to Fort Carson went smoothly. She'd be delivering on base at Evans Army Community Hospital. They settled into their room, and Elvin fell asleep briefly.

"Babe. Babe, are you awake?" Shadrack whispered.

He was nudging her gently. She kept her eyes firmly shut, hoping he might realize that waking his wife right now wasn't one of his better ideas.

"Elvin. It's Monday morning. Patriot's Day. It's on. We should watch."

The instant he said it, she opened her eyes, scanning the room to see where the television was. Shadrack smiled, grabbing the remote and flipping to the coverage which was just starting. On the screen were swaths of blue and yellow, along with the white unicorn that symbolized the running of the Boston Marathon.

"I can't believe I'm in labor on Marathon Monday," Elvin mumbled.

"Epic, just epic," Shadrack answered. "Feeling okay? This will get us through the next two hours, right?"

"I'm doing okay. No pain yet, so let's do this thing," Elvin responded. "We have friends in the race. We've gotta watch. The baby can wait until the race is done."

By noon the marathon was wrapping up. It had indeed been a great way to kill a couple hours, but she could feel her body cramping as the winners were interviewed. Hours of contractions began, and an epidural by the evening. The baby was descending properly, and the doctors vowed that everything looked good. The couple knew that the epidural helped with pain but slowed the labor. It would be a full night of counting, breathing, contractions, and Jell-O.

The sun rose on the morning of April 19, 2022. A new doctor, a team of eight to ten nurses, and a medical student entered the room.

"Elvin, it's go time. You're about to push that baby out," the doctor said.

Shadrack stood, his eyes focused on the doctor's expression, which was confident and eased his alarm at the rate this was about to happen.

"What? I'm next? Already?! I'm not ready," Elvin exclaimed.

She lifted herself onto her elbows, looking over at her husband.

"You can do this," he said, seriously.

"You're ready and we're all here for you," the doctor assured her.

He took one more check of her heart rate as the team got into place circling Elvin's bed. They counted down from ten as she pushed, cheering between repetitions.

"You're doing great, Elvin!"

"That was an amazing push, Elvin!"

"You're crushing this, Elvin!"

The entire thing seemed like a race. Her own personal cheerleading squad. She paused, thinking of her own mother and her own birth. How different it must've been. How silent and lonely. How scary.

After seven pushes and nearly at the finish line, the room got quiet. In contrast to the cheers, the silence sent panic through Elvin's body as she searched the face of the doctor for answers. Instructed to push one more time, the baby came out. It was a boy, and he wasn't crying. His limp body was placed on Elvin's chest only for a moment before he was taken away by the doctor and nurses to a different part of the room.

"What's going on?! Tell me! Oh my God tell me what's happening!" Elvin screamed.

She pushed again, releasing the placenta from her body as the doctor instructed.

Still no crying. The team was hovered around the baby in the corner, taking directions from the doctor who was doing a dance between Elvin and the baby.

"Dad, let's go," one of the nurses said, gesturing to Shadrack.

And with that, the room emptied except for the doctor, who returned to sew Elvin and listen to her wails. He worked in a matter of moments and without words, then left her alone to get back to the baby in another room.

"Tell me! God help my baby! Please tell me what's happening. Someone tell me! Shadrack!"

Down the hall, she wondered if the team with her baby could hear her begging and crying at the top of her lungs.

"I need to see my baby! Somebody take me to my baby!"

Elvin turned onto her side looking at the door, willing it to open with Shadrack holding their son. She was sobbing as a nurse checked her vitals and stroked her back.

"Oh God please tell me he's okay! I need him to be okay. I'll do anything if my baby is okay!"

Only a few minutes had passed but it seemed like fifteen years. A medical student entered the room, assuring her that everything was stable. The baby was going to be fine and was hooked up to oxygen.

"Show me! I want to see him for myself. I want to hear him. Now, now, now!"

Elvin was unhinged, desperate to leave the room, but held back by the nurse.

The medical student left, returning less than a minute later holding her phone. It was a photo of the baby, connected to oxygen. Elvin held the phone in her hand, shaking as she looked at the image.

"I want to go see him," she said.

"They're still doing some tests, but I'm sure you can see him soon," the medical student replied.

Another few minutes passed and Shadrack returned with a wheelchair. Her legs were still numb from the epidural, so he helped load her down and wheeled her several doors away. The baby was hooked up to wires and oxygen and held by a nurse behind glass but looked alive and better than he had.

"He's okay, Elvin," said Shadrack, resting his hand on her shoulder.

Elvin was sobbing uncontrollably, her entire body still shaking. She couldn't take her eyes off the baby.

"He's going to be okay," Shadrack repeated.

"God, I'm on my knees. Thank you, God, for saving him for me," Elvin cried.

Her body heaved as Shadrack bent over and put his arm around her.

"I thought we lost him, Shadrack. I thought we lost him."

She glanced at her husband and saw that he was crying, too. For the first time, she realized he must've been just as terrified as her.

They sat for a long time, looking at their son. Hours later, he was in the room with her, breastfeeding. His entry into the world had been harrowing, but he looked like a survivor.

Two days later, Mylo Kiptoo Tirop went home.

"So, this blood draw will be quick, but there will be screaming, so which one of you can handle a little bit of that?" the nurse asked.

Five days had passed, and Shadrack, Elvin, and Mylo were back at the hospital for a blood draw.

"I'm the new dad in town. I've totally got this," Shadrack replied, taking the bundle in his arms.

Mylo peeked out from the baby blanket as the nurses prodded him trying to find a vein. He squirmed and began to whimper. One minute turned into two as the nurses struggled to find a proper injection point. From the corner of her eye, Elvin sensed movement. She turned her head upward and saw Shadrack swaying back and forth. He had lines of sweat running down both sides of his face.

"Oh, good God, Shaddy, give him to us," Elvin said.

She took Mylo and gave him to a nurse, then steadied her husband who'd slumped over in the chair.

One of the nurses jumped up and stuck her head out the door, yelling, "Dad down! Dad's down in here! A little help, please!"

Nurses rushed in, bringing candy, water, and a cool rag for Shadrack's forehead.

Having served in supporting roles for both Kipchoge and his five-day old son, it was apparent now which one was the greater star in Shadrack's life.

The American flag hung adjacent to the long table at the Pentagon. Speaking behind microphones were several members of the Army, each in their dress uniforms with stripes indicating rank. The soldiers were all women, and fielding questions on the Army's latest policy. The Army Parenthood, Pregnancy and Postpartum Directive had been developed following a grassroots effort by a Facebook group called Army Mom Life. Its stated goal was to support the unique challenges faced by soldiers navigating pregnancy and parenthood.

It was, according to one of the soldiers who helped develop the policy, a move that would help soldiers continue to feel supported and gain promotions while managing the difficulties of new parenting.

"The Army spends a lot of money on soldiers to train them and keep them in the force, so I think it's going to be extremely impactful with retention. I also think it's going to be huge for recruitment as well because our civilians are going to see us be able to make the force more modern," the soldier who championed the policy stated.

Included in the policy were provisions allowing for body composition and physical fitness testing exemptions for pregnant and postpartum soldiers for 365, rather than 180 days, the provision of lactation breaks and designated lactation areas for soldiers regardless of time after the child's birth, and family readiness planning. It also allowed for the designation of "No-Hat, No Salute" areas in which soldiers wouldn't be required to salute to superiors when holding a child in their arms.

The Secretary of the Army, after speaking a few words, picked up a pen and signed the directive in front of the gathered audience. Christine Wormuth was the first woman to serve in the role.

As with all new policies, this one would take time to distribute and implement. The Army was a massive machine with a million moving parts. In the meantime, Army parents would continue as they always had in managing their families, their careers, and in the case of Elvin, her life as a professional athlete.

Secretary Wormuth grinned as the crowd clapped at a step forward for the Army. An assistant picked up the document from the signing table, tucking it into a briefcase. It would be stamped hours later with the date of signing.

It matched the date on Mylo's birth certificate: April 19, 2022.

They were now a family of three, upending the routine of the past seven years. Shadrack had decided to make the leap away from the track and focus on the roads. His end game was the marathon, a distance he hoped to explore for many years. If things came together as he planned, the 2024 U.S. Olympic Marathon Trials were calling his name. Behind him was the support of a new agent and a new sponsor, Puma. The years with Nike, like his years with the Army, had been positive and served a purpose. He hoped his relationship with both the marathon and with Puma would be long-lasting. Soon he'd travel to Iten for a training block in Kenya. He hoped it would be one of many for their family. With so many hands in Kenya to help care for Mylo, it would be good for all of them to spend short chunks of time in Kenya over the coming years.

For Elvin, the postpartum journey brought a wealth of challenges. She'd also begun to think about the 2024 U.S. Olympic Marathon Trials and running there with Shadrack would be a wonderful goal. Mylo was thriving, but her delivery had required stitches that needed to be re-sewn several months after his birth. The procedure stretched her recovery time, adding to her anxiety about getting back into race shape. Not only was she juggling parenting and the need to attend to basic military duties, but she was also still a professional athlete with time standards to hit to stay in the WCAP unit.

She began to watch what she ate more than before.

She struggled with the decision on whether to breastfeed or bottle feed. Breastfeeding would require her to consume more, but she worried that would lengthen the period it would take to lose the pregnancy pounds.

Concerns about how her new body looked in her duty uniform sent her into a spiral.

Other pro distance runners who had babies seemed to be bouncing back in no time at all. Social media images of them on long runs pushing fast paces added to her stress.

Shadrack saw her scrolling one night. He held a sleeping Mylo while she lay next to him on the couch pumping breast milk. The freezer in their living room was half full of tiny bags of milk already.

"I'm a little concerned about your scrolling. Your brow always furrows, and you make annoyed sighs when you're on Instagram. Maybe take a break from that. Just talk to me," he said.

"It's just so frustrating," Elvin said, laying the phone down. "How are all these other runners able to get back in shape so quickly? They are practically going to the track straight from giving birth. It's messing with my head. What if WCAP kicks me out of the program because I'm not meeting benchmarks?"

"No. There's no way. You're too valuable. Your value goes way beyond your running, too, by the way. They know that."

"I agree, but we both know it's about the numbers. I must be able to get back to the times I was running a couple years ago. I don't know how to do that. I'm being crazy strict with my food intake and nothing's happening."

"Elvin, you had a hard birth. Your body is not the body of anyone else. It'll take time to get back to where you want to be, and even then, it might not feel the same. You're perfect just the way you are. As for the food nonsense, it feels like you've been in America too long. This country has changed how you look at food. Don't limit yourself like that. It freaks me out," Shadrack said.

Mylo stirred and Elvin stuck out a teething toy for him to grab.

"I told you about Sammy, didn't I?" Elvin asked Shadrack. "She and I have had a couple chats. She knows I've had a hard time postpartum with food and body image. We both agree that we wish we'd had more support and resources to deal with our body stuff."

"You told me. I'm glad we're going to see her next week. The two of you need a few moments together," Shadrack said.

"I've told her a few times about how proud I am of her. I really am, Shaddy. There's so much to navigate for us. Women. In the military. Trying to remain at the top of our athletic potential. It's a lot. She made a choice to take care of herself. That's easier said than done in our positions."

"Babe, I know, and I'm sure she feels the same pride for you."

"She does. She told me she doesn't know what it's like to come back to running post-pregnancy but can imagine it's been a challenge. I told her I thought it would be a breeze and that it hasn't been."

"There are better days ahead. Change takes time. Things will improve for women in your shoes, Elvin. For now, all you can do is pave the way as best you can. Use your voice."

Elvin looked at Shadrack, holding their son who was a mass of thigh rolls and big cheeks. A thick pile of tight black curls at the top of his head had been trimmed in the back and along the sides. He drooled, looking up at Shadrack and then at Elvin.

What if they hadn't seen each other on that field in Terre Haute, Elvin wondered? Where would they be? There was nobody else who could soothe her the way Shadrack could. Nobody who knew the color of Gogo's eyes nor the way the light flickered across the hillside from Kapchorwa in the noon sun. And she was certain that nobody on earth could understand him the way she did. Nobody who could put up with his crazy altitude tents or his obsession with staying in traditional mud huts when they were in Kenya. Nobody who could flow so effortlessly with her between the four languages they spoke. Kalenjin, English, military, and running.

"I know you're right. Thanks for having my back, Shaddy. I'll take him now. And screw it. Maybe some more dinner. I'm so damn hungry."

Elvin reached over, taking Mylo in her arms, and offering her breast.

In June 2023, Sammy and Karl stood next to the track at Mesa Ridge High School. Shielding their eyes from the sun, they looked up and saw Shadrack, Elvin, and Mylo cresting the hill that edged the track.

"You made it," Sammy shouted up to Elvin.

Mylo was in his mother's arms and squirmy. Sammy had met him once before, but it was Karl's first time.

"Isn't he to die for?" she asked Karl.

"He's pretty damn cute," responded Karl.

Setting up just beyond the start line was a sports photographer. He was there to get action photos of all three athletes, a task made easier because they'd only be pretending to be working out hard, and not actually sweating. Sammy had been cleared by her therapist to spend just a few minutes in front of the camera. Her days in the military were almost done, and she'd no longer be required to pose or stretch or submit her body in any way other than on her own terms.

Elvin reached Sammy and handed Mylo to Shadrack so she could give her friend a warm hug.

"I've been thinking of you so much," Elvin said. "I'm so proud of you for asking for help. I want to be here for you if I can."

"I want to be here for you, too," Sammy responded. "We both know that we've learned over time to toughen up, but sometimes you gotta listen to your gut, right?"

"Yes, absolutely," Elvin said.

Shadrack shifted Mylo from one hip to the other, calling out to Elvin and Sammy to join him on the track. The group approached the photographer just as the sound of hissing began. At first, its origin wasn't clear, but the unmistakable sight of sprinkler heads lifting from the turf on the infield caught everyone's attention. Water sprayed in all directions and the group shrieked, taking cover, and grabbing camera equipment for safety. Mylo broke into a grin at the sight of adults running wild.

Water dripped from duffel bags and the bleachers, but their clothes had remained dry. The sprinkler system settled into a pattern, at least for the next few minutes, and the group scrambled to take photos before its trajectory moved again.

The photographer lined up Shadrack, Elvin, and Sammy side by side in Team USA jerseys.

"Okay, you guys, we've worked together before, so you know the drill. We'll take a bunch of shots today, but to start, give me your best 'badass look' and lean into each other."

The trio struck a pose, holding a serious expression for a moment, lips pursed, and arms crossed solemnly. Then, unable to take themselves seriously, all three burst into laughter. Bouncing off the cement bleachers, their joy could be heard at the far end of the track.

Outside on the front sidewalk, Mylo was taking tentative steps. At fourteen months, he'd mastered crawling and had progressed to a faster and more efficient way of getting from point A to B. Shadrack came out of the house, taking up a post in front of him to get video.

Elvin walked behind, letting him use her fingers when he wanted. Mostly, he didn't.

Mylo took a few steps, fell onto his bottom, pondered a moment, then got up again. He seemed to prefer walking outside to the hard floors inside, and a fat diaper cushioned his fall. Eventually, Elvin came around front, watching with Shadrack as Mylo continued toward both, relentlessly falling, pausing, and getting up again as they cheered like the crazy new parents they were.

The sun began to set, but Mylo continued his practicing. A breeze blew from the mountains to the west as he sat on the sidewalk contemplating his next move. Turning his head, he looked towards the mountains and the breeze. This pause seemed longer than the rest, and Elvin wondered if he was done walking for the night. She searched his face for signs of crabbiness or perhaps hunger and saw none.

Instead, he looked back at his parents . . . smiling, then rising.

Author's Note

I started running when I was seven years old. It was 1977. Title IX had been enacted five years prior and my mother had just turned thirty years old. Having watched her beloved older brother forge a path in sports and then in sports journalism for a career, she decided to pick up a pair of running shoes to be a little more sporty herself. Soon we had a new copy of the Jim Fixx book, *The Complete Book of Running*, on our coffee table.

Mom trained on the long dirt roads circling our farmhouse in rural Wisconsin. The loops she ran were flat, and the house was always within view, allowing her to leave us without a babysitter and keep watch for a random house fire or other monkey business. One time she looked back and saw my sister and me, skinny limbs flying as we jumped out the bathroom window. Eventually, Mom just took us with her on runs to keep us out of trouble.

I didn't know until much later that both my mother's long runs and her eventual career in journalism were revolutionary at the time. She became a public information officer in the athletic department at a D3 college, a groundbreaking task for a woman in the 1970s. It also allowed her to continue following in her brother's footsteps. My mother's job was to get stories, both of sport and humanity. Once, when she asked her male supervisor about her byline, he told her, "Write whatever you want to. Just don't call yourself a sportswriter."

I unknowingly avoided many of the challenges young women and girls face as they're growing in the sports they're passionate about. More interested in theatre than sports in high school, I stopped running competitively through the throes of puberty. This allowed my body to shift without the glare of performing in athletics magnifying those shifts.

Picking up running at the very end of high school once again, I remembered how much I loved it.

At the end of my senior year of high school, my mother took my sister and me to the United States Olympic Track and Field Trials in Indianapolis. We watched Florence Griffith-Joyner set a blistering world record in the one hundred meters. The electricity of being at the track was addictive. I'd seen Joan Benoit win gold in the first women's Olympic marathon at the 1984 Los Angeles Olympics a few years earlier. If these women could make a life in running, the least I could do was give it a try in college, I thought. I announced my intention to walk onto the cross-country team as a freshman at Syracuse University.

"Oh Jesus, Janie," my uncle Bill told my mother before I left. "Don't let her do it. It'll chew her up and spit her out."

At the time, my uncle was the sports editor at the *Los Angeles Times*. He was a tireless advocate for women on his sports staff, but his niece running D1 college athletics scared the daylights out of him. He knew how cutthroat it could be. We've laughed at this story since then, but in a very real sense, he was spot-on to be concerned. Upon entering the world of college sports, I joined a system full of women silently grappling with disordered eating, stress fractures, and challenges with body image. I could've easily ended up in trouble. The saving grace was a college coach who cared for the well-being of his athletes beyond just our finishing places or times.

During my sophomore year, Coach brought each of the women athletes a pair of tight, bun-hugging shorts and awkwardly said, "I think you're going to see most of your competitors wearing these now."

We could tell that even *he* was trying to figure it out.

"Coach, you must be kidding. They look like diapers," one of the women on my team responded.

"You're gonna be on the line with Vicki Huber and the Villanova women," he said, a reference to the intense level of competition we faced in our conference.

We looked at him, deadpan.

"No way, Coach. Our butts are gonna be hanging out. How is *that* going to make us faster?" I asked.

He took a moment, looking at all of us and making the sort of lightning speed calculation that college coaches must make all the time.

"Aw hell, wear whatever you want on the bottom. Whatever you're most comfortable in," he said, tossing the bun huggers into a pile on the floor.

In return for his advocacy and priority of our comfort and emotional well-being, I was gifted with a lifetime love of running.

With a serious dose of naivete about the level of machismo that existed in the professions I was entering, I made my way through college and into the working world. I was almost always in orbits that were traditionally male dominated.

A sports journalism program.

Law school.

Coaching young runners.

A deep dive into the writing of a book on high-altitude mountaineering, a community awash with male egos the size of Texas.

Given the gift of Title IX and the "Women-can-do-anything-men-can-do" attitude born in the 1970s, I thought little of the subtle limitations forever being placed on me in the worlds in which I worked. When it finally became clear to me how hard I was working to be taken seriously, I still fell short in my understanding. I didn't realize the shortcomings of Title IX, nor the ways in which women were made to feel like they'd crossed an imaginary finish line when in fact, so many women had been left behind. Women of color and women with disabilities among them. I also didn't understand the layers of race, gender, and body image that were affecting the way others were or were not entering sports.

Angst about my career and bad romances took my attention away from the issues touching sports, and in particular, running. I was too busy trying to make it in worlds that didn't seem meant for me. Too busy to notice that there were millions behind me who hadn't even entered the conversation yet. I suppose now it's easy to say that I was doing the best I could. Somehow it still stings that I wasn't more aware.

Not until my own daughter began to mature with a voice of her own has it become apparent how stilted my reality was. Her voice, loud and confident, has revealed the ways in which her gender and status as a female of color have held her back. The fight to show up as who she is and be valued wholly is the challenge ahead for her and all of us.

A few years ago, my sister and I cleaned out my mother's desk. We'd just moved her into a memory care facility, her mind now riddled with Parkinson's Disease–induced dementia. Digging through her stack of writings, I discovered an essay she'd crafted long ago. It was unpublished but had been painstakingly self-edited many times over. The margins were filled with notes, the ending changed several times. The title of the piece was, "Why I Will Never be a Sportswriter." I felt a little something tear inside me.

In another drawer my sister found a letter from an attorney dated in the mid-1980s. It was a summary of their consultation and his legal opinion as to why, despite years of struggling in a male-dominated newsroom, he did not feel she had sufficient evidence to bring forth a claim of sex discrimination in the workplace. The letter was there, forty-plus years later, mixed among the Valentine's Day cards and art projects we'd made, a touchstone of a life well-lived and well-fought. The contrast between the life my mother lived and the one my daughter is presently living hits me frequently and in funny ways like this. Progress can seem so slow and yet looking back I see the huge strides women and people of color have made to get this far. I believe it's possible to be both grateful for the progress and overwhelmed by what's left to achieve.

After the publication of my mountaineering book *Edge of the Map*, I knew I was back to sports writing for good. I'd taken a twenty-five-year hiatus since college, but I'd missed it. With one sports book under my wings, I began looking for a new story to share. Uncle Bill once again stepped up with insight, this time aware that once I set my mind to something, it was best to give advice and then get out of my way. He connected me tc an Olympic historian who suggested I investigate the Army's World Class Athlete Program.

"You should really check it out. The distance runners are based in Colorado Springs and you're a runner. It's a natural fit. And a damn good story. Can't believe it hasn't been told yet," the historian said.

A few weeks later I found myself in the bleachers at Mesa Ridge High School in Colorado Springs. It was a month before the rescheduled Tokyo Olympics in the summer of 2021.

Laughter from the parking lot alerted me to the arrival of the WCAP runners. From my perch in the bleachers, I could see a stream of them, each carrying a water bottle and joking as they entered the stadium. Nobody noticed me at first and I sensed relief, anxious to blend in. Their legs were taut, muscles defined as some of them sat to change into their racing spikes. I listened to a mix of English and Kalenjin, all of it peppered with lightness as they joked with each other.

Several of the runners stepped to the starting line, getting a few words from Coach Scott Simmons who stood holding a stopwatch. The pack took off on a 400-meter lap that took less than seventy seconds. I'd been running all my life but had never seen running look so fluid and effortless. I realized I'd stopped breathing as the pack came down the home stretch, worried that if I exhaled, I'd miss a moment of magic. As the runners paused between laps, I got my bearings and scratched some notes on a notepad.

Noticing me high up in the stands, a tall athlete with street clothes stepped up, sitting just below me. I nodded at him.

"Hey there . . . who are you?" he asked.

He had a British-Kenyan accent, and was lanky, with an easy smile.

"I thought I could blend in," I laughed.

"Yeah . . . unlikely! We're a small group. I tore my calf muscle a few months ago, so I'm just here to support the team. They're starting to taper with the Olympic Trials just a few days away. What about you . . . what's your deal?"

"I'm Johanna . . . a writer," I paused.

"Oh, a writer. Well, I can give you a play by play as they run, if you want. I can tell you all their names and events, but you won't remember any of them. I know because neither did I when I first came here. You American women all looked the same to me. You were all blond to me. But I've learned. I can see the differences now. You will too, if you're here long enough," he said.

"Well, let's start with you. You haven't told me your name," I inquired.

"Shadrack. I'm Shadrack."

I've run a bunch of marathons, but there's one that stands out. It wasn't my fastest. Hell, I think it was my slowest. But it was easily my favorite and the one I describe as transcendent. In April 2018 I stood on the starting line of the Boston Marathon in Hopkinton, Massachusetts. It wasn't my first time running in Boston, and I thought I was prepared for anything. Until I wasn't.

The day before the race, the weather forecast told us it was going to be a historic run. A torrential downpour and headwinds of up to thirty-five-miles per hour. It was weather none of the participants could have imagined, but now on the starting line, there we were, one giant mess of soaking, freezing humanity. Some of us shaking our heads. Some of us shivering. All of us bearing witness to the ridiculousness of our sport.

My pit crew consisted of my two college besties, Ann and Jenn. We'd been on the cross-country team together and they knew how to meet my needs in the final miles of this marathon. They'd been here before and were seasoned in their supporting roles.

I saw them before they saw me, as I approached our designated check-in spot at mile twenty-two. Their faces were lined with urgency and concern as they looked for me in the throngs of misery passing in front of them. Their umbrellas had been whipped inside out by the wind, and their layers of clothes had been soaked through. Screaming over the gusts, I waved my arms until they spotted me.

"Jo! Oh my God, Jo! Over here!" Jenn yelled, wildly motioning me over.

I made my way a few more meters through the puddles to the two of them, blocked from me and from the racecourse by metal barricades. I was fully sobbing now, tears and rain mixing in long streaks down my face. Ann put her arm around my shoulder, shouting above the wind,

"Oh, good lord, Jo! This is nuts! Do you want to keep going? You can stop! You don't have to do this!"

I wasn't sure why I was crying until the words left me. I raised my voice and responded in a short burst, "Not stopping! Joy!"

They paused and looked at each other as if they needed translation.

"What?! What the hell did you say? Can't hear you!" Ann shouted over the rain and wind.

"I said joy! Every step! Every step is pure joy!"

I was speaking my truth, and it shocked both them and me. I was overcome with gratitude even during the suffering. Gratitude that my body could move this way and endure. The stunned looks on their faces made me smile. I began to laugh, knowing how utterly deranged I must look and sound, standing there in hurricane-like conditions, jointly bawling and laughing with four-point-two miles left in the journey.

"You're flat-out crazy!" Jenn yelled as she began laughing with me.

I reached over the metal barrier for a tight, three-way embrace. I could feel their bodies shaking from the cold but also now from their own tears.

"Jo!" Ann yelled as I stepped back into the racecourse to begin running again.

I turned around to see them both smiling as they clung to each other and watched me run away.

"Des Linden won!" Ann screamed.

I smiled and gave a weak thumbs up, continuing forward, and shouting back, "I'll see you at the finish line!"

Acknowledgments

My gratitude for those who helped me put together this book starts with the people in my life who've embraced my love of running. My parents, Jane and Tony Garton, along with my sister Britt, the late Coach Joe Perez of Appleton East High School and Coach Richard Coleman, formerly of Syracuse University, who each allowed me to grow in the sport of running in healthy and positive ways.

Special thanks to Retired Colonel Sean Ryan who became a trusted adviser from day one. To Mark Ryan, Jim Ryan, Genie Ryan, and Quincy Ryan for sharing their stories with me. Karl Schultz, Don Sims, and Retired Colonel C. Eldon Mullis were especially valuable, along with Sergeant Major Jennifer Williams, US Army Retired, who stepped in to tirelessly respond to inquiries big and small.

I'm deeply grateful for my writing group, Carrie Esposito, Anjuli McReynolds, M. C. Platt, Carolyn Wilson-Scott, and Melissa Yoder. These five women are a constant source of inspiration, laughter, and insight. I'll wrap my arms around each of them and the stories they tell for the rest of time.

The family and friends of Elvin Kibet, Shadrack Kipchirchir, and Samantha Schultz always responded with enthusiasm to my many questions. This tribe includes Elaine and Dave Achterberg, Mandy and Chelsea Achterberg, Hanna Rustin, Hannah Moen, Hugo van den Broek, Scott Jones, Sherry Vonriesen, Augustus Maiyo, Emmanuel Bor, Hillary Bor, Paul Chelimo, Chelelgo Tallam, Salina Kosgei, Alfred Yego, Lawi Lalang, Benard Keter, Stephen Sambu, Stanley Kebenei, Lenny Korir. Elvin's and Shadrack's parents and siblings were incredibly generous with their time and tales. Rose and John Tirop, Peter and Grace Kibet, along with Elvin's siblings Hilda, Sylvia, Robert, Valentine, Ivy, Collins,

Caroline, Ian, and Daisy and Shadrack's siblings Titus, Florence, Irene, Erick, Nicholas, Sheilah, Damaris, and Dennis . . . thank you for sharing your loved ones with the world.

As I worked on the book, I was supported by a group of sports journalists, sports media members, agents, attorneys, sports scientists, and coaches who are the finest at what they each do, including Bill Dwyre, Rich Perelman, Chris Chavez, Sarah Lorge Butler, Lance Rosen, Hawi Keflezighi, James Li, Dave Smith, Scott Simmons, Nicholas Garton, Sarah Gearhart, Jonathan Gault, Rodger Kram, Kathrine Switzer, Carla Benton, Erin Dawson, Stacy Creamer, Matt Fitzgerald, M. J. Grogan, Evan Hayes, Matt Hart, Melissa Ludtke, Jo Lannin, Michael Hunnisett, Brian Finman, Niul Manske, Amanda Luedeke, Renee Landegger, Iain Hunter, and George Hirsch.

My cheerleaders during this process included Alison Levine, Vanessa O'Brien, and Lisa Thompson who helped me navigate both adventuring and authoring. My agent Linda Konner provided wisdom and patience in the early stages. Christen Karniski at Rowman & Littlefield saw the beauty in this story and wanted to bring it to the page. My publicist Samantha Lien has been with me for nearly a decade and brings so much light and joy to the world in important ways and to the daunting process of marketing my work. I'm so lucky to have found you, Sami.

The number of books by and about female athletes and athletes of color multiplied at the conclusion of my writing and provided me with valuable knowledge. In particular, *Running While Black* by Alison Mariella Desir, *Good for a Girl* by Lauren Fleshman, and *Up to Speed* by Christine Yu. The alliances we make when adding more stories to our genre will be valuable for those writers coming behind us, and I'm humbled to add my voice to this mix.

This manuscript was put together in three different countries over many years, and an intense four months at the end. Offering the quiet and views I needed to create the pages of this book, I'm indebted to the Kerio View Lodge in Iten, Kenya, and Fig Tree Camp in the Maasai Mara. A special shout out to the hippos who stood watch over me as I finished the book's Kenya chapters. Our neighbors Eduardo and Marilu-isa in Playa Grande, Costa Rica, for their thoughtful Gatorade runs. And to Deirdre Garton, for letting me crash and enjoy her lake room for the final days of revisions.

Finally, to Elvin, Shaddy, and Sammy for opening their homes and their hearts to me, and for answering every single question I had over the course of several years. To Elvin for feeding me endless piles of chapati and chai, to Sammy for leading me through yoga classes, and to Shaddy for driving me all over rural Kenya and caring for me so well when my weak American tummy turned upside down. You are the definitions of grit, compassion, and grace and I'm lucky to call all three of you friends forever.

And most of all, to my family. My husband Ernie, son Will, and daughter Eden. Thank you for your understanding as I checked out to focus on these words. You champion me in ways more valuable than finishing times or Olympic gold medals and I love you all deeply.

Selected Bibliography

Chapter Two

"Africa: 101 Last Tribes - Kalenjin People." AFRICA | 101 Last Tribes, n.d. https://www.101lasttribes.com/tribes/kalenjin.html.

"EarthWord: Graben." EarthWord: Graben | U.S. Geological Survey, October 12, 2015. https://www.usgs.gov/news/earthword-graben.

"Encyclopedia of World Cultures." Encyclopedia.com, July 6, 2023. https://www.encyclopedia.com/humanities/encyclopedias-almanacs-transcripts-and-maps/nandi-and-other-kalenjin-peoples.

Finn, Adharanand. *The Rise of the UltraRunners: A Journey to the Edge of Human Endurance*. New York: Pegasus Books, 2021.

A History of the Kalenjin People. HomeTeam History, 2020. https://www.youtube.com/watch?v=Z1RfLcs6HGA.

"Kalenjin Age Sets: Latest Developments." Kenyalogue, February 8, 2023. https://kenyalogue.com/kalenjin-age-sets-latest-developments/.

"Worldmark Encyclopedia of Cultures and Daily Life." Encyclopedia.com, n.d. https://www.encyclopedia.com/humanities/encyclopedias-almanacs-transcripts-and-maps/kalenjin.

Chapter Three

"Birth and Naming Traditions in Kenya." *Spirit in Action*, Oct. 29, 2020, www.spiritinaction.org/post/birth-and-naming-traditions-in-kenya.

"Definitions for Kipchirchir." Definitions.Net, www.definitions.net/definition/Kipchirchir.

"Popular Kenyan Runners -What's in Their Names?" *Enda Sportswear*, Oct. 7, 2020. www.endasportswear.com/blogs/news/popular-kenyan-runners-whats-in-their-names.

Chapter Four

"Iten: It's More Than Just a Name." Medium, April 17, 2018. https://medium.com/enda-sportswear/iten-it-s-more-than-just-a-name-361b03df4ebb.

Chapter Five

"KenSAP Home Page." KenSAP, n.d. https://www.kensap.org/.

Running. "Rarefied Air: Eight Days at Kenya's High-Altitude Training Camp." *Canadian Running Magazine*, October 17, 2018. https://runningmagazine.ca/the-scene/rarefied-air-eight-days-at-lornah-kiplagats-high-altitude-training-camp-in-kenya/.

Chapter Six

Al Jazeera English. "A Sense of Community: Iten, Kenya - Where Female Runners Are Fighting to Win On and Off the Track." YouTube, November 3, 2022. https://www.youtube.com/watch?v=LDqU5No_YzI.

"Beyond the Block A: Kenyan Connection." University of Arizona Athletics, May 28, 2020. https://arizonawildcats.com/news/2019/11/5/cross-country-beyond-the-block-a-kenyan-connection.aspx.

Clemens, Jon. "A Guide to the College Recruitment Process." *Runner's World*, March 3, 2022. https://www.runnersworld.com/advanced/a20790868/a-guide-to-the-college-recruitment-process/.

"Frontline/World. Kenya—Run, Lornah, Run. Interview with Alexis Bloom and Cassandra Herrman: High-Altitude Women." PBS, n.d. https://www.pbs.org/frontlineworld/stories/kenya/producers.html.

"Interview with Lornah Kiplagat: Training for Change." PBS, n.d. https://www.pbs.org/frontlineworld/stories/kenya/kiplagat.html.

"Kenya—Run, Lornah, Run." PBS, n.d. https://www.pbs.org/frontlineworld/stories/kenya/thestory.html.

"Kenya Runner's Death Highlights Pressures Faced by Female Athletes." France 24, October 22, 2021. https://www.france24.com/en/live-news/20211022-kenya-runner-s-death-highlights-pressures-faced-by-female-athletes.

Lomong, Lopez, and Mark A. Tabb. *Running for My Life: One Lost Boy's Journey from the Killing Fields of Sudan to the Olympic Games*. Nashville, TN: Nelson Books, an imprint of Thomas Nelson, 2016.

"Lornah Kiplagat Biography, Olympic Medals, Records and Age." Olympics, n.d. https://olympics.com/en/athletes/lornah-kiplagat.

"Lornah Kiplagat." New York Road Runners, n.d. https://www.nyrr.org/about/hall-of-fame/lornah-kiplagat.

Sullivan, Tim. "Sullivan: Running Coaches Find Shortcut in Kenya." *Courier Journal*, November 20, 2015. https://www.courier-journal.com/story/sports/college/2015/11/19/sullivan-running-coaches-find-shortcut-kenya/75965118/.

Chapter Seven

Anderson, Owen. "Eating Practices of the Best Endurance Athletes in the World." ACTIVE.com, November 1, 2017. https://www.active.com/running/articles/eating-practices-of-the-best-endurance-athletes-in-the-world.

Carey, Nessa. *The Epigenetics Revolution: How Modern Biology Is Rewriting Our Understanding of Genetics, Disease, and Inheritance*. New York: Columbia University Press, 2013.

Epstein, David J. *The Sports Gene*. Rearsby: Clipper Large Print, 2013.

Epstein, David. "Sports Genes." Vault, May 17, 2010. https://vault.si.com/vault/2010/05/17/sports-genes.

Finn, Adharanand. *Running with the Kenyans: Discovering the Secrets of the Fastest People on Earth.* London: Faber, 2013.

Finn, Adharanand. "The Secret Is That You Think There's a Secret." *Guardian*, April 26, 2011. https://www.theguardian.com/lifeandstyle/london-2012-olympics-blog/2011/apr/26/running-with-the-kenyans.

Fisher, Max. "Why Kenyans Make Such Great Runners: A Story of Genes and Cultures." *The Atlantic*, April 17, 2012. https://www.theatlantic.com/international/archive/2012/04/why-kenyans-make-such-great-runners-a-story-of-genes-and-cultures/256015/.

Galbraith, Andy. "Can Genetics Explain the Success of East African Distance Runners?" *Conversation*, October 6, 2022. https://theconversation.com/can-genetics-explain-the-success-of-east-african-distance-runners-62586.

"Eliud Kipchoge: Daily Routine." Balance The Grind, October 18, 2022. https://balancethegrind.co/daily-routines/eliud-kipchoge-daily-routine/.

Karimi, Faith, and Idris Mukhtar. "The Reasons Why Kenyans Always Win Marathons Lie in One Region." CNN, November 6, 2019. https://www.cnn.com/2019/11/06/africa/kenya-runners-win-marathons-trnd/index.html.

Kiplagat, Sam. "Understanding Kalenjin Initiation Rites." *Star*, February 23, 2016. https://www.the-star.co.ke/sasa/2016-02-23-understanding-kalenjin-initiation-rites/.

Moore, Richard. "The Sports Gene: What Makes the Perfect Athlete by David Epstein—Review." *Guardian*, August 22, 2013. https://www.theguardian.com/books/2013/aug/22/sports-gene-david-epstein-review.

Onywera, Vincent O. "Scientists Are Closer to Pinning Down Why the World's Best Marathon Runner Is So Good." *Quartz*, May 26, 2019. https://qz.com/africa/1628684/why-kenyans-keep-winning-marathons-long-distance-races/amp.

Parameswaran, Gokul. "The Secrets of the Kalenjin People." Right for Education, December 7, 2020. https://rightforeducation.org/2020/12/07/the-secrets-of-the-kalenjin-people/.

Pitsiladis, Wilber. "Kenyan and Ethiopian Distance Runners: What Makes Them So Good?" *International Journal of Sports Physiology and Performance*, n.d. https://pubmed.ncbi.nlm.nih.gov/22634972/.

Price, S. L. "Is It in the Genes?" SI Vault, December 8, 1991. https://vault.si.com/vault/1997/12/08/is-it-in-the-genes-studies-have-found-physical-differences-that-might-help-explain-why-blacks-outperform-whites-in-certain-sportsbut-scientists-are-wary-of-jumping-to-conclusions.

Reynolds, Gretchen. "How Exercising Now Could Benefit Your Future Grandchildren." *Washington Post*, November 25, 2022. https://www.washingtonpost.com/wellness/2022/09/28/exercise-genetics-grandchildren/.

Ross. "The Kenyan Success Genetic Controversy." *The Science of Sport*, May 12, 2014. https://sportsscientists.com/2013/04/the-kenyan-success-genetic-controversy/.

"Run, Lornah, Run—Interview with Alexis Bloom and Cassandra Herrman: High-Altitude Women." PBS, n.d. https://www.pbs.org/frontlineworld/stories/kenya/producers.html.

Sanil, Sharan. "Here's How Eliud Kipchoge Went from Selling Milk for a Living to Creating Epic Marathon History." www.mensxp.com, October 12, 2019. https://www.mensxp.com/sports/other-sports/57596-here-s-how-eliud-kipchoge-went-from-selling-milk-for-a-living-to-creating-epic-marathon-history.html.

"The Secrets to Long Distance Running - [p]Rehab Running." [P]rehab, October 4, 2022. https://theprehabguys.com/the-secrets-to-long-distance-running/.

"Talent or Skill?: Homing in on the Elusive 'Sports Gene.'" NPR, August 5, 2013. https://www.npr.org/2013/08/05/209160709/talent-or-skill-honing-in-on-the-elusive-sports-gene.

Warner, Gregory. "How One Kenyan Tribe Produces the World's Best Runners." NPR, November 1, 2013. https://www.npr.org/sections/parallels/2013/11/01/241895965/how-one-kenyan-tribe-produces-the-worlds-best-runners.

"What Makes Kenyans Superior Runners? It's Not the Genes." PodiumRunner, August 17, 2020. https://www.podiumrunner.com/culture/its-not-the-genes/.

Zaske, Sara. "Twin Study Links Exercise to Beneficial Epigenetic Changes." WSU Insider, December 6, 2022. https://news.wsu.edu/press-release/2022/12/06/twin-study-links-exercise-to-beneficial-epigenetic-changes/.

Chapter Eleven

Barker, Sarah. "How a Small-Time Training Group and an Army Program Changed American Distance Running." Deadspin, September 7, 2017. https://deadspin.com/how-a-small-time-training-group-and-an-army-program-cha-1797614412.

Barrett, Carrie. "Good for a Girl - a Woman Running in a Man's World." Purple Patch Fitness, January 16, 2023. https://www.purplepatchfitness.com/podcast-transfer/episode-249-good-for-a-girl-a-woman-running-in-a-mans-world-interview-with-lauren-fleshmen.

Cullen, Margie, and Anne Marshall-Chalmers. "Female High School Runners Say Unhealthy Training Pressure Is Pushing Them Beyond the Breaking Point." *Runner's World*, November 18, 2022. https://www.runnersworld.com/women/a41845898/high-school-running-pressure/.

Davant, Jeanne. "New Sign a 'Stake in the Ground' for Olympic City USA Brand." *Colorado Springs Business Journal*, April 5, 2019. https://www.csbj.com/premier/businessnews/new-sign-a-stake-in-the-ground-for-olympic-city-usa-brand/article_70b50cfa-a462-520e-8033-47a24ec7800e.html.

Désir, Alison Mariella. *Running While Black: Finding Freedom in a Sport That Wasn't Built for Us*. New York: Portfolio / Penguin, 2022.

Dooney, Emma, and Jenny Bozon. "Red-S: The Condition All Runners Need to Know About." *Runner's World*, May 30, 2023. https://www.runnersworld.com/uk/health/a33589189/red-s-relative-energy-deficiency-running/.

"Fighting for Equity in Sports." NPR, January 10, 2023. https://www.npr.org/2023/01/09/1147813367/fighting-for-equity-in-sports.

Fleshman, Lauren. *Good for a Girl: My Life Running in a Man's World.* London: Virago Press, 2024.

Fletcher. "U.S. Citizenship Through Military Service." Military OneSource, April 7, 2023. https://www.militaryonesource.mil/financial-legal/legal/us-citizenship-through-military-service/.

Fox, Collin. "Restore Mavni for Legal Aliens to Enter the Military." U.S. Naval Institute, August 29, 2022. https://www.usni.org/magazines/proceedings/2021/august/restore-mavni-legal-aliens-enter-military.

"Half of Girls Quit Sports by the End of Puberty*: New Always® #LikeAGirl Video Examines Cause." Businesswire, June 28, 2016. https://www.businesswire.com/news/home/20160628005793/en.

"How Olympic Athletes Make a Living." Sports Management Degree Hub, July 14, 2021. https://www.sportsmanagementdegreehub.com/olympic-athletes-salaries/.

Konheim, Orrin. "U.S. Army's World Class Athlete Program Puts Runners on Fast Track to Citizenship." Landscape, August 21, 2017. https://andscape.com/features/u-s-armys-world-class-athlete-program-puts-runners-on-fast-track-to-citizenship/.

Laframboise, Michelle A., Cameron Borody, and Paula Stern. "The Female Athlete Triad: A Case Series and Narrative Overview." *Journal of the Canadian Chiropractic Association*, December 2013. https://www.ncbi.nlm.nih.gov/pmc/articles/PMC3845471/.

Mardini, Yusra. *Butterfly: From Refugee to Olympian, My Story of Rescue, Hope, and Triumph.* New York: St. Martin's Griffin, 2022.

"Relative Energy Deficiency in Sport (RED-S)." Boston Children's Hospital, n.d. https://www.childrenshospital.org/conditions/red-s.

Schaefer, Jenni, and Thom Rutledge. *Life without Ed: How One Woman Declared Independence from Her Eating Disorder and How You Can Too.* New York: McGraw-Hill, 2014.

"Some Veteran Pro Runners Are Making Less Money This Year, and They're Ditching the Sport." *Runner's World*, November 2, 2021. https://www.runnersworld.com/news/a36385189/how-much-do-pro-runners-make-sponsorships-contracts/.

Steinhauer, Jennifer. "As Military Addresses Diversity, Republicans See Culture War Target." *New York Times*, June 10, 2021. https://www.nytimes.com/2021/06/10/us/politics/military-diversity.html.

Swarner, Ken. "A Soldier & A Runner." *Runner's World*, June 14, 2019. https://www.runnersworld.com/advanced/a20784625/a-soldier-a-runner/.

Thames, Alanis, and Jonathan Abrams. "Female College Athletes Say Pressure to Cut Body Fat Is Toxic." *New York Times*, November 10, 2022. https://www.nytimes.com/2022/11/10/sports/college-athletes-body-fat-women.html.

Thorpe, Helen. *Soldier Girls: The Battles of Three Women at Home and at War.* Waterville, ME: Thorndike Press, a part of Gale, Cengage Learning, 2015.

"WCAP Home Page." Army WCAP, n.d. https://www.armywcap.com/.

Yu, Christine. *Up to Speed: The Groundbreaking Science of Women Athletes.* New York: Riverhead Books, 2023.

Chapter Fifteen

"What Is WCAP?" Army WCAP, n.d. https://www.armywcap.com/about.

Chapter Sixteen

Antush, Maxx. "The Rise of Super Shoes (Carbon-Fiber Plated) & the Fall of World Records." Fairhaven Runners, October 15, 2021. https://fairhavenrunners.com/coach-corner/the-rise-of-super-shoes-carbon-fiber-plated-the-fall-of-world-records/.

Gault, Jonathan. "Paul Chelimo Proves Everyone Wrong (Including Letsrun.Com) Once Again to Win the U.S.'s First Olympic 5,000 Medal in 52 Years." LetsRun, February 12, 2017. https://www.letsrun.com/news/2016/08/paul-chelimo-proves-everyone-wrong-including-letsrun-com-win-u-s-s-first-olympic-5000-medal-52-years/.

NBC Sports. "41-Year Old Lagat's Incredible Final Kick Claims Olympic Spot in 2016." YouTube, June 14, 2020. https://www.youtube.com/watch?v=noQStd-gUfQ.

Strout, Erin. "For Bernard Lagat's Coach of 20 Years, Tears of Joy." *Runner's World*, September 17, 2020. https://www.runnersworld.com/news/a20808570/for-bernard-lagats-coach-of-20-years-tears-of-joy/.

Chapter Eighteen

Burgess, Matt. "The Incredible Science Behind Eliud Kipchoge's 1:59 Marathon." *Wired UK*, October 14, 2019. https://www.wired.co.uk/article/eliud-kipchoge-ineos-159-marathon.

"Eliud Kipchoge." Inch Magazine, n.d. https://www.ineos.com/inch-magazine/articles/eliud-kipchoge/.

Gearhart, Sarah. *We Share the Sun: The Incredible Journey of Kenya's Legendary Running Coach Patrick Sang and the Fastest Runners on Earth*. New York: Pegasus Books, 2023.

Ineos. "Ineos 1:59 Challenge Live." YouTube, October 12, 2019. https://www.youtube.com/watch?v=k-XgKRJUEgQ.

Kipchoge: The Last Milestone. United Kingdom: Ridley Scott Creative Group, 2021.

Chapter Nineteen

3AE Gameplay. "Women 10000m Finals | U.S Track & Field Olympic Team Trials." YouTube, June 26, 2021. https://www.youtube.com/watch?v=F_cCw4NnCeU.

"Athlete Biological Passport." World Anti Doping Agency, January 5, 2022. https://www.wada-ama.org/en/athlete-biological-passport.

Chapter Twenty

Army Publishing Directorate, n.d. https://armypubs.army.mil/.

Goucher, Kara, and Mary Pilon. *The Longest Race: Inside the Secret World of Abuse, Doping, and Deception on Nike's Elite Running Team*. New York: Gallery Books, 2023.

Lorge Butler, Sarah. "Kara Goucher's Book Offers Rare Insight into Elite Athlete Contracts." *Runner's World*, May 26, 2023. https://www.runnersworld.com/news/a44006099/gouchers-book-offers-insight-into-athlete-contracts/.

Lorge Butler, Sarah. "What's Behind the Elite Runner Baby Boom?" *Runner's World*, April 11, 2023. https://www.runnersworld.com/runners-stories/a43555425/elite-runner-baby-boom/.

Montaño, Alysia, Max Cantor, Taige Jensen, and Lindsay Crouse. "Nike Told Me to Dream Crazy, Until I Wanted a Baby." *New York Times*, May 12, 2019. https://www.nytimes.com/2019/05/12/opinion/nike-maternity-leave.html.

Rich Roll Podcast. "Contracts, Pregnancy, and the Life of a Female Athlete| Lauren Fleshman X Rich Roll." YouTube, July 2, 2021. https://www.youtube.com/watch?v=RzffdReKrGA.

Strzalkowski, Bianca. "New Army Policy Seeks to 'Normalize Parenthood' for Soldiers." *Reserve & National Guard*, August 10, 2022. https://reservenationalguard.com/parenting/new-army-policy-seeks-to-normalize-parenthood-for-soldiers/.

Wood, Monica. "Changes in Army Policies on Parenthood, Pregnancy and Postpartum Makes It Easier for P3T to Help Soldier-Mothers Stay Fit." *Army*, June 14, 2022. https://www.army.mil/article/257529/changes_in_army_policies_on_parenthood_pregnancy_and_postpartum_makes_it_easier_for_p3t_to_help_soldier_mothers_stay_fit.

About the Author

AUTHOR PHOTO BY ANDREA FLANAGAN

Johanna Garton began running on the dirt roads surrounding her family's farmhouse in Wisconsin at age seven. She continued through college, where she competed for Syracuse University as a walk-on. She's run more than twenty marathons, including five finishes at the Boston Marathon. Her book *Edge of the Map* tells the story of American high-altitude mountaineer Christine Boskoff and is currently being developed into a feature film. Johanna is a sportswriter and high school cross-country coach who lives in Denver with her family. Find her online at johannagarton.com